PENGUIN BOOKS

THE GREEN FLAG: VOL. THREE
Ourselves Alone

An author, journalist and broadcaster, Robert Kee has worked for many years for both ITV and BBC television on current affairs series, such as *Panorama* and *This Week*, and on other programmes, including a number of documentaries. He has been a special correspondent for the *Sunday Times* and the *Observer*, and was literary editor of the *Spectator*.

The Green Flag has been continuously in print since 1972. The other two volumes in his monumental history of Irish nationalism are *The Most Distressful Country* and *The Bold Fenian Men*, also published by Penguin. Robert Kee made a thirteen-part series for BBC television based on *The Green Flag*. Entitled *Ireland: A History*, it received great critical acclaim and was widely shown both here and in the United States. He is also author of *Trial and Error* (1986, Penguin 1989), *Munich: The Eleventh Hour* (Hamish Hamilton 1988), published to commemorate the fiftieth anniversary of the Munich Agreement, and *The Picture Post Album* (1989).

The Green Flag
Volume Three:

Ourselves Alone

Robert Kee

PENGUIN BOOKS

PENGUIN BOOKS

Published by the Penguin Group
Penguin Books Ltd, 27 Wrights Lane, London W8 5TZ, England
Penguin Books USA Inc., 375 Hudson Street, New York, New York 10014, USA
Penguin Books Australia Ltd, Ringwood, Victoria, Australia
Penguin Books Canada Ltd, 10 Alcorn Avenue, Toronto, Ontario, Canada M4V 3B2
Penguin Books (NZ) Ltd, 182–190 Wairau Road, Auckland 10, New Zealand

Penguin Books Ltd, Registered Offices: Harmondsworth, Middlesex, England

First published in a single volume (with *The Most Distressful Country* and
The Bold Fenian Men) under the title *The Green Flag* by
Weidenfeld and Nicolson 1972
Published in Penguin Books 1989
3 5 7 9 10 8 6 4

Printed in England by Clays Ltd, St Ives plc

To the memory of my father,
Robert Kee (1880–1958),
and of my mother,
Dorothy Frances Kee
(1880–1964)

Contents

	Preface	ix
1	Executions and Negotiations	1
2	Rebellion to De Valera's Election at Clare (July 1917)	17
3	The New Sinn Fein (July 1917–April 1918)	30
4	Conscription Crisis to General Election (December 1918)	44
5	Sinn Fein in a Vacuum (January–May 1919)	55
6	Michael Collins and Others (April–December 1919)	67
7	The Campaign of Killing (1919–20)	77
8	Enter Black and Tans (1920)	92
9	Murder by the Throat (1920)	108
10	War and Truce (1921)	124
11	Treaty (1921)	145
12	Nemesis (1922–23)	158
	Epilogue	174
	References	179
	Index	193

IRELAND

50 miles
80 km

Lough Swilly · Rathlin I.

DONEGAL · Derry · LONDONDERRY

TYRONE · Larne · ANTRIM

BELFAST · Bangor

Dungannon · Lisburn

FERMANAGH · ARMAGH · DOWN

SLIGO · LEITRIM · MONAGHAN · Newry

Cavan · Dun Laoghaire

MAYO · Ballaghaderreen · CAVAN · LOUTH

Westport · Ballinalee · Dundalk

ROSCOMMON · Drogheda

Tourmakeady · LONGFORD · MEATH · Balbriggan

· Tuam · Trim · Ashbourne

WESTMEATH · Ashtown · Howth

GALWAY · Athlone · Maynooth · Clontarf

Galway · OFFALY · DUBLIN · Dun Laoghaire

(KING'S Co.) · KILDARE

Curragh · Kilcoole

Ennistymon · LEIX · WICKLOW

Lahinch · CLARE · (QUEEN'S Co.)

Miltown · Ennis · Woodenbridge

Malbay · Thurles · Arklow

· Limerick · Kilkenny

Solohedbeg · TIPPERARY · KILKENNY · CARLOW

LIMERICK · Cashel · Enniscorthy

Knocklong · Tipperary · WEXFORD

Banna Strand · Kilmallock · Carrick

· Ardfert · on Suir · Wexford

Fenit · Mitchelstown

· Tralee · Malloy · Fermoy · WATERFORD

KERRY · Clunbanin · Waterford

· Killarney · Clonmult

Macroom · CORK · Midleton

· Kilmichael · Cork

Bealnablath · Cross Barry

Bantry · Bandon · Kinsale

... The study of Irish history does not excite
political animosity but leads to the very
opposite result. Thoroughly to appreciate the
history of this or any country it is necessary to
sympathise with all parties ...

    A. G. Richey, from *A Short History of the
Irish People*, 1869

... My God, I thought that I would never live
to see what is happening today under an Irish
government. When we look back on the
days when we were oppressed by England it
would look like Paradise if we could get
the same sort of oppression now.

    John Dillon, 9 January 1925

Preface to Volume Three

When I finished writing *The Green Flag* in the Spring of 1971 the latest of the ancient troubles of Ireland had already been continuing for nearly two years. It was not part of my scheme then to include any account of them, and it is not now. They are still confused, unresolved and impossible to treat with the historical detachment which I hope is part of the character of this book. What I have tried to do in *The Green Flag* is to unfold as dispassionately as possible a narrative of earlier events (principally from 1789 to 1925) of which some knowledge is indispensable for any understanding of what has happened or may happen in Ireland. Knowledge and understanding do not in themselves provide solutions but there can be no solutions without them. I cannot help hoping that this new edition will, however indirectly, contribute something to an ending of the horror which the events of recent years have brought to the United Kingdom and Ireland.

The present volume, *Ourselves Alone*, is concerned with the modern growth of that extreme Irish republicanism which won freedom from British rule for twenty-six counties of Ireland in 1921, and which today pursues the same goal for all Ireland in the remaining six. The narrative begins with the aftermath of the Dublin rebellion of 1916. It describes how the aims of the unrepresentative few who brought about that rebellion came to be accepted, with some misgivings, but the majority of the people of Ireland. It tells in detail the story of the so-called war of Independence of 1920–21, of the Anglo-Irish treaty, of the split in the I.R.A. and of the Civil War that followed, leading to the compromise of 1925 which was to be blown apart in our own day.

The first inspiration for *The Green Flag* came from a magical valley in Co. Wicklow to whose resident spirit I send across many years gratitude and affection. Among others who gave me help I should like to thank particularly Mrs Ralph Partridge, Sir Nicholas Henderson, the late Dr P. M. Turquet, my wife Cynthia, my son Alexander, Miss Marguerite Foss and Mrs Topsy Levan: also the staffs over many years of the British Museum Reading Room, the British Museum Newspaper Library at Colindale, the London Library, and of the National Library of Ireland.

ROBERT KEE
January 1976

1

Executions and Negotiations

On the Sunday afternoon of 30 April as the last group of organized rebels, under MacDonagh at Jacob's Biscuit factory, were about to surrender, still almost intact as a fighting force, Birrell wrote his last report before resignation to Asquith. 'It is not an *Irish* rebellion,' he summarized. 'It would be a pity if *ex post facto* it became one, and was added to the long and melancholy list of Irish rebellions.'[1]

It now seems astonishing that the danger should have been so accurately predicted – and not only by Birrell – and yet the very action most likely to enhance it was allowed to take its course. The same day Dillon wrote to Redmond in London, from Dublin: 'You should urge strongly on the government the *extreme* unwisdom of any wholesale shooting of prisoners. The wisest course is to execute *no one* for the present. This is the *most urgent* matter of the moment. If there were shootings of prisoners on any large scale the effect on public opinion might be disastrous in the extreme. *So far* feeling of the population in Dublin is against the Sinn Feiners. But a reaction might very easily be created.'[2] A little further on in his letter he repeated: 'Do not fail to urge the government not to execute any of the prisoners. I have no doubt that if any of the well-known leaders are taken alive they will be shot. But, except the leaders, there should be no court-martial executions.'

Perhaps this preparedness to accept as inevitable the executions of some leaders shows that even Dillon underestimated the infinitely precarious balance of feeling in Ireland. Redmond, in London, clearly did. He saw Asquith at once and thought he was doing the right thing by securing agreement that while 'the real ring-leaders' would have to be dealt with 'in the most severe manner possible' the rest would be treated with leniency.[3] Two days later, however, when definitely informed by Asquith that some executions would be necessary, he did make a protest.[4] On the same day, 3 May 1916, Pearse, MacDonagh and Clarke were shot at dawn in a yard at Kilmainham gaol.

A priest was allowed to give Holy Communion to them a few hours before the executions. Assuming that the established custom in such matters would be observed, the priest who attended Pearse and MacDonagh reassured them that he would be close to them in their last moments even though they would be unable to see him because of their blindfolds. The thought made them happy.[5] But the military refused to allow it, and ordered the priest to leave the building so that he was not with them when the time came.

Probably Pearse, MacDonagh and Clarke were in too great a state of spiritual and patriotic exaltation to be much affected by this cruelty, but it was symbolic of the military's insensibility in such a highly sensitive situation. The insensibility with which they were now allowed to proceed seems all the more curious for the fact that Sir John Maxwell himself, who had arrived as Commander-in-Chief in Ireland at the end of Easter Week with full military powers, clearly had some appreciation of the delicacy of the atmosphere, and was prepared to receive at least advice from Dillon.[6] But his awareness was accompanied by that arrogance often inseparable from even high military intelligence. In later refusing the right of burial in consecrated ground for Pearse's body he was able to write brusquely: 'Irish sentimentality will turn these graves into martyrs' shrines to which annual processions will be made which will cause constant irritation in this country.'[7] He seems to have thought that quick-lime would be enough to dispel 'Irish sentimentality'. But it had failed in the case of Allen, Larkin and O'Brien and many others. He can hardly have supposed that when Pearse himself spoke of 'the fools' leaving extreme nationalists their Fenian dead, he was thinking literally of their corpses.

On 4 May four more executions after courts-martial were carried out – on Joseph Plunkett, Edward Daly, Michael O'Hanrahan and William Pearse, Patrick's younger brother. All were allowed to see priests shortly before their execution, and this time, it seems, the priests were allowed to stay with them to the last, though military clumsiness was not entirely absent. One of the men was brought to Confession in handcuffs and unable to remove his hat until they were unlocked.[8]

Plunkett, however, had been allowed to marry the girl he was engaged to by the light of a candle with a warder for witness in the prison chapel in the early hours. He at least, the elegant tubercular poet who had walked about the General Post Office during the Rising with a bangle on his wrist and a Mauser at his belt[9] could properly be described as one of the leaders. As a member of the IRB's military council he had helped draft the original plans for an insurrection and had signed the Proclamation of the Republic.[10]

Daly had had nothing to do with the planning of the rebellion though he was the son of an old Fenian, and had merely carried out his military duties as a Volunteer Commandant under orders. He had, however, done so in effective fashion from his command in the Four Courts area, and since the government knew nothing about the IRB's manipulation of the Volunteers it was not unreasonable for them to suppose him a leader.

The same could just be said of Michael O'Hanrahan, a literary man who had been a clerk at Volunteer headquarters. But if leading Volunteers were going to be executed on these grounds alone the indications were of a massive number of executions to come.

Willie Pearse seems to have been shot for no other reason than that he had taken part in the rebellion as a Volunteer and was Pearse's brother. Though devoted to his brother he had known nothing of his schemes for turning blood-red poetic fantasies into reality. But the military seem to have thought they had already been lenient enough for that particular day – which, by their own lights, they were. Simultaneously with the announcement of these four executions, they revealed that seventeen other courts-martial sentences of death, which had been confirmed, had been commuted to penal servitude.

Asquith, the Prime Minister, was himself uneasy, but not uneasy enough. As so often throughout the history of the Union, responsible English statesmen even when compelled to take Ireland seriously still accorded her a secondary priority. Thus, though even on 3 May Asquith told Redmond that he had given the War Office orders from the start 'to go slowly', and that he was himself shocked by the news of the first three executions, he would not absolutely promise that there would be no more, merely expressing that as 'his desire and intention'.[11] Now four more men had been executed. Nor was Asquith the only man to be weak or mistakenly flexible in a disastrously deteriorating situation. Redmond himself told Asquith that he would probably resign if there were any more executions.[12] Asquith told him that he had wired Maxwell that there should be no more. But Asquith's wire went unrespected. Redmond did not resign.

The next day, 5 May, another man, John MacBride, was executed. Though he had taken part in the rebellion and was a rank-and-file member of the IRB with some two thousand others, he, like almost all of them, had absolutely no prior knowledge of the plans for the rebellion. His well-known predilection for drink preserved him especially from any confidence on the part of the leadership. He had, however, led an Irish Brigade – composed mainly of Americans – against the British in the Boer War.* Unlike another Irishman, Arthur Lynch, who had done the same and later renounced his separatist views and become an MP, MacBride, who had enjoyed since 1911 the post of water bailiff to the Dublin Corporation, had remained true to 'the cause'. It is difficult not to think that he was shot partly as a simple act of revenge by the military for an offence for which the common law had long forgiven him, though he had continued to wage war in speech against the British, urging his hearers at a Manchester Martyrs' commemoration at Kilkenny in 1909 to 'do all in your power to prevent your countrymen from entering the degraded British Army'.[13] Undoubtedly, too, he had refused to show any signs of contrition at his court-martial. He had, he

* See *The Bold Fenian Men*, Volume 2 of *The Green Flag*, pp. 147–8.

told the court, stared down the barrels of British rifles far too often in the past to be afraid of death.[14] And thus it may be assumed he bore himself at the end. He, too, in the words with which Yeats was soon to express his emotion at these strange events, had 'resigned his part in the casual comedy. ... A terrible beauty is born.'

Anyone with any sense of the workings of Irish history, particularly if also aware of that ambivalence which had underlain many attitudes even of downright hostility to the rebellion while it was going on, could have foretold what the long-term effect of these wholly unpredictable day-by-day executions was likely to be. Already a Capuchin Father noticed that the feeling among the working classes of Dublin was becoming 'extremely bitter' over the executions, 'even amongst those who had no sympathy whatever with the Sinn Feiners, or with the rising'.[15] Before long, as one Irishwoman was later to put it, the Irish people began to feel that they were 'watching a stream of blood coming from beneath a closed door'.[16] The fact that on the same day as MacBride's death the commutation of death sentences on two other Irish Volunteers, including William Cosgrave, was announced was not the fact that counted.

And yet even now, for most people the whole situation was immensely complicated and opaque. British statesmen and military men were not in the habit of thinking of Ireland in the light of the workings of past history. General Maxwell, with only the government's incomplete and over-simplified knowledge of the background to the rebellion at his disposal, saw it primarily as a German manoeuvre in the Great War which was at that moment going badly for England. Quite incorrectly, but sincerely, he thought that the Germans had inspired the rebellion and that what seemed like Casement's attempt to land with German arms to lead it was the corner-stone of the enterprise.[17] After all, the Republican Proclamation which Pearse had read out to such an apathetic audience from the front of the Post Office had actually mentioned with pride support from the Germans as 'gallant allies in Europe'.

Now every indication was that the vast majority of the Irish people found the thought of such support repellent. Some 90,000 Catholic Irish had joined the British Army from Ireland since the beginning of the war and far more had already died in the war than had died fighting the British Government in the past hundred years. Elements of seven Irish regiments had taken part in the suppression of the rebellion itself and there had, of course, been other Irishmen in non-Irish regiments.* Some of the sharpest fighting in Easter Week had been between the Royal Irish Regiment and the rebels at the South Dublin Union, and between the Dublin Fusiliers and the rebels at the barricades in Cabra Road. In his order of the day of 1 May

* For instance, among the Lancers, who had been the first military casualties of the rebellion. (*Rebellion Handbook*, p. 56.)

1916 Maxwell had singled out for praise 'those Irish regiments which have so largely helped to crush this rising'.[18] He may well have felt he had a duty to his own Irishmen to fulfill in enforcing at least some of the rigour of the law.

Moreover, in addition to pressure from Asquith and the Home Rule Nationalists to stop the executions, Maxwell was also under strong pressure in the opposite direction from Unionists. A memorial presented by 763 'influential' people in Dublin protested against any interference with the discretion of the C-in-C in Ireland and the operation of martial law.[19] Altogether, by his own lights, Maxwell was by no means unreasonable in the circumstances of the time in thinking he was being lenient in shooting only fifteen rebels over the period of nine days beginning on 3 May and commuting other death sentences to penal servitude. But where Irish nationalism was concerned nothing could be safely judged only by the light of reason, as Redmond and Dillon were well aware. And it was on this factor that Pearse in particular had been counting.

On Saturday, 6 May, no other executions were announced. Instead, eighteen death sentences were commuted to penal servitude and only two of these sentences as severe as life, one of which was that passed on Constance Markievicz. Dillon crossed to London that night with a draft resolution for the Irish party in his pocket condemning the insurrection, but protesting 'in the most solemn manner against the large number of military executions ...' continuing, '... We solemnly warn the government that very serious mischief has been done by the excessive severities.... And that any further military executions will have the most far-reaching and disastrous effects on the future peace and loyalty of the Irish people.'[20] Redmond had already told Asquith of a cable received from the president of the Irish League of New York, a loyal supporter of Redmond's and of the British war effort, saying that the first executions had revolted the American Irish who had condemned the rebellion itself.[21]

On Sunday the 7th there were rumours of more executions pending the next day. Redmond sent an urgent message to Asquith 'at his place in the country'. Asquith sent what he called 'a strong telegram' to Maxwell saying that he hoped the shootings, except in some quite exceptional cases, would stop. The next day Cornelius Colbert, Edmund Kent (Eamonn Ceannt), Michael Mallin and Sean Heuston were shot.

Colbert, a clerk in a bakery and yet another of the rebellion's poets, had been an active organizer of the Fianna Eireann, the nationalist boy scouts. Heuston, a railway clerk, another prominent figure in the Fianna, had held the Mendicity Institution bravely for three days during the Rising. He was shot sitting on a soap box.[22] Ceannt, a Dublin Corporation clerk, had been a member of the IRB's military committee since its inception in May 1915 – though the authorities had no such precise information – and one of the signatories of the proclamation; he had also been the commander of the garrison in the South Dublin Union. Mallin, a silk weaver with five children, had been second-in-command of Connolly's Citizen Army and in charge of the St Stephen's Green garrison during Easter Week.

Connolly himself was tried and sentenced to death the next day, 9 May, Maxwell noting laconically, in reply to Asquith's feeble demurs, that though his bullet wound had fractured the ankle bone he would recover 'in ordinary circumstances' in three months. He informed the Prime Minister that Connolly would be shot at dawn on 11 May. Sean MacDermott would be shot at the same time. 'They will be the last,' Maxwell conceded.[23]

Meanwhile, however, on 9 May Thomas Kent, a Cork Volunteer who had resisted an attempt to arrest him at his home near Fermoy two days after the rebellion in Dublin was over and had killed a policeman, was shot in Cork.

On 11 May, in a last desperate attempt to prevent further executions, Dillon moved the adjournment of the House of Commons. Bitterly he seems to have sensed that it was too late and that untold damage was already done. He who with Redmond stood to lose his whole political future from the rebellion showed how the executions had already begun to affect him. He lost control of himself and cried out to a hostile House:

I say I am proud of their [the rebels] courage and if you were not so dense and stupid, as some of you English people are, you could have had these men fighting for you ... it is not murderers who are being executed: it is insurgents who have fought a clean fight, however misguided, and it would have been a damned good thing for you if your soldiers were able to put up as good a fight as did these men in Dublin ...[24]

Even Asquith himself was now disturbed, if only by his own ineffectualness, and announced, while knowing quite well that Connolly and MacDermott were to be executed on the following day, that he was going to Dublin to investigate the future.

In the early morning of 12 May Connolly, after receiving Holy Communion, was put on a stretcher and taken by ambulance from Dublin Castle to Kilmainham. There in the yard he was placed in a chair and gripping the arms of it held his head high to the end.[25] Sean MacDermott had written to his family, '... you ought to envy me. The cause for which I die has been rebaptized during the past week by the blood of as good men as ever trod God's earth.... It is not alone for myself I feel happy, but for the fact that Ireland has produced such men.'[26]

Many of them expressed in their last words the same confidence that their deaths were a sort of triumph, thus retrospectively at least subscribing to Pearse's theory of the blood sacrifice. 'People will say hard things of us now,' Pearse himself had written to his mother two days before his execu-

tion, 'but we shall be remembered by posterity and blessed by unborn generations. You too will be blessed because you are my mother.'[27] Scan Heuston
wrote to his sister, a Dominican nun, 'If you really love me, teach the
children the history of their own land and teach them the cause of Caitlin ni
Uallachain never dies.'[28] Ceannt, who expressed resentment that Pearse had
surrendered so early, nevertheless accepted that Pearse's ultimate objective
had been achieved. 'Ireland has shown she is a Nation,' he wrote the day
before he died. '... And in the years to come Ireland will honour those who
risked all for her honour at Easter in 1916.'[29]

Meanwhile, no one knew for certain that the volley of the firing squad
which had killed Connolly had been the last. Courts-martial were proceed-
ing. Death sentences continued to be announced though simultaneously with
their commutation to penal servitude. But this was no guarantee that executions were over. Seven commuted death sentences had been announced the
day before Connolly and MacDermott were shot, among them one on
Edward de Valera, the rebel Commandant of Boland's Mills – one of the
many examples of Redmond's successful personal intervention with
Asquith.*[30]

Eight more commuted death sentences were announced a few days afterwards. There had been over 3,000 arrests altogether, a number of them
irrelevant, and though nearly 1,000 men and women were released within
six weeks, more than 1,500 prisoners had been taken across the Irish Sea
by 10 May. 1,867 were eventually interned there altogether, either in
criminal prisons or at a special camp at Frongoch in Wales.[31]

On 30 May the findings of a court-martial on John MacNeill, who had
been arrested a month earlier, were announced. The man who had known
nothing of the planning of the rebellion and had done everything in his
power, short of betraying his comrades, to prevent it once he had discovered
what was afoot, was sentenced to life imprisonment and sent to Dartmoor.

In the special Irish situation an extremely tense and sensitive emotional
atmosphere had been created by these measures, though in any normal situation they might indeed have seemed lenient on the part of a hard-pressed
government in time of war. But even so it cannot be said that they need
inevitably, in themselves, have led to the pronounced swing round of public
opinion to the rebels' way of thinking which took place. They merely created
a needlessly favourable climate for such a transformation.

Other influences less noble than martyrdom or even patriotism, which
even before 1916 had helped to create a very slight shift of opinion towards

* It has often been said that de Valera, who was born of an Irish mother and a
Spanish father in America and lived there until he was two, was saved as a result of
American diplomatic intervention But there is no evidence for this and de Valera was
not technically an American citizen See Alan J. Ward, *Anglo-American Diplomatic
Relations* (London, 1969), pp 117-18 Gwynn states that Redmond stressed to Asquith
de Valera's American extraction.

extreme Irish nationalism, were now accentuated. As one witness before the Royal Commission of Inquiry into the rebellion put it, the country people were doing extremely well with their farms and were 'fat and prosperous'. 'A great many farmers' sons,' he added, had been 'joining the Sinn Fein movement, and ... using it as a kind of umbrella in excuse for not fighting.'[32] Extreme nationalism made it patriotic as well as advantageous not to want to join up. Now, with the British Army's need for men growing more and more desperate and the possibility of an extension of conscription to Ireland, the ideals of young heroes like Sean Heuston and Con Colbert undoubtedly offered some who might not normally have been drawn to Irish patriotism a happy conjunction of patriotism with self-interest.

Even so, these were all no more than conditioning factors in the situation, though conditioning factors, after so much Irish history, of particular force. The really decisive factor would be such political action as the British Government might now decide to take. The omens for a successful political manoeuvre could hardly be good in the atmosphere provoked by the manner of executions and deportations, but clearly something new had to be done, and quickly. The whole future of England's relationship with Ireland, which only eighteen months before had seemed about to be so happily resolved after seven centuries, now hung more precariously than ever in the balance.

In the prevailing political circumstances it is difficult to see that Asquith had any chance of success. He was already personally on the defensive within his own Coalition Government. That government contained men like Walter Long, Lord Selborne and Lord Lansdowne, the corner-stone of whose political faith was their opposition to Home Rule. It had for several months even contained Carson himself who had resigned only to be able to put pressure on Asquith more effectively. In a coalition situation Asquith had no parliamentary need to placate Redmond and the Irish nationalists, who were in any case themselves politically ham-strung by their patriotic commitment through Redmond to the war effort. But Asquith did need to placate the Unionists. Thus from now on almost every action he took almost inevitably made the situation worse, even those which in themselves were right.

His personal visit to Ireland on the eve of Connolly's and MacDermott's execution was a case in point.

In announcing his decision to go he had declared that the government recognized that the system under which Ireland was governed had 'completely broken down', and that what was essential was the creation 'at the earliest possible moment of an Irish government responsible to the Irish people'.[33] In other words, by their rebellion, republicans had brought the reality of Home Rule nearer. This was in itself already something to make that vast majority of the population who were Home Rulers look on the republicans with less hostility, and to begin a blurring of distinction between the two. The very importance of a visit from the Prime Minister at such a time, with non-republican feeling deeply disturbed by the executions, also lent importance to the republicans. Asquith even visited rebel prisoners in gaol in Dublin, finding them 'very good-looking fellows with such lovely eyes',[34] and the effect of his visit on them was, according to their gaolers, instantaneous. He had scarcely left the prison when, the warders maintained, the rebels who had been hitherto despondent and in tears began 'insulting their guards, throwing up their caps and shouting victory'.[35]

After his return to London he told the House of Commons that there was now 'a unique opportunity for a new departure for a settlement of outstanding problems'.[36] He had used the same phrase the day before in writing to one of his ministers and asking him to accept special responsibility for finding 'a permanent solution', by which he meant some way of immediately implementing Home Rule which would be acceptable to all. The minister who accepted this challenge was David Lloyd George.[37]

Not all the omens were bad. The Unionists through influential personalities of their press – Garvin of the *Observer* and Northcliffe of the *Daily Mail* – had expressed a willingness to go back to the Ulster deadlock of 1914 and see if some practical acceptable compromise could not be found.[38] Moreover, there was a direct reason why all British patriots should want to resolve the Irish difficulty now that the rebellion had shown that the passage and suspension of the Home Rule Act in 1914 had been inadequate. This reason was the need to placate public opinion in the United States of America, which country was then still neutral in the Great War, but sorely needed as an ally.

At the end of Easter Week the British Ambassador in Washington had been able to write that American public opinion had been on the whole totally opposed to the rebellion. Nineteen days later, however, after the executions, he was reporting a dangerous change.[39] He was substantiated by other observers. One Home Ruler had written to Redmond three days earlier from Vermont: 'The present wave of fury sweeping through Irish America originated with the executions and not with the rising ... pro-Ally Irishmen, who were calm and sorrowful at the rising ... have become hysterical during the protracted week of executions.'[40] Another Irishman reported from Chicago on 24 May that where the '"Irish Rebellion", so-called' had excited only contempt and derision, after the executions 'a feeling of universal sympathy among the entire American people sprang into action at once'.[41]

In Ireland itself the same very sharp transformation of opinion which Dillon and others had already noted was continuing. 'It would really not be possible to exaggerate the desperate character of the situation here.' Dillon, who had returned to Dublin, wrote to Redmond while Asquith was still there. 'The executions, house-searching throughout the country, wholesale arrests ... *savage* treatment of prisoners, including a very considerable number of those who had no more sympathy with Sinn Fein than you have, have exasperated feeling to a terrible extent.'[42] And Redmond himself was already entertaining, in the absence of some settlement, 'very grave doubts as to the future of the Irish party'.[43] Personally he was in a very depressed state. His son had just left for the Front and he repeatedly talked of the possibility of retiring from politics altogether.[44]

It was therefore in an atmosphere of some urgency that Lloyd George began his work. The known force of his own personal ambition made it likely that, having accepted the task, he would do his utmost to succeed. Typically, he did too much. Taking care to keep Carson and Redmond apart, but conferring with each individually and giving favourable reports of his discussions with each to the other, he succeeded in obtaining an initial agreement between the two which looked like early success.

The same concessions in principle which had been made by each side before the war still stood. That is to say, the Ulster Unionists conceded the principle of Home Rule for the rest of Ireland if they themselves were excluded; the Nationalists conceded the principle of exclusion for a limited time of those Ulster counties with Protestant majorities. The difficult points at issue were still those which had brought the Buckingham Palace Conference to deadlock and which had been put into cold storage by the device of passing the act but with a suspensory act. These points concerned both area and time. The Ulster Unionists held out for exclusion of all nine counties of the province on a permanent basis. The Nationalists could only accept the exclusion of the four majority Protestant counties (Derry, Antrim, Down and Armagh) and only on a temporary basis. It was this deadlock which, in a fashion typical of his personal political technique, Lloyd George soon appeared to be overcoming.

The solution which both Redmond and Carson agreed to recommend to their supporters was as follows: Home Rule was to be put into operation at once for twenty-six of Ireland's counties, while the other six, in Ulster (Derry, Antrim, Down, Armagh, Tyrone and Fermanagh) would be excluded. This involved a final concession by Carson that not the whole province of Ulster but only six counties would be excluded; Donegal, Cavan and Monaghan were to be 'surrendered' to Home Rule. Similarly, the proposal demanded from Redmond the concession that the two Ulster counties of Tyrone and Fermanagh, each of which had Nationalist majorities, would be surrendered to the Unionists. Each leader now agreed to recommend these concessions to his supporters. In neither case was it anything like a foregone conclusion that he would be able to force them through. The really crucial point, however, on which ultimately any such agreement would have to stand or fall, was the question of whether such exclusion was going to be temporary or permanent. And on this a curious vagueness supervened.

What had happened was that Lloyd George by keeping the two negotiators apart had allowed each to receive a different impression and believe that the other had agreed to what he wanted. For good measure Lloyd George told Redmond, who had insisted that no further concessions should be demanded of the Nationalists, that he 'placed his life upon the table and would stand or fall by the agreement come to'.⁴⁵ In the agreement the provisional nature of the exclusion arrangement was indeed outlined. But this was done in ambiguous terms which might have made negotiators less desperate for a settlement than Redmond and Dillon suspicious. The exclusion of the six counties was to remain in force for the duration of the war and up to one year thereafter, but, if Parliament had not by that time made further permanent provision for the government of Ireland, the arrangement was to continue in force until it had. An Imperial Conference was also to be called at which the permanent settlement of the Irish question should be considered.⁴⁶

All this was undoubtedly interpreted by the Nationalist leaders as meaning that the exclusion was to be only temporary. Yet, even so, and even with the self-sacrificing support of Joe Devlin, the Belfast Nationalist leader, and the sanction of a threat of resignation from Redmond, the leaders only just succeeded in getting the very reluctant agreement of the Ulster Nationalists, and thereafter that of the party as a whole, to the temporary abandonment of the substantial Nationalist minority in Ulster with its actual majority in two counties. Carson had an equally difficult time in getting his supporters in Ulster to agree to 'the clean cut' – the surrender to Home Rule of Donegal, Cavan and Monaghan with their substantial Protestant minorities. He had, however, as a result of his meetings with Lloyd George, a written assurance in his pocket of which the Nationalists were in total ignorance and without which he would have accomplished nothing. This assurance ran: 'We must make it clear that at the end of the provisional period Ulster does not, whether she wills it or not, merge in the rest of Ireland.'*⁴⁷

It seems improbable that a man even of Lloyd George's consummate political guile could have kept the discrepancy in the proposal concealed for long. He presumably thought there was a chance of keeping it concealed long enough to be able eventually to convince Redmond and Dillon of the need to accept a *fait accompli*. But Redmond and Dillon had already strained their supporters' loyalty to the absolute limit. The dénouement came abruptly without their having to consider the possibility of trying to strain it even further.

Though Carson stuck loyally to his new position, a massive opposition to the whole scheme for putting Home Rule into operation at all was now mounted by the English Conservative Party and many of its leaders inside the coalition cabinet. 'They are all in it,' Lloyd George wrote disarmingly

* Clearly, in this letter, Lloyd George meant by 'Ulster' only the six counties.

to Dillon, 'except Balfour, Bonar Law and F. E. Smith. Long has behaved in a specially treacherous manner. He has actually been engaged clandestinely in trying to undermine the influence of Carson in Ulster.... He told them there was no war urgency, no prospect of trouble in America.... I could not think it possible that any man, least of all one with such pretensions of being an English gentleman, could have acted in such a way.'[48]

But Lloyd George, without any such pretensions, was hardly acting better and both doubtless were doing what they thought best. Long had many other English gentlemen to support him. Lord Selborne at least resigned from the cabinet at the prospect of having to be a party to the immediate implementation of Home Rule. Bonar Law had to bow before the Conservatives of the Carlton Club, who were unable to give him their support for the proposals. On 11 July Lord Lansdowne, another member of the cabinet, finally forced Lloyd George's hand when he stated in the House of Lords that in his view any proposed alteration to the Act of 1914 would be 'permanent and enduring'.[49]

The cat was now out of the bag. If Lord Lansdowne's views (and Walter Long's) did not represent those of the cabinet then Asquith would have to have their resignations. But on the defensive as he already was in his own cabinet for his conduct of the war, and with the high hopes with which the Battle of the Somme had begun a fortnight earlier disappearing into the mud, Asquith was in no position to face the break-up of his government. On 22 July Redmond was informed of the cabinet's decision that the proposed settlement was to be permanent. Two days later, in the House of Commons, Redmond, marking the collapse of the negotiations, accused the government of entering on a course which 'is bound to do serious mischief to those high Imperial interests which, we were told, necessitated the provisional settlement of this question ... they have taken the surest means to accentuate every possible danger and difficulty in this Irish situation'.[50]

Asquith wrote a wretched private letter to Redmond: 'My dear Mr Redmond, I am more afflicted than I can say (in the midst of many other troubles and worries) by the breakdown of the negotiations.... I think it is of great importance (if possible) to keep the negotiating spirit alive ...'

There was in fact at that very moment something Redmond might have persuaded Asquith to do which could at least temporarily have ameliorated the disastrous situation. But ironically even Redmond himself was not sufficiently attuned to the new mood in Ireland to perceive what this was. He seems to have accepted from the first days of May that Roger Casement would have to be executed as the rebels' chief contact with Germany. And, though much had changed since those first May days, it does not seem to have occurred to him that this attitude to Casement might need to be adjusted to that change.

On 29 June, after a trial in which the prosecutor was F. E. Smith, a man who had himself organized armed resistance to the Crown only two years before, Casement was convicted of high treason and condemned to death. There can, of course, be no doubt that, legally, the verdict against Casement was correct, for all the ingenious word-play with the ancient statute under which he was tried, indulged in by his advocate, Serjeant Sullivan, a constitutional Irish Nationalist of some spirit. Casement's own eloquent plea that he owed allegiance only to his country Ireland was, as he well knew, technically irrelevant, and even less eloquent than it might have been if he had not only a few years before felt sufficiently a liege man of George v's, however Irish, to accept a knighthood from him. His argument, too, that he had in fact come to try to put a stop to the rising, though perfectly true, was nothing like so convincing as he seemed to think it, for if the German help which he had worked for had been forthcoming he would have wanted the rising to proceed. He had conspired with the king's enemies in time of war and had tried to turn the king's soldiers against him. He had done so for the loftiest of reasons and in full knowledge of the risk he ran. That he was a courageous, sincere and even noble, if disturbingly lonely man is unquestionable. It is equally unquestionable that no shadow of legal injustice was done to him at his trial, however personally distasteful and discreditable F. E. Smith's role may appear. Whether or not, in the light of the earlier executions and Irish and American reaction to them and particularly in the deteriorating atmosphere after the collapse of the Lloyd George negotiations, it was politic to proceed with the death sentence was a different matter.

The fact that, after the rejection of Casement's appeal, the cabinet with due deliberation could come to a unanimous decision that it was right to execute him, may now seem incredible. On the very day after Asquith had written his pathetic 'negotiating spirit' letter to Redmond it even reaffirmed this decision. Once again, a British government which boasted as one of its unalterable principles the connection with Ireland, was to show that it had no true contact with Ireland at all.

Admittedly, some members of the cabinet had had their doubts about the matter, and had for a time seized at a most curious straw – a diary of Casement's – to try to get them out of their difficulty. When it proved inadequate they put it to a less creditable use.

By some means, which to this day have not been authoritatively established, this diary of Casement's came into the government's possession, possibly sold to them by the disreputable sailor, Adolf Christensen, whom Casement had adopted as his servant companion.* Ninety-five per cent of the material of these diaries consisted of humdrum recordings of day-to-day movements and occurrences. But the remaining five per cent appeared to indicate unmistakably a compulsive and obsessional homosexual activity of a promiscuous

* See *The Bold Fenian Men*, pp. 244-5.

nature, crudely described. A certain amount of circumstantial evidence exists to suggest that Casement may indeed have been a repressed or even a practising homosexual. It has also been suggested that the compromising passages were forged interpolations introduced by the British Intelligence Chief Admiral Hall (who undoubtedly showed the diaries to the press and influential people even before the trial). While this suggestion is not wholly impossible the authenticity or otherwise of the diaries is of less immediate concern to the historian than the further uses to which they were now put.

The government seems first to have tried to use the diaries officially to get Casement's defence lawyers to plead insanity on his behalf. Serjeant Sullivan properly refused to look at them, though one of his juniors did so, and the issue did not figure at the trial. Even after Casement's conviction, but before his appeal had been heard, some members of the cabinet, including incidentally Lord Lansdowne, thought it would be better to confine Casement as a criminal lunatic on the strength of the diaries rather than let him be 'canonized as a martyr both in Ireland and America'. But when a medical report had been received on the diaries to the effect that their author was 'abnormal but not certifiably insane', pages from the 'black' diaries were circulated and used to discourage sympathy for Casement in the minds of those urging the government for a reprieve. Among those so affected, to their discredit, were the Archbishop of Canterbury and John Redmond.[51]

On 3 August, just after nine in the morning, Casement, pinioned in the traditional fashion, was taken to the execution shed at Pentonville to be hanged. After a month's instruction he had been received into the Roman Catholic Church the day before, and the priest who had given him his first and last Communion that morning was allowed to remain with him to the end. The priest wrote afterwards: 'He marched to the scaffold with the dignity of a prince and towered over all of us ...'[52]

His last request to his cousin, Gertrude Bannister, had been 'don't let me lie here in this dreadful place – take my body back with you and let it lie in the old churchyard in Murlough Bay'.[53] A request for his body was made at once by Miss Bannister to the Home Office, but the British Government did not feel able to give it up again for another fifty years. Roger Casement, as predicted, became the sixteenth martyr of Easter Week at once.

Yeats was soon to write with more truth than accuracy (for Casement, of course, had been hanged):

> Oh but we talked at large before
> The sixteen men were shot,
> But who can talk of give and take,
> What should be and what not
> While those dead men are loitering there
> To stir the boiling pot?

You say that we should still the land
Till Germany's overcome;
But who is there to argue that
Now Pearse is deaf and dumb?
And is there logic to outweigh
MacDonagh's bony thumb?

How could you dream they'd listen
That have an ear alone
For those new comrades they have found,
Lord Edward and Wolfe Tone,
Or meddle with our give and take
That converse bone to bone?

It was the failure to achieve a settlement in the new situation created by the actions of Pearse and his companions that was now the real turning-point in the Nationalist Party's future. The suspicion that had lain over Home Rule ever since it had been placed on the statute book, and which had been aggravated when Carson and Smith had joined the government, and allayed only by the confident reassurances of Redmond, was now openly confirmed. It was not to go through. The Parliamentary Party were revealed in this last opportunity as unable to win Home Rule after all without permanently partitioning Ireland. In the new atmosphere created by the rebellion, the demand for Home Rule was now too firm to be disappointed much longer.

As early as June, T. P. O'Connor had been telling Lloyd George that the executed men were already passing into legend, with their scrupulously upright characters, their devoted Catholicism and in many cases their abstinence from drink. He recounted the story of a little girl who was said to have asked her mother for a new hat and, when the mother refused, to have prayed to 'St Pearse' until the mother relented.[54] The fact that the story was being told was what was significant. While martial law persisted masses for the dead men's souls were increasingly becoming a form of political demonstration in support of their ideals.

In September 1916 Dillon made a considered survey of the political situation in Ireland. After admitting that the party had been losing its hold on opinion unawares ever since the formation of the coalition, he wrote that its strength was now entirely of a negative character, due to the fact that there was no alternative either in leadership or policy. 'But,' he continued, 'enthusiasm and trust in Redmond and the party is *dead* so far as the mass of the people is concerned.'[55]

There was, however, an alternative leadership with an alternative policy. It was not immediately available. The bulk of it was in British prisons. But at this emotional moment in Irish history it could have had no more favourable starting-point.

2

Rebellion to De Valera's Election at Clare (July 1917)

It is sometimes said that it was the Dublin rebellion of 1916 and the subsequent executions which dramatically swung Irish majority opinion away from the goal of constitutional Home Rule nationalism in favour at least of a Fenian republican separatism to be achieved, if necessary, by bloodshed. This is a most misleading oversimplification. There is a sense in which that turned out to be the sequence of events, though whether Irish majority opinion was ever in favour of bloodshed to achieve nationalist aims is highly questionable. But certainly that sequence of events was no simple product of cause and effect.

It was neither the Fenian tradition nor Griffith's Sinn Fein which the rebellion and the executions immediately stimulated but the Home Rule movement itself. This fact is of the greatest importance in understanding the hybrid and even confused nature of much Irish opinion over the next few years. It is often forgotten that in the first by-election fought in Ireland after the rebellion – more than six months later, in the very representative nationalist constituency of West Cork in November 1916 – a man describing himself as a Sinn Feiner came easily bottom of the poll to two rival Home Rule candidates.* There can be little doubt that if the Home Rule Act as passed by Parliament had been put into effect immediately after the rebellion, it would have remained, at least for the foreseeable future, the measure of Irish nationalism which the vast majority of Irish nationalists were content to settle for. What the rebellion and the executions did was to give the demand for Home Rule a new and desperate urgency which, when frustrated by Lloyd George's post-rebellion manoeuvres, burst its bounds.

The thinking of the vast majority of Irish nationalists in the late summer of 1916 went something as follows: A Home Rule Act for all Ireland,

* See below. p. 20. The contest was between an unofficial United Irish League candidate (pro-Redmond, pro-Home Rule), an All-For-Ireland League candidate (anti-Redmond, pro-Home Rule) and an unofficial All-For-Ireland League candidate who declared himself a Sinn Feiner, though opposed to physical force. (*Irish Independent*, 11, 15 November 1916.)

without any mention of separate treatment for any Ulster county, had been passed by Parliament and signed by the king two years before. Ireland's contribution to the war effort and not least her repudiation of the 1916 rebellion, which had been partly suppressed by Irish troops, gave her a moral right to have the Home Rule Act put into legal effect forthwith. (It had, after all, been agreed in 1914 to suspend it only for twelve months, or, if the duration of the war were longer, only until its end. Few had thought it would last so long.) The shedding of blood in the common cause was taken to have redeemed Ireland from any Amending Bill. But the only response her sacrifice had elicited from the government was an actual diminution of the Home Rule Act involving the exclusion of six Ulster counties and the repudiation of the basic nationalist idea of an undivided Ireland. In other words all the government offered was a simple return to the pre-war situation. Ireland's gesture for the common cause might just as well never have been made. Reasonable, however, as the Home Rule case might seem morally, it was wholly out of touch with current political reality. Ulster Unionists, as a result of the coalition, had a far stronger control over the government than they had ever had in 1914. And the susceptibilities or even the moral rights of Irish nationalism were not considerations in which they were interested. The only future for Irish nationalism in fact now lay in coming to terms with this reality one way or the other – either by accepting it with the sacrifice of six counties it entailed, or by working out clearly and precisely what contesting it would involve and deciding to accept that or not as the case might be. Very few Home Rulers had yet done this.

Meanwhile, Redmond's own continued preparedness to accept, for a 'temporary' phase, an exclusion of six Ulster counties strained far more seriously than ever before the ties of loyalty binding the movement to him as its leader. Indignant protests against the whole principle of partition now poured in from responsible local bodies and authoritative moderate nationalists all over Ireland. Disapproval came too from the many staunch Southern Unionists it threatened to isolate. The *Irish Times*, the leading organ of Unionist opinion in Ireland, while saying that the situation was so difficult that Home Rule must wait until the end of the war, had totally rejected the idea of a divided Ireland as any sort of possible solution. Unionists, it said, accepted that the Home Rule Act was on the statute book and realized they must accept the inevitable; they were 'patriotic Irishmen and intended to live in their country unless and until they were driven out by intolerable misgovernment'. But,

If we are to have self-government, Ireland must be a self-governing unit. That instinct is implanted deeply in the heart of every thoughtful Irishman, Unionist or Nationalist. In the first place the country is too small to be divided between two systems of government. In the next place, the political, social and economic qualities of North and South complement one another; one without the other must be miserably incomplete. For Southern Unionists ... the idea of the dismemberment of Ireland is hateful. ... In a word, the permanent partition of our country is inconceivable.[1]

If these were the feelings of Southern Unionists, those of Irish Nationalists of every description can well be imagined. As an orthodox Home Ruler had written, 'a thrill of horror and amazement' had been felt throughout the land at the new exclusion proposals.[2] He said that it was Redmond's lack of contact with opinion in Ireland that had already made possible 'the unholy alliance of Sinn Fein and Liberty Hall', but insisted that, should he now fail to save his reputation as leader, 'there are men enough left in Ireland still to carry on the constitutional fight, who, with God and justice on their side will act with courage and refuse at any cost, all and every invitation to compromise'.

Just over a week later this correspondent wrote again to the *Irish Independent* saying that the formation of some new organization in Ireland was imperative, and the following day another correspondent also called for a national organization for those Nationalists who had 'lost confidence in the leaders of the so-called Nationalist party'.

An 'Anti-Partition League' was formed and, on the day of Casement's execution, at the beginning of August 1916, it changed its name to the Irish Nation League. But there were as yet no new leaders to lead these newly-impassioned Home Rulers, some of whom in their anger were already beginning to enlarge their concept of what Home Rule should mean to 'Colonial Home Rule', or a position analogous to that of Canada or Australia within the Empire. Without leaders and without any precise new policy, a stronger popular nationalist spirit than ever before was now abroad. Spontaneous searching for a new policy and new methods began to take place at the grass roots of the old movement. 'People are beginning to think and act for themselves,' wrote the *Galway Observer*, unconsciously evoking again Davis's old slogan of Sinn Fein. And the *Mayo News*, independently and without any need of help from Griffith or Sinn Fein, said of the Nationalist Party that they 'would have been much better employed in the last month cutting turf at home than promenading in the House of Commons'. Indeed, the paper thought it might well be better for Ireland not to send her representatives there at all but rather to 'take a lesson from the Covenanters by binding our Parliamentary representatives to form themselves into a National Council to promote National interests without any regard to the antics of the Westminster Parliament'. The new Irish Nation League, said the paper, would have to decide whether or not Irish representatives should sit at Westminster.[3]

Throughout this new ferment Redmond had remained silent, and when he did finally choose to break his silence it was on 6 October, the anniversary of Parnell's death, a day inevitably evoking some comparisons with that earlier Home Rule leader's firmness and intransigence. Redmond's speech was embarrassingly unimpressive. He referred to his vigorous critics as 'about the vilest excrescence that ever yet appeared in the body politic in Ireland', and at the end of his speech ostentatiously tore up a list of questions that had been handed to him and threw the fragments on the floor.⁴ In what now seems an almost unbelievable failure to gauge the mood of the moment he complacently confided: 'Now I will tell you a secret about myself. For the last six weeks or two months I have been practically out of public life. I have been lying in the purple heather and trying to entice the wily trout out of the water, and trying to circumvent the still more wily grouse. I have really seen little of the newspapers.'⁵ He seemed totally unaware that the time had gone by when he could live off political capital like that. Three weeks later the expanding Irish Nation League promulgated in Dublin its constitution and objectives. Its first aim was 'to secure the National self-government of Ireland without any partition of the nation', and its provisional constitution declared that Irish MPs should 'if called on to do so, withdraw from Westminster'.

And yet some indication of the size of the political capital which Redmond and the old Parliamentary Party had accumulated over so many years was demonstrated the following month in the by-election at West Cork, the first since the rebellion. The result was actually a gain for the pro-Redmond candidate over the other (independent) Home Ruler, the narrow victory being made possible by the intervention of the self-styled Sinn Feiner. The significance of the result in the light of later developments undoubtedly lies in the strength revealed of Home Rule nationalism whether or not discontented with Redmond. In the course of the by-election the anti-Redmond candidate – F. J. Healy, one of Tim Healy's brothers – powerfully expressed the nature of anti-Redmond Home Rule sentiment at that time. Speaking of the 150,000 Irish soldiers (90,000 of them Catholics) who up to that date had served in the war, he declared: 'I glory in their fame. I take pride in their glory; but was it fair for a man who boasts himself leader of the Irish people not to tell these men on their way to Flanders, "I have blown the bugle for you, and when you come back, your country will have shrunk from thirty-two counties to twenty-six."?'⁶

Such representative indignation was easily enough expressed. It was less easy to see how the British Government could ever be persuaded to revert to that thirty-two county concept on which every Home Rule Bill had been based. It became less easy than ever the following month when, in a political crisis over the conduct of the war, Asquith was ousted as Prime Minister by Lloyd George, the very man who had given Carson the pledge of per-manent six-county exclusion. Carson himself entered the government. Walter

Long, the staunch Ulster Unionist supporter, became Colonial Secretary, and Curzon, Milner and Bonar Law, all of whom had urged Ulster resistance to the point of defiance of the constitution in 1914, became members of the War Cabinet.

Later in December the new Prime Minister, as a Christmas gesture of goodwill designed to encourage the Americans to enter the war, released those 560 rebellion prisoners who had not been specifically sentenced by court-martial, but were being held in Britain without trial. They were all back in Ireland by Christmas Day. Their release caused no great stir in Ireland though there were some cheers for them at the quayside and on arrival at their homes. Among those few who had been held in Reading gaol and who looked wan and sickly as a result was Arthur Griffith, the founder of the pre-war Sinn Fein organization. Most of the internees had been held at a camp at Frongoch in Wales, and were in good health. Among them was a young man of twenty-seven from West Cork named Michael Collins, of whom few people in Ireland had ever heard. He was disappointed to find that in Clonakilty, the town nearest his home, only two people wanted to shake him by the hand.[7]

Collins had started his career as a clerk in the British Civil Service and had lived in London for nine years until the beginning of 1916, latterly working as a bank clerk for an American company in the City. He had become a London member of the IRB in 1909, and, having got wind of the coming rising, and not wishing to be conscripted in England under the new Con-scription Act, had returned to Ireland in January 1916. He had taken part in the Rising and had been in the burning Post Office with the leaders to the end. In a letter from his prison camp at Frongoch in Wales a few months later, while expressing personal admiration for some of the leaders, especially Connolly and MacDermott, he strongly criticized the actual conduct of the Rising as being 'bungled terribly' and suffering from 'a great lack of very essential organization and cooperation'.[8] He was himself, within four years, to become the most effective organizer of armed rebellion in Irish history.

The political climate to which the prisoners returned had changed drama-tically since that day eight months before when they had been marched off to the Dublin quays, sometimes to the jeers, sometimes merely to the curious stares of the Irish people. But the returning men themselves could present as yet no clear-cut offer of leadership. Their views as to future policy varied considerably. They included exponents of the orthodox constitutional Sinn Fein doctrine of pre-war days as preached by Griffith; they included Irish Volunteers who had simply obeyed orders at Easter, but whose views were more accurately represented by MacNeill than by the signatories of the Republican Proclamation; they also included other Volunteers, many of them under-cover members of the IRB like Michael Collins, who were determined to bring about an Irish Republic at all costs. They had virtually no organization at all, apart from such reorganization of the IRB as had taken place at Frongoch with Collins's participation and that was by definition secret and aloof. Collins himself now became Secretary of the National Aid Association, a body which Tom Clarke's widow Katherine had organized on the prisoners' behalf while they were away and which provided a further temporary framework in which extremists could work. But nothing like a coherent political organization yet existed to coordinate the new mood.

However, an opportunity for political action very soon presented itself. J. J. O'Kelly, the old Member of Parliament for Roscommon who had first sounded out Parnell for John Devoy, had died. A by-election was due there at the beginning of February 1917. A candidate to stand against Redmond's man in the constituency was found in Count Plunkett (a Papal count), father of that Joseph Mary Plunkett who had been executed after the rebellion and of two other sons then in English gaols. The Count had himself just suffered the indignity of being expelled from the Royal Dublin Society for his sons' activities. It shows the confused and blurred nature of Irish nationalist opinion at this time that the man who defended him staunchly at the Royal Dublin Society and led the unsuccessful vote against expulsion was a supporter of his Redmondite opponent in the by-election.[9] Griffith, Collins and other returned prisioners threw themselves energetically into the election to try to capture anti-Redmond Home Rulers' votes for Plunkett.

Plunkett stood on no very clear policy at all, stating frankly that his claim on them was 'as the father of his dead boy and his two sons who were suffering penal servitude'.[10] Griffith was unable to persuade him to declare that if elected he would refuse to attend at Westminster and it was in fact urged on Plunkett's behalf, at one election meeting at least, that his return would not only be good for Ireland but for the Irish party's influence on English politics.[11] The nearest thing to a policy for Ireland that was put forward on his behalf was the argument that he would be the ideal man to represent Ireland at the International Peace Conference which would follow the war.[12] But the bulk of dissident Nationalist votes were concerned about only one thing: namely, voting *for* a man who would not accept the partition of Ireland in any form whatever, and *against* a party which had shown itself too easily duped into doing so.

A number of practical factors were to Plunkett's disadvantage. His opponent, the party candidate, was a local man well known in the constituency. Moreover, Plunkett himself, who had been deported after the rebellion, remained in England sick until only a few days before polling. It was here that the energy put into his campaign by Griffith and Collins and other recently released Irish Volunteers stood him in good stead. They had bad weather to contend with and much of the constituency was snow-bound. But there was a noticeable enthusiasm at many of Plunkett's meetings and the opinion on the eve of the poll was that he would win.

He won, but the size of his majority amazed everyone. He received almost twice as many votes as Redmond's man. It was only at a celebration rally after the result that Plunkett declared that he had been considering whether or not to represent the people of Roscommon 'in a foreign parliament', but had decided that his place was beside them in their own country, 'for it is in Ireland that the battle of Irish liberty is to be fought'. How exactly it was to be fought, no one was too particular to inquire. At the conclusion of the rally, the crowd sang Davis's old song: 'The West's Awake'.[13] Press comment throughout Ireland was to the effect that the writing was now on the wall for Redmond's party. Nevertheless, there was still no proper organization with which to oppose him. 'There now exists,' wrote Collins at about this time, 'a wilderness – ripe for any advancement along the road to salvation.'[14]

There were certainly some signs that the IRB itself was at work. On Easter Monday 1917 a Republican flag (the orange, white and green tricolour) was flown at half-mast over the ruins of the GPO, and many holiday-makers passing down O'Connell Street raised their hats to it or waved handkerchiefs. Small posters reproducing the wording of the 1916 Republican Proclamation appeared all over the city with the words at the bottom: 'The Irish Republic still lives.' The Dublin mob responded with a certain amount of haphazard stone-throwing at police and troops.[15] But if the party were going to be challenged on a nation-wide scale, and if that mass opinion which had shown itself ready to be wooed away at the Roscommon by-election was to be successfully wooed all over Ireland, something much more effective and politically mature than this sort of activity had to be devised.

Ten days after Easter an 'Irish Assembly' was convened by Count Plunkett at the Dublin Mansion House. Over 1,200 delegates attended, and sixty-eight public bodies were represented, together with forty-one of Griffith's Sinn Fein clubs. The dominating note struck was the need to submit Ireland's case to the Peace Conference at the end of the war and to form some sort of organization for the next General Election. However, the most that could be practically agreed about such a future organization was that an organizing committee should be formed to establish it. At the same time there was an affirmation proclaiming Ireland a separate nation and asserting her right to freedom from all foreign control and denying the authority of any foreign parliament in Ireland.

This was, of course, taking the Irish national demand far beyond the Home Rule Act on the statute book. It might reasonably have been wondered how a British Government, which would not even agree to implementing that act without excluding six Ulster counties, was going to be brought to accept a far wider measure of independence without the same exclusion.

But the prevailing mood was not one to be precise about the future. In so far as doubts arose, they were generally silenced by the notion that an international Peace Conference summoned to conclude the war for the rights of small nations would impose its will on Britain to give Ireland the freedom she demanded. Certainly there was a total refusal to accept publicly even the possibility that physical force against the British Government might be required.

The *Irish Independent*, Ireland's biggest daily newspaper, which while deploring the rebellion and standing for Home Rule had long dissociated itself from Redmond, loosely referred to the men who had met in the Assembly as 'what is now known as the Sinn Fein party'. But a party organization and, more important, detailed policy, still had to be constructed. Meanwhile, the *Independent* itself gave an example of the prevailing mood of imprecise and optimistic thinking among nationalists. For it too extended its own national aims from the limited Home Rule of the act on the statute book to 'Colonial Home Rule' on the Canadian or Australian pattern. Again, it was not made clear how a British government which could not accept the lesser measure without partitioning the country could ever be brought to accept the greater. The paper was even less precise than Sinn Fein, going so far as to repudiate specifically the nearest thing the new 'Sinn Fein' grouping had to a constructive policy, namely that of abstention from Westminster. Plunkett had now declared this to be an indispensable commitment for all members of such new organization as might form his committee.

In this imprecise and optimistic national mood a further electoral test now presented itself – a by-election at Longford. Here the candidate chosen by Plunkett's committee, with the organizing experience of the Roscommon election behind them, was not even one who was able, as Plunkett had been, to put in an appearance at the last moment. For he was Joe MacGuinness, at the time a prisoner serving penal servitude in Lewes gaol for his part in the rebellion, and his name went before the electorate in the simple slogan: 'Put him in to get him out!'

MacGuinness, a Longford IRB man, had no wish to let his name go forward in the election at all. He felt that to do so would be to compromise the traditional republican attitude of contempt for parliamentary methods. And his refusal to stand was backed up by almost all his fellow-prisoners in Lewes gaol.[16] Michael Collins, however, in the interests of strengthening the Republican hold over the developing political movement, blandly ignored MacGuinness's refusal and went ahead with the election campaign on his behalf. Collins's preoccupation as a Republican at this time was with the need to preserve the new political movement from the relatively moderate ideas of Arthur Griffith, with whom he had been having some 'fierce rows'.[17] He now implored his only supporter among the prisoners in Lewes, Thomas Ashe, the rebel commander in the fight at Ashbourne in 1916, not to let them think that 'Master A.G. is going to turn us all into eighty-two-ites'.*

In fact, many old-style Sinn Fein devotees worked hard together with Griffith and Collins in the Longford election. Collins himself made use of his IRB control over the re-forming Volunteers to provide a body of enthusiastic campaign workers to rival the Redmond party machine. But perhaps the most decisive and, for the future, a most significant intervention on Mac-Guinness's behalf came from another quarter. It came in the form of a letter to the press on the eve of polling day from the Archbishop of Dublin, Dr W. J. Walsh himself. The Archbishop solemnly warned anyone who thought that partition had been abandoned as practical policy by the politicians that he was living in a fool's paradise.[18] Between two candidates, one of whom represented Redmond and the other of whom was in Lewes gaol, there could thus be little doubt as to who the Archbishop preferred. The new movement, embryonic, imprecise and even self-contradictory as it might be, now had all the indispensable respectability of the Catholic Church behind it.

The electrifying result of the by-election after a recount was that MacGuinness had won by thirty-eight votes over the Redmond candidate. Flags, illuminations, bonfires, blazing tar barrels and the singing of national songs took place all over Ireland in celebration of the victory.

A few days later the British Government and Redmond made one more attempt to reach an agreement over the Irish national demand. Redmond's political manoeuvrability had now been considerably circumscribed by the prevailing mood in Ireland. Clearly he could no longer afford to consider partition on any terms, and when the first half of Lloyd George's new offer proved to be one again involving exclusion of the six north-west counties of Ulster – to be reconsidered after a period of five years – Redmond had no alternative but to reject it out of hand. But the second instalment of Lloyd George's offer broke new ground. It had actually originated in a proposal of Redmond's.

Redmond, in rejecting partition this time, had let it be known that in his view the only hope was some sort of conference or convention at which Irishmen of both North and South should by themselves work out their own solution. Picking up this suggestion Lloyd George declared that if such a convention could reach 'substantial agreement' then he would accept whatever the terms of that substantial agreement might be. It was a tailor-made Lloyd George formula, combining surface plausibility with apparent concession while throwing the onus of success on to other shoulders than his own. Appearances were then of particular importance to Lloyd George, for with the United States at last entering the war in April 1917, it was urgently necessary, as the British Ambassador in Washington constantly reminded

*i.e., believers in the 1782 Constitution of King, Lords and Commons of Ireland.

him, to make the American contribution effective by showing that the war really was one for the sanctity of engagements and the independence of small nations.[19]

But beneath the surface plausibility, the chances of success for the convention, which was to meet in Dublin from July 1917 to April 1918, never looked bright. From the start, the two positions which needed to be reconciled – those of the Ulster Unionists and of all Irish nationalists – were totally irreconcilable. The government had driven Redmond up to and possibly beyond his farthest practical limit of concession long ago in 1914; it was now virtually impossible that he could carry Irish opinion with him on any form of exclusion of Ulster counties, however limited in time and place. At the same time, with Carson and so many other staunch Unionists in the government, the government was less than ever in any position to force any further concession from the Ulster Unionists beyond the abandonment of the three Ulster counties they had so reluctantly agreed to in 1916.*

The only possible room for manoeuvre left lay between the Nationalists and the Southern Unionists. The Southern Unionists did not want partition, partly on patriotic principle, and partly out of self-interest, for they did not wish to find themselves overwhelmingly isolated in a Catholic Ireland. It was Redmond's one remaining hope that if he could reach agreement with their leader, Lord Midleton, Southern Unionists themselves might bring pressure on the Ulster Unionists to abandon their inflexible attitude. Alternatively, it was possible that if agreement were reached between Redmond and the Southern Unionists, Lloyd George might interpret this as sufficiently close to 'substantial agreement' to put pressure himself on the Ulster Unionists to close the final gap.

But before the convention could get down to its deliberations a further event occurred to make them seem blighted.

Another by-election was pending, this time in East Clare, and another of the 1916 prisoners was selected as the Sinn Fein candidate to stand against Redmond's man there. This prisoner was the last of the surviving commandants of Easter Week, Eamon de Valera, whose death-sentence had been commuted to twenty years' imprisonment. The very day after it was announced that he would be standing, de Valera was included in an amnesty along with the 117 remaining other prisoners of Easter Week – an amnesty granted as a gesture of goodwill by the Lloyd George Government to create a favourable climate for the convention.[20]

This time, often to their amazement, the released prisoners received a rapturous welcome in Ireland. They were escorted through the streets of

---

* In fact, in the same month in which Carson joined the government, Lloyd George and the rest of the cabinet had been prepared to put Home Rule for all Ireland into effect at once with the sole proviso of a further review of the situation in five years' time. The proposal was vetoed by Carson; Lloyd George promptly dropped it.

Dublin by enthusiastic crowds. cheering and waving small orange, white and green tricolours.[21] The *Westmeath Independent* noted that 'Sinn Fein. whatever it may ultimately end in, for the present has caught the fancy of the country. Sinn Fein clubs are springing up as mushrooms.'

One specific thing at least which 'Sinn Fein' stood for was made clear by de Valera, who got down to electioneering in East Clare the day after his return. It was not himself they were supporting, he declared. but the principle for which he stood – the complete independence and liberty of Ireland.[22] Both he and MacNeill who campaigned for him totally repudiated Lloyd George's 'Convention'. How precisely 'Sinn Fein' intended to bring Ireland's complete independence and liberty about was left vague. De Valera's opponent in Clare, a popular local man named Lynch, in fact challenged him to say whether he was for the policy of revolution or for what was known as constitutional Sinn Fein. What, he demanded, was his alternative to a programme involving violence? And a speaker campaigning for Lynch in Ennis chided the Sinn Feiners with the 'audacity' of asking the electors to endorse a policy that was not yet formulated. But that, of course, was a large part of 'Sinn Fein's' attraction. The disgruntled electors themselves were not too clear where they wanted to go. and audacity was about all they demanded.

Griffith, speaking at a Westmeath Sinn Fein Convention during the Clare election, made the chief issue whether to seek for Ireland's independence at the inevitable post-war Peace Conference or in the English Parliament. This, he said, would be the main issue at the next general election.[23] The idea of appealing above the British Government's head to an International Peace Conference was indeed a sweepingly idealistic one suitable to the prevailing Irish mood. But de Valera, electioneering in Clare, kept even vaguer options open. They were not dependent on the Peace Conference alone, he said at Corofin on 1 July, '... they expected something good from it, but while waiting they would be able to do a good deal in making John Bull uncomfortable'.[24] Some days later, however, he complained that his opponents were trying to frighten the voters by saying he meant to lead the young men into an abortive rebellion and declared that the formation of a representative National Council to select delegates to the Peace Conference was the immediate political task. He told how a voter had said to him:

'Mr de Valera, I would vote for you but for fear you are going out in rebellion in a week or two!'

He replied: 'Can anyone be so stupid as to believe that?' adding that there was no fear of another Easter Week as it had accomplished its purpose.[25] The policy of abstention from Westminster was little mentioned.

The tall, austere, bespectacled figure of the young de Valera quickly impressed the Clare electorate personally, though almost all they knew about him was his record in the rebellion of the year before. Additional glamour attached to him from two small incidents during the campaign. Once narrowly escaping a collision between his motor-car and a runaway horse and trap, he jumped out and gave chase and captured the animal. On another occasion he gave prompt assistance to the occupants of a trap whose restless horse was threatening to overturn them.[26]

Two special features of the campaign were remarked. The first was the conspicuous number of young and middle-aged priests attending de Valera meetings; it was to one of these that an English correspondent heard an old farmer put the question: 'Is there another rising in the air, Father?'

To which the priest replied with great seriousness: 'God forbid, Pat! We want no more bloodshed and we won't have it.'[27]

The second feature of de Valera's campaign was the excellence of the Irish Volunteer organization which supported him. On polling day Sinn Fein had a large number of motor-cars at its disposal and Volunteers from other districts entered the constituency to help escort Sinn Fein voters to the polls – a precaution which paid off, for a number of attacks with sticks and stones were made by Redmond's supporters on the occupants of Sinn Fein cars, and the *Irish Independent* reckoned there would have been bloodshed but for the Sinn Feiners' restraint.

The most optimistic Sinn Fein forecasts of the result were that from the electorate of eight thousand de Valera might get a majority of about one thousand. Such would have been a remarkable victory indeed. In fact the result was a landslide, giving de Valera a majority of almost three thousand over the Redmondite candidate.*

The *Cork Examiner* described it as the most surprising result since the ballot had been instituted. De Valera, appearing on the steps of the court-house at Ennis in Volunteer uniform, told the huge crowd waving Republican flags: 'You are worthy descendants of the Claremen who fought under Brian Boru, with the same spirit in your hearts today that your fathers had a thousand years ago!'

In paying a tribute to those who had helped organize the campaign, he echoed the sort of ambivalent language that O'Connell had employed on the occasion of another famous Clare election. Of the Volunteer effort he said they had showed they could have a little military organization, and 'these habits of discipline and organization were worth more for a nation than anything else'.[28]

In Dublin the news of the result was received with wild enthusiasm. Hand-kerchiefs were waved, walking-sticks and hats flung in the air, and motor

---

* The figures were: de Valera 5,010
Lynch 2,035

S.F. majority 2,975
Eighty-seven per cent of the electorate voted.

and horse traffic brought to a standstill.[29] The rejoicings throughout the rest of Ireland were, according to the *Irish Independent*, 'unprecedented in the history of Irish political contests'.[30] Symbolic of the deep emotional springs that were touched by the event was a pietistic visit by Carlow Sinn Feiners to the croppies' grave there.*[31]

* See *The Most Distressful Country*, Volume 1 of *The Green Flag*, p. 103.

3

The New Sinn Fein
(July 1917–April 1918)

Precision about the exact political future was still comfortably avoided. In personally pinning his colours to an Irish Republic, de Valera seemed to do so undogmatically.

'Until the Irish people declare that another form of government is more suitable,' he said at Mullingar soon after his victory, 'the Irish Republic is the form of government that the Sinn Feiners will give allegiance to.'[1] And though Redmondite Nationalists might complain with reason that when 'asked to say in simple words how the Irish Republic is to be raised on the ruins of the British Empire, he takes refuge in vague and impalpable generalities',[2] his argument that for Ireland's case to be heard at the Peace Conference she should first claim total independence seemed reasonably flexible to many old Home Rulers. The dominant political note of the day after the East Clare election was that Ireland was declaring for 'independence' not by revolution but by resort to the Peace Conference. As to what 'independence' itself actually meant to most new Sinn Fein supporters a writer in the *Irish Independent* of 14 July 1917 was accurate in saying that at that time 'Dominion Home Rule within the Empire would be accepted with practical unanimity by Nationalists and possibly a substantial section of Unionists would also vote for it'. The correspondent of the *Westminster Gazette*, analysing the East Clare election result, wrote that while the young genuinely did want total independence, the older voters did not think it feasible but had been content to vote for it, arguing that 'the more they ask for the more likely they are to get "Colonial Home Rule", a phrase now common in the mouths of moderate Irishmen everywhere – even in Unionist circles'.[3] He added that the Sinn Fein policy of abstentionism from Westminster hadn't really worried moderates at all, because the Irish party at Westminster had proved so totally ineffective against a combination of the two British parties anyway. He predicted, incidentally, that there would be no split between the de Valera–Volunteer type of Sinn Fein and the Griffith–Plunkett type until after the end of the war.

And if any moderate Irishman, disillusioned with Redmond, should momentarily raise an eyebrow at the way in which young men at the end of Sinn Fein meetings increasingly arranged themselves in military forma- tions and marched off in fours singing national songs into the countryside, he could find reassurance enough in de Valera's definition of the recon- structed Volunteer body's task, namely that they would be 'the best protec- tion that England could not come and rob them' of their rights.' This was, after all, the very purpose behind the mass Volunteer movement of 1914 in which all ardent Home Rulers had joined after the Curragh mutiny. And when at the beginning of August 1917 Colonel Maurice Moore again pre- sided over an Irish National Volunteer Convention of 176 companies in Dublin, he called for a healing of the split of three years before and a reconciliation with the Irish Volunteers, implying that it was logically one movement again. The reality of his contention received some substantiation from the British Government ten days later when the Irish National Volun- teer headquarters in Parnell Square, Dublin, were raided together with Catholic halls all over the country, and the rifles and other arms in them seized. The arms of the Ulster Volunteer Force in the North were, of course, not touched, and the *Irish Independent* remarked: 'This fact like the immun- ity enjoyed by the UVF in the past is setting people furiously to think.' If there was to be one law for the Unionist and a different law for the Nation- alist, it seemed all the more logical for all Nationalists to be in the same boat.

The result of yet another by-election, this time in Kilkenny, declared just before the raids, had shown a further consolidation of the new nationalist front. The Sinn Fein candidate, William Cosgrave, had been fairly confidently expected to win, but even so it had hardly been expected that his victory, which turned out to be a two-to-one majority, would be so decisive, and once again there were enthusiastic celebrations in many parts of Ireland involving Volunteer parades and the singing of national songs in which the song of the 1916 rebels, 'The Soldier's Song', increasingly figured.

The increasing efficiency and self-confidence of the newly reconstructed Volunteers was indeed beginning to disconcert the authorities. Predictable counter-measures were set in motion by them with the inevitable result of increasing their prestige among all Nationalists still further. Arrests for drilling began. Austin Stack, the commandant of the Tralee Volunteers, who, faithfully observing orders, had failed to rescue Casement from his police cell in the town the year before, was arrested and sentenced to two years' hard labour for wearing Volunteer uniform at a demonstration at Ardfert on the first anniversary of Casement's execution. Three thousand Volunteers of whom two hundred were on bicycles and three hundred on horses had attended the ceremony and the road from Tralee to Ardfert had been thronged all day, with orange, white and green colours visible every- where. Sean MacEntee, the former Redmond supporter sentenced to death after the rebellion, was now court-martialled for a recent speech at Drogheda in which he, however, maintained he had simply advocated peaceful means to obtain a Republic, telling the meeting that Ireland's status would be recognized at the Peace Conference and that any further resort to violence and rebellion would not be necessary.[5] Also re-arrested at this time, for a speech at Longford, was Collins's associate, Thomas Ashe, who after his release with all the other 1916 prisoners in June had been elected President of the Supreme Council of the IRB.[6] By the middle of September 1917 there were over thirty such Volunteers, or Sinn Fein prisoners, in Mountjoy gaol serving sentences from six months to two years for drilling or making so-called seditious speeches.

The Volunteers were controlled, in so far as they were centrally controlled at all, by their own executive which included Collins and the reconstituted IRB machinery. But more often than not they acted with local individual spontaneity, and they now lent assistance to the new political movement in a form even more valuable than the practical organization they had been supplying at elections. They began to provide martyrs. For the repression they invited from the authorities aroused old emotional springs of Irish nationalism at the very moment when the mass of public opinion might otherwise have paused and wondered whether there really was anything coherent enough to follow in the new leaders after all. A number of contemporary political commentators had already noted that Sinn Fein's failure to produce a really positive national policy was giving rise to serious second thoughts.[7] But it was at this very moment that something happened to swing sympathy towards Sinn Fein more markedly than ever before.

The prisoners in Mountjoy gaol, curiously perhaps in view of the Sinn Fein insistence that there was no need for a further resort to arms, were demanding for themselves treatment as 'prisoners of war'. An explanation was that since no such special status as 'political prisoner' was recognized by the authorities, 'prisoner of war' was the only recognizable status by which they could be distinguished from common criminals. The prison authorities adhered strictly to their own regulations which recognized no distinction between anyone sentenced by the courts and placed in their custody. The Volunteer prisoners, however, refused to work or wear prison clothes and eventually, after some smashing of cell windows and organized singing of national songs, resorted to the old suffragette weapon of the hunger strike. The prison authorities again applied their own regulations and began what was officially described as 'artificial' or forcible feeding. Some forty prisoners were soon being subjected to the procedure. Large protest meetings were addressed in Dublin by de Valera, by Cathal Brugha, recovered from his wounds of Easter week, and by Griffith who did not hesitate to make clear in the course of them that he had disapproved of the rebellion.[8]

The warders in Mountjoy were not brutal, but did their duty. The practice of regulation forcible feeding involved the strapping of a prisoner to a chair at the elbows and below the knees, the placing of an eighteen-inch rubber tube either via the mouth, or if the prisoner refused to open his mouth, via the nostrils down his throat and the pumping of two eggs beaten up in a pint of warm milk into the stomach by some twenty to thirty strokes of a stomach pump.[9] The whole business took between five and ten minutes. The prisoner usually vomited at first when the tube went down his throat. If fed through the nostrils, the nose and throat invariably bled.

Austin Stack, then the official leader of the prisoners in Mountjoy, thus described at the time what happened to him personally on Tuesday, 25 September, at the hands of the doctor in charge that day. This doctor was by all accounts more than usually maladroit.

He got the tube down eventually. I was unable to see as water was running from my eyes, and with the pain and a kind of vomiting I could not see what was going on. When he took up the tube I vomited about a quarter of a pint of liquid. I thought I had been fed then; when the doctor came again and asked me to open my mouth I said, 'What for? Haven't I been fed?' He said: 'No, not yet.'

While the doctor made another attempt, Stack thought he 'seemed to be using more force than skill, grinding his teeth practically'. His finger reached down his throat almost to his neck. When the operation had been completed Stack heard a warder call out. 'Ashe next'.[10]

Thomas Ashe had spent fifty hours the previous week deprived of his boots, bed and bedding as a punishment for insubordination. However, the prison medical officer had passed him as fit: '... fit for close confinement, fit for scale punishment no. 1 and 2. Also deprivation of mattress, fit for restraint in handcuffs, waist belt, muffs, restraint jacket or jacket in splints.'[11] Ashe had first been forcibly fed on Sunday, the 23rd, when like every other prisoner he found the experience very unpleasant and painful. He told the doctor he was sorry to see him reducing a noble profession to the level of an executioner. Stack had given orders to the prisoners not to resist the operation physically. The only struggle was between the doctor and the tube. When Ashe was released from the chair after following Stack on Tuesday, 25 September, he felt ill and weak and another doctor, meeting him on his way back to his cell, allowed him to be released at once to the Mater Hospital. Within hours he was dead.

At the autopsy a bruise was found on his neck, presumably evidence of the clumsiness of the feeding doctor's exertions. Grazes and scratches also found on his cheeks were probably caused when his beard was shaved after death. The coroner's jury – which contained a number of Unionists – eventually found that Ashe had died of heart failure and congestion of the lungs, and condemned forcible feeding as 'inhuman and dangerous'.[12] Every detail of what had been done to Ashe and was being done to the other prisoners could be read by the public in the inquest reports in the newspapers.

Arrangements for Ashe's funeral were made by Michael Collins and the IRB through their cover organization, the long-standing Wolfe Tone Memorial Committee, and the occasion was made one in the tradition of the great patriotic funerals of the past: T. B. McManus, Parnell and Rossa. In fact it was generally admitted that the funeral was even more impressive than Parnell's. After Ashe's body had lain in state the day before in the City Hall, from which troops were removed for the first time since the rebellion and replaced by Volunteer guards in uniform, and where last respects were paid to Ashe by a large Volunteer contingent headed by de Valera and a group of the Citizen Army led by Constance Markievicz, the funeral took place at Glasnevin cemetery on 30 September 1917.

Almost all Dublin was in mourning, and a procession estimated at between 30,000 and 40,000 followed the coffin through the crowded streets, the hearse itself being flanked by Volunteers in uniform with rifles reversed. Immediately behind it came about 150 clergy, then 8,000 members of the Irish Transport Workers' Union, 10,000 members of various trades bodies, 9,000 Irish Volunteers, most of them in uniform and, of some significance in denoting the unanimity of the reaction of Irish Nationalist opinion to Ashe's death, a large body of the Irish National Volunteers, previously Redmond supporters, under Colonel Moore. Constance Markievicz led a Citizen Army contingent, wearing full uniform with a revolver in her belt. Orange, white and green colours were extensively worn, even by the Dublin Fire Brigade. At the cemetery three volleys were fired over the grave by a Volunteer firing party and Collins delivered the only funeral oration. It was a very short one. After a few words in Irish he said, 'Nothing additional remains to be said. That volley which we have just heard is the only speech which it is proper to make over the grave of a dead Fenian.'[13]

The efficiency and order displayed throughout the proceedings were remarkable evidence of Collins's organizing ability. The various Volunteer contingents from many parts of Ireland drilled freely and marched in military formations to and from their various assembly points in defiance of all the regulations and regardless of the presence of the police. A film taken of the volleys fired over the graveside by the Volunteers was developed in motors on the way back to the city and was on view in Dublin the same night. The whole event testified strikingly to the growing power, both emotional and material, of the new movement.

The day of the funeral de Valera, speaking at Ennis, recalled the dead man's role at Ashbourne the year before and allowed himself to strike his most belligerent note since his release. Nothing but freedom, he said, would satisfy the Irish people and they were ready to perish one after the other rather than submit to be conquered. 'I feel as certain as I stand here that I shall see, before my day comes, Ireland free!'[14]

All commentators agreed that a new and much-needed stimulus had been given to the Sinn Fein movement. 'The circumstances of his [Ashe's] death and funeral', wrote the London *Daily Express*, 'have made 100,000 Sinn Feiners out of 100,000 constitutional nationalists.' The *Daily Mail* remarked that a month earlier Sinn Fein, despite its success at the by-elections, had been a waning force. 'It had no real practical programme, for the programme of going farther than anyone else cannot be so described. It was not making headway.... Sinn Fein today is pretty nearly another name for the vast bulk of the youth of Erin.'

Because of the war and the abrupt drop in emigration, there was a far higher proportion of that youth in Ireland than there had been for generations.

While the Volunteers grew bolder in public – 1,500 of them parading and marching through Cork with officers and many of the rank and file wearing uniforms and bandoliers – the political half of the movement set out to give itself a more plausible coherence at a great convention in Dublin at the end of October 1917. It was attended by about two thousand people, including delegates from over a thousand Sinn Fein clubs. All it really revealed was a commendable degree of professional skill in political management. Where a contest had been anticipated between de Valera, Count Plunkett and Griffith for the presidency of the new Sinn Fein organization which was here formally constituted, all the public saw was a display of brotherly sweetness and light as both Plunkett and Griffith stood down by agreement in de Valera's favour. The formal Sinn Fein constitution revealed itself as no more free of unresolved ambiguities than the movement had been since its inception. But it was to Sinn Fein's advantage to offer as vague and wide a political platform as possible. Thus, while it was known that Sinn Fein stood for 'total independence' and de Valera himself and many of his Volunteer comrades for a Republic, the wording of the new constitution was designed to placate moderates when it declared that Sinn Fein aimed 'at seeing the international recognition of Ireland as an independent Republic, and, having achieved that status, the people might by referendum, choose their own form of Government, when they would deny the right of the British, or other foreign Government to legislate for Ireland'.

A further aim was 'to make use of every available means to make impotent the power of England to hold Ireland in subjugation by military force or otherwise'. This significantly produced one of the few discordant notes in the meeting.

One of the several priests present moved an amendment to this part of the constitution to the effect that after the words 'every available means' should be added the words 'which in the judgement of the National Council are deemed legitimate and effective'. As the rule stood, he said, it might cover anything 'from pitch and toss to manslaughter' and they did not want Sinn Fein sullied by 'any crime or outrage'.[15]

This touched on the most awkward area in the minds of many who, while prepared to vote for Sinn Fein, feared that some of the Volunteer activists in the movement would lead Ireland into fresh violence. Another priest seconded the amendment, saying it was a slander to say, as some people did, that they were a secret society.

Now the movement had just benefited from a great access of public support, largely thanks to the discipline and organizing ability of a secret society deep in the heart of it, though this fact was, of course, unknown to all but a handful in that convention hall. And Collins and other IRB men and Volunteers had no squeamishness whatever about any methods that might be required to win an Irish Republic. But the majority of the Convention's opinion was almost certainly behind the sense of the two priests' amendment. For when voting took place for the twenty-four members of the Sinn Fein executive council MacNeill, who had opposed the rebellion of the year before and believed that the Volunteers should resort to violence only in their own defence, easily headed the poll by more than two hundred votes over his closest rival, the more uncompromising Cathal Brugha. Collins, himself not yet widely known, only just scraped on to the council in twenty-fourth place.[16]

De Valera's first major political task therefore was to placate the moderate majority in his movement while leaving as free a hand as possible to those who gave that movement effectiveness and practical organization. Now in the cooperative mood of this first convention the two priests' amendment presented him with no very severe test. He declared righteously that they were not going to truckle to anyone who insinuated such things as that they were really a secret society.[17] And inasmuch as de Valera himself now saw no need for the IRB, and declined to remain a member of it after the rebellion, this was an honest expression of intent, though he must have known something of the extent of Collins's activity and have been aware of its value to the movement.

He kept a wary option open, however, on the use of violence itself, adding that 'available means' meant 'justly available in the minds of all Irishmen'. Cathal Brugha followed him in reply to the amendment. Brugha also disapproved of further use of the IRB, on the grounds that now that there was an open Republican party, with its open Republican army (the Volunteers), secrecy was unnecessary and dangerous. But he was in fact as implacable in his belief in unsanctioned violence as any Fenian who had ever sworn allegiance to an Irish republic, as his record the year before proved. Nevertheless, he now echoed the overall mood of the conference by saying that they did not intend to meet English rule by assassination.[18] The Sinn Fein

Convention concluded in an impressive display of superficial unanimity with the Chairman, Griffith, maintaining that they would never break the moral law, and a tumult of cheering greeting MacNeill's election to the Council at the head of the poll.

A few days later de Valera was telling a meeting at Baillieboro' that there were no differences in Sinn Fein. 'They were all out for one and the same thing – to get international recognition for a free and independent Republic. The methods ... were any methods and means in accordance with the moral law and the will of the Irish people.' On the question of physical force he maintained that Irishmen had a perfect right to arm and defend themselves against any attempt to impose conscription on Ireland:

> Nothing would please John Bull better than that they should put it into their minds that physical force in any shape or form was morally wrong. ... As to the word 'constitutional', they had no Constitution of Ireland. The English Constitution was not theirs and they were out against it. What he understood as Constitutionalism was that they should act in accordance with the will of the Irish people and the moral law. Their movement was constitutional in that sense.[19]

With such skilled ambivalence did the new movement more or less successfully conceal for the time being its crucial discrepancies.

As a self-sufficient organization the Volunteers held a convention of their own, at the same time as the Sinn Fein Convention. Further to convey an impression of unified identity for the whole Sinn Fein movement, de Valera was elected President of the Volunteers as well as of Sinn Fein, while Brugha, Sinn Fein's Vice-President, was made Chief of Staff. But the unity was far more apparent than real. Brugha himself was a split personality in his dual role. For all his moderation towards a Sinn Fein Convention he was always to regard the Volunteers as an instrument for wresting an Irish Republic from England by physical force. Furthermore Collins, with identical views, was now officially made the Volunteers' Director of Organization. And utilizing the IRB network which Brugha thought redundant, Collins was increasingly to become the effective force in the central control of the Volunteers, placing other competent activists in key posts.

A letter for which Collins and the Volunteer Executive had been responsible a few months earlier caused some embarrassment when it came to light in the late autumn of 1917, inducing a critical priest from Wexford to raise that question which, he said, every man and woman in Ireland should ask themselves, namely: 'What does Sinn Fein stand for?'

'The principle duty of the executive,' this Volunteer executive letter dated 22 May 1917 had declared, 'is to put them [the Volunteers] in a position to complete by force of arms the work begun by the men of Easter Week ... the Volunteers are notified that the only orders they are to obey are those of their own executive.' They were reminded that in the past the conjunction of Fenianism with constitutional politics had led to the abandonment of physical force as a policy and were warned to join Sinn Fein only in order to propagate the principles of their own organization which was the only one to which they owed allegiance.[20]

De Valera applied himself to this difficulty with that evergrowing combination of dexterity and single-minded integrity which was to be his particular political talent. He pointed out with technical correctness that the letter had not been written by the present executive and that he had himself been in Lewes gaol at the time, but then added typically that there was in fact nothing in that document that he himself would not put his name to and that it was Sinn Fein's own policy to proclaim that only sovereign independence would satisfy the aspirations of the Irish people.[21] The need to discuss the crucial issue of physical force was thus somehow obviated.

Within the Volunteer movement itself there was little doubt both among the organizers and the younger and active rank and file that physical force would in the proper time be used to assert Ireland's sovereign independence. Sinn Feiners who were not Volunteers were sneered at.[22] To reassure opinion de Valera would himself point out in public that the Volunteers were a completely distinct and separate organization from Sinn Fein, as if this and his own dual role somehow clarified rather than obscured the political future. But the truth was that the situation carried real dangers. The Volunteers themselves, drilling, studying manuals of British field tactics, starting up their own local companies quite independently of any central organization, even unashamedly shocking the local Sinn Fein supporters by their audacity, were going their own way from early 1917 onwards, sometimes unamenable even to their own executive's discipline in Dublin.[23]

De Valera's attempt to reassure public opinion over the opaqueness of the political future was by no means wholly successful. The Irish correspondent of the *Westminster Gazette* commented that any Irish Parliament would split into several groups and that 'of the Sinn Fein voters at elections there are a large number who deprecate under any circumstances, barring attempted conscription, a resort to armed force'.[24] Cardinal Logue warned that 'an agitation ill-considered and Utopian' had sprung up and was spreading, and that if persevered in it would 'entail present suffering, disorganization and danger and is sure to end in future disaster, defeat and collapse'.[25] To redress the balance de Valera strove to win over more constitutional Nationalists by saying that though some who lived for their national interests might still feel bound up with the British Empire, this was no reason not to agree to differ about ways and means with other Nationalists and still march shoulder to shoulder with them.[26] But *The Times* noted that in Mr de Valera's 'scholastic hands' Sinn Fein was losing much of its political force.[27] And a correspondent wrote to the *Irish Independent* warning of the consequences of Sinn Fein trying to win Irish independence on the field of battle, saying that it could not be done, but would bring upon Ireland 'dire misfortune and untold horrors, and ruin and devastation, and the demon of civil strife'.[28]

From the beginning of 1918 raids for arms by independent groups of Volunteers began to be reported from different parts of the country. At the end of January a stud farm near Bansha in County Tipperary was raided by about twenty masked men calling for 'arms for the Irish army', but otherwise behaving in a scrupulously correct manner, taking neither valuables nor money and apologizing to the owner's secretary.[29] A month later more masked men – including one of Count Plunkett's surviving sons – cleared the armoury and one thousand rounds of ammunition from Rockingham House near Boyle. Other Volunteers had long been buying or stealing individually British service rifles from individual British (often Irish) soldiers. In February 1918, a new activity loosely carried out under the auspices of Sinn Fein but recalling more ancient aspects of the Irish struggle began to disturb many moderates in the movement.

In the name of necessary precautions against famine, parties of men in the countryside, but particularly in the west of Ireland, began driving cattle off private grass land and commandeering it in the name of the Irish Republic and ploughing it up for food cultivation. Compensation was offered to the landlord and was often agreed, but where there was a dispute the last word tended to lie with whoever could produce the bigger battalions. Ironically, one such dispute took place on the land of the first ever President of Sinn Fein, Edward Martyn, the friend of Yeats and Lady Gregory, at Tulyra in County Galway. Martyn got an injunction from the courts to prevent local Sinn Feiners ploughing up his land after he had freely offered them one field which they had turned down as unsuitable.[30] Evidence that there were stronger, more independent forces at work in this activity than those merely of the Sinn Fein political movement was revealed when the Standing Committee of Sinn Fein, after conceding that most cattle drives were 'no doubt justifiable', declared that some had taken place without due regard to the circumstances and that 'foolish or indiscreet action' was to be deplored. By the end of the month County Clare had to be declared a special military area and the town of Ennis itself was under curfew with troops lining the streets.

Not only the government but the local Sinn Fein Executives themselves tried, increasingly in vain, to keep things under some sort of control. But a lawlessness reminiscent of the old days of the Land League or even the Defenders was soon rife in that part of Ireland. Offences up before the Clare Grand Jury at the beginning of March included cattle-driving, raids for arms, ploughing-up of poor people's land, firing into houses and intimidation. Two men in Kerry were even arrested under the old Whiteboy Act. And a man living with his wife and child in a remote part of County Roscommon woke to find that a warning grave had been dug on his land.[31]

Though some of this activity gained crude popular support for the movement and sympathy for the Volunteers in the countryside – crudest when, as in a few cases, individuals were actually able to help themselves to land – the growing signs of anarchical violence were an embarrassment to Sinn Fein and a liability to its attempts to woo moderate but disgruntled Home Rulers. At the beginning of March the headquarters staff of the Volunteers had directed not only that the raiding of houses for odd guns was strictly prohibited but that Volunteers should not take part in cattle drives as such because these were 'neither of a national or a military character'.[32] A week later Collins himself, speaking in County Longford, expressly stated that the raids on homesteads by Sinn Fein or Volunteers were not only not sanctioned but carried out in direct opposition to the leaders. But the rest of his reproof was hardly an assurance to the moderates. If, he said, the Volunteers wanted arms they would not have to resort to such methods of raiding farmhouses for useless old shotguns and rusty weapons.[33] Drilling and the acquisition of arms by more sophisticated means in fact proceeded apace. Raids unauthorized by headquarters also recurred from time to time.

All this activity led to a substantial increase in the number of arrests made for offences such as illegal drilling, unlawful assembly, raiding for arms and cattle-driving. Prisoners in court who were almost always members of the Volunteers usually refused to recognize the court's authority, declaring that they were soldiers of the Irish Republic, and generally disrupting proceedings by singing 'The Soldier's Song', smoking and refusing to remove their hats. In the middle of March two of Collins's key men in the organization, Oscar Traynor and Richard McKee, received three months' hard labour for illegal drilling.

That the organization itself was continuing both to recruit successfully from the numbers of young men in the country who in more normal times might have been emigrating, and to increase its efficiency, was displayed convincingly at three more by-elections that took place in the early part of 1918. These also served to give some indication of the degree of success Sinn Fein was having in winning over disgruntled Home Rule supporters, though their results represented something of a check to its hitherto annihilating progress.

The electors in fact, if they were beginning to see reasons for disillusionment with Sinn Fein's lack of constructive policy or alarm at its anarchical tendencies, were in something of a dilemma. For the only political alternative, the old Nationalist Party, had done nothing to restore its fortunes in the Convention summoned by Lloyd George, which had made no relevant progress and was soon to founder totally in disaster. The negotiations themselves had run a predictably calamitous course. Quite apart from the inbuilt irreconcilability of the two chief attitudes to be negotiated, the total boycott of the Convention by Sinn Fein had further seriously undermined its plausibility from the beginning. However, Redmond by great perseverance did succeed finally in reaching agreement with Midleton and the Southern Unionists. But he achieved it only at the price of new concessions over a Home Rule government's power to impose taxes. At a time when opinion was moving beyond the concept of Home Rule altogether a further diminution by Redmond himself even of such Home Rule as was at least on the statute book seemed preposterous. Moreover, Redmond had risked the concession without any categorical assurance from Lloyd George that the government would back the Nationalist and Southern Unionist agreement against the Ulster Unionist demand for permanent exclusion. The furthest Lloyd George had gone was to say that if in the end the only opposition to Home Rule for all-Ireland came from the Ulster Unionists then he would 'use his influence with his colleagues ... to accept the proposal and give it legislative effect'.[34]

Once again, it was a palatable Lloyd George formula without substance. The Prime Minister's 'colleagues' when he gave that assurance included Carson and Bonar Law. More and more Redmond seemed manoeuvred out of the political ring altogether. We now know that the Ulster Unionists in the Convention had all along had a definite assurance from the government through Carson that they were not to be bound by any majority vote and that 'without their concurrence no legislation was to be founded on any agreement between the other group in the Convention'.[35] In other words Lloyd George's promise of legislation on 'substantial' agreement allowed substance only to the Ulster Unionists. Any new ground that might have been opened up by the Convention had really been cut from under it from the beginning. It finally collapsed altogether in April 1918. Midleton, the Southern Unionist leader, afterwards asserted that the Southern Unionists would never have participated in the Convention at all if he had realized that it was thus committed in advance to Partition.

Redmond, humiliated and defeated, did not live to see the Convention's formal closure. After a short illness and an operation for gallstones he died in London in March 1918, a saddened and bitterly disappointed man, confronted with the ruin of all his patient hopes. Staunch and generous-hearted, he had brought the cause of a popular and practical Irish nationalism inherited from O'Connell, Butt and Parnell to an apparent triumph in the Home Rule Act of 1914 and had seen his triumph turn to ashes.

The immediate effect of his death was to cause a by-election in Waterford – the second of three which Sinn Fein had had to fight in the early part of 1918.

None of these three by-elections could be said to provide a particularly representative cross-section of the country as a whole. And since Sinn Fein lost all three of them they drew consolation from that fact. All three defeats were at the hands of the old Home Rule Nationalist Party, but two were in

Ulster where that party's organization had for obvious defensive reasons long been more vigorous than in other parts of Ireland. Sinn Fein, on the other hand, had to build an organization from scratch there, which it did as in the 1917 by-elections by bringing in large numbers of Volunteers from Dublin and the South. On polling day in the South Armagh by-election in February there were twenty Sinn Fein motor-cars operating whose drivers carried special licences authorizing them 'to drive and use a motor-car in the performance of the duty assigned to him. In the name of the Irish Republic – Signed Eamon de Valera, 31st Jan. 1918.'[36]

At the last election in South Armagh there had been a Unionist vote of 1,600 there. This time the Unionist candidate withdrew, and since the Sinn Fein candidate, the IRB man Patrick McCartan, lost by 1,019 to the Nationalist in a not greatly reduced poll, it was not unreasonable to deduce that possibly the Nationalist had won only thanks to the Unionist vote, and certainly that Sinn Fein had not done badly in the circumstances.

The same sort of deduction could reasonably be made in the other two by-elections. The second defeat, in Waterford, the seat made vacant by John Redmond's death, was inflicted by his son, who campaigned in British uniform with a black armband for his father on his left arm. Not only could he command in that constituency the strongest personal loyalties of the old party but he could be reasonably sure of the greater part of the three to four hundred estimated Unionist voters in Waterford. Moreover, like all the by-elections fought before the General Election in 1918, it was fought before the extension of the franchise to all men of twenty-one and over and to women of thirty – so that Sinn Fein did not have the advantage of its undoubted wide support among the young.

De Valera, Griffith and Darrel Figgis of the Howth gun-running adventure bore the brunt of the campaigning for Sinn Fein in Waterford. De Valera made the tart point that there was little likelihood of the Parliamentary Party obtaining Colonial Home Rule when they had failed to get 'even the miserable Bill that is at present on the statute book'.[37] Captain Redmond's main line of attack was that Sinn Fein meant 'anarchy and destruction'. When de Valera charged him with being an English officer Redmond replied that he was an Irish officer and that anyway he had a high regard for English officers who fought for their country but none for a hybrid American who would not fight for the Stars and Stripes.[38]

There was a certain amount of violence in the election, the Sinn Fein candidate being hit on the head with a stick by a soldier when travelling on an outside car with de Valera and having to have his wound dressed in hospital. De Valera himself had a large block of wood thrown at him on one occasion and a number of Volunteers were severely beaten up. Captain Redmond won by 478 votes in a total poll of just over 2,000.[39]

Taking into account the Unionist votes, the old franchise and the personal element in this constituency. it was by no means a decisive defeat for Sinn Fein. And when the Mayor of Kilkenny hoisted the municipal flag over the Town Hall there to celebrate Redmond's victory, the local Volunteers in a confident counter-demonstration seized the building, hoisted the orange, white and green tricolour in its place and held the building for a day. Equally indicative of an old order changing was the actual hauling down at Baltinglass of a green flag hoisted there to celebrate the Nationalist victory and its burning amid the cheers of the crowd.

A further defeat for Sinn Fein in the Ulster constituency of East Tyrone was hardly regarded as a setback for they had not even intended to contest the election at first, but on deciding to test the strength of Sinn Fein support there won over 1.200 votes in a poll of about 3.000. The following Sunday a body of about five hundred Volunteers carried out manoeuvres in the Dublin mountains quite unhindered and undismayed.

The recent by-elections demonstrated that Sinn Fein, while not perhaps gaining democratically and even causing a certain number of second thoughts among potential supporters, was still a very vital political force. If its strength lay perhaps more in the enthusiasm of the Volunteers than in its electoral policies, from now on things were to be made easier for it by the British Government.

4

Conscription Crisis to General Election (December 1918)

By April 1918 the disaster suffered by the British armies in France as a result of the German March offensive was the War Cabinet's chief preoccupation. The situation was desperately serious and replacements for the extremely heavy casualties were imperative. The cabinet understandably began to reconsider whether conscription should not, after all, now be extended to Ireland. The decision to do this was announced on 9 April.

The predictable effect was to unite the whole of nationalist Ireland against the measure, and strengthen Sinn Fein, the newest political force in the field, with all the vigour of the new protest. The blurring of all nationalist feeling into a Sinn Fein image – the very objective for which de Valera and others had been striving for the past nine months – was now virtually achieved in a matter of days.

Lloyd George, incredibly, offered as a sop to such sentiment a simultaneous Home Rule Bill on the partition principle. Never perhaps had British insensitiveness to Ireland been more blatantly illustrated. The effect was to add insult to injury on a gigantic scale. The very words with which the Prime Minister chose to introduce this part of his measure rang with the bitterest irony in former Home Rulers' ears after what had happened in the past four years.

'When the young men of Ireland are brought into the fighting line,' he declared, 'it is imperative that they should feel they are not fighting for establishing a principle abroad which is denied to them at home.'

This had been the essence of Redmond's case and of many tens of thousands of his followers in supporting the war effort and volunteering for the British Army. Now the British Government, having rejected that case, when the Irish were enlisting voluntarily, was prepared to concede it in order to purchase their agreement to compulsion.

As the Irish bishops under Cardinal Logue immediately declared in unanimously condemning conscription: 'Had the Government in any reasonable time given Ireland the benefit of the principles which are declared to be at stake in the war, by the concession of a full measure of self-government, there would have been no occasion for contemplating forced levies from her now.'[2] Local public bodies from all over Ireland condemned conscription as 'unjust', 'tyrannous', 'fatuous' and 'insane'. On 16 April, the day on which the new Conscription Bill passed through Parliament, the Irish Nationalist Party left the House of Commons in a body in protest and returned to Ireland. Such a leaf out of the Sinn Fein abstentionist book could hardly fail to add to the credit of Sinn Fein plausibility.

On 18 April an unprecedented type of conference took place at the Mansion House, Dublin, at which all sections of nationalist opinion were represented: Devlin and Dillon for the Nationalist Party, de Valera and Griffith for Sinn Fein, Healy and William O'Brien for the dissident element in the old Home Rule Party and three representatives for Labour. After adjourning to consult personally with the Catholic hierarchy which was simultaneously meeting at Maynooth, the Conference issued the following unanimous declaration: 'The attempt to enforce conscription will be un-warrantable aggression which we call upon all true Irishmen to resist by the most effective means at their disposal.'[3] The Catholic hierarchy themselves issued a statement saying that conscription thus enforced was 'an oppressive and inhuman law' and that the Irish people had a right to resist it by all means consonant with the law of God.[4]

In such an atmosphere a greater degree of tolerance at least inevitably developed in the attitude of moderate Sinn Feiners towards the activities of the Volunteers. The first two Volunteers had in fact been killed in a raid for arms on a police hut in County Kerry four days after the announcement of conscription for Ireland.[5] Near Dublin masked men held up a motor-car in which a load of 250 lb. of gelignite was being transported and removed it. In Tipperary on the initiative of a local Volunteer, Dan Breen, raids on private houses were stepped up in spite of all the headquarters executive's previous orders. 'We generally went at night and asked for the arms,' he wrote afterwards. 'Those who would have liked to refuse knew they dare not. Many others gave them willingly, and some even sent us word to call for them.'[6] In County Cork a young Volunteer named Liam Lynch, who was to become one of the most uncompromising militant republicans of the next few years, though he had not in fact committed himself to the Republic until after the 1916 rising, chose this moment of the conscription crisis to give up his regular job and devote himself entirely to preparation for an eventual armed struggle.[7]

When canvassing for the next pending by-election began early in May – a contest between Sinn Fein and the party in East Cavan which broke the temporary alliance achieved over conscription – the Volunteers were out in force in support of the Sinn Fein candidate who was Arthur Griffith himself. One thousand Volunteers paraded in the town of Cavan and two thousand in Kilnaleck at the very start of the campaign which did not promise to be anything like a walk-over. Not only was the old Nationalist Party well-organized as in all Ulster constituencies, but there were reckoned to be some 1,000–1,500 Unionists out of an electorate of 9,000, many of whom in the absence of a Unionist candidate would cast an anti-Sinn Fein vote for the party. But political circumstances were strongly in Griffith's favour. With the conscription crisis at its height it was a bad moment for the party to try to make an issue of the British Parliament's importance to Ireland as against the Sinn Fein policy of abstention and an appeal to an eventual Peace Conference. More important, the British Government once again played into Sinn Fein's hands, for when polling day came in the middle of June Griffith himself, together with most of the other new leaders, including de Valera, was again in prison in England.

The *Manchester Guardian* appears to have got wind of what was about to happen when on 12 May a new Viceroy, Lord French, and a new Chief Secretary, Short, arrived in Dublin to take up their appointments. It wrote that the government was preparing for 'some very evil work in Ireland.... If not restrained it will within a few short weeks undo, and much more than undo, all the progress which has been made since Mr Gladstone first undertook the work, in the pacification of Ireland.' It went on to say that the government was about to produce an Ireland 'more ungovernable except by main force, more exasperated in feeling, more alienated than any with which this country has had to deal since the Rebellion of 1798'.[8]

The prediction was soon to come horrifyingly true.

Within five days of his arrival, French, the new Viceroy, issued a sensational proclamation declaring that there was in Ireland a 'German Plot', and that Sinn Fein had been found to be in treasonable communication with the German enemy. Drastic measures, the proclamation insisted, would have to be taken to put down 'this German Plot, which measures will be solely taken against that Plot'. Seventy-three of the leading Sinn Fein political activists, including Griffith and de Valera, were arrested during the night.

It was an indication of how far the government was out of touch with Irish opinion, at this critical stage, to think that the majority of the Irish people would be convinced by such reasoning. In fact, of course, the effect was highly favourable to Sinn Fein, for the immediate conclusion drawn was that the government had struck at Sinn Fein because they were the really powerful force in the anti-conscription movement. While it must be remembered that, from the British point of view, this action took place at perhaps the most critical point in the whole war, with the German armies driving forwards in an offensive that was within days to have Rheims half-encircled and constitute a menace to Paris itself, yet even the most loyal government supporters found the allegation of a plot hard to swallow. Wimborne, the replaced Viceroy, made no secret in the House of Lords of his scepticism, and when the government responded to various challenges by producing its evidence the plot looked thinner than ever. Much of the 'evidence' consisted of a repetition of the long-known contacts between the 1916 rebels with Germany before the rebellion; and those details which were concerned with communications on Irish affairs between the German Embassy in Washington and Berlin *after* April 1916 all referred to dates on which de Valera and all the other Sinn Fein leaders had been in English gaols or internment camps. The only direct evidence adduced personally against de Valera was a public speech he had made in which he had said the Volunteers must be ready to take advantage of any German invasion of *England*.

There was, however, one additional item of evidence that did seem relevant. In the second week of April a member of Casement's pathetic Irish Brigade, named Dowling, had been picked up on the west coast of Ireland after landing from a German submarine in a collapsible boat. He had brought a message from the Germans intended for the Sinn Fein leaders, inquiring about their plans and offering assistance. Dowling had been arrested before the message could be delivered. In fact, though some individual Volunteers knew of Dowling's pending mission, the mission itself was clear enough evidence that de Valera and his colleagues were *not* in contact with the Germans, for the essence of the message was that the Germans were in the dark. But used in conjunction with earlier events and de Valera's public statements, the government, perhaps understandably, thought it provided an adequate excuse to try to stifle the whole Sinn Fein movement. More subtle acquaintance with the emotive factor in Irish history might have made them weigh more carefully the long-term disadvantages of such action.

From this moment onwards Sinn Fein began to make further electoral advances. Polling in the East Cavan by-election took place on 19 June. The fact that the Sinn Fein candidate, Griffith, was now in gaol, though the government had announced that none of the prisoners would be tried, was of course a great additional asset to him. The Sinn Fein campaign organizers had been confidently expecting to win by a majority of 500. There was a high poll. When the result was announced, Griffith had a majority of 1,204. Again, bonfires blazed that night on the surrounding hills and all over Ireland.

The arrests had also brought about one other result that was to have great importance for the future. Advance warning of the impending arrests given by a nationalist-minded detective at Dublin Castle, named Kavanagh, had reached Michael Collins. Collins had passed it on to the Sinn Fein Executive, which had been meeting that night in their headquarters at 6, Harcourt Street, Dublin. Most of the leaders decided to accept arrest, correctly assessing that this would work politically to Sinn Fein's advantage.[9] Only those who were thinking militarily rather than politically about the future decided to avoid arrest and these included Collins himself, his close IRB friend

Harry Boland and Cathal Brugha. The result was to give the surviving organization of Sinn Fein a more militant and uncompromisingly republican leadership beneath the surface – an influence not in itself weakened by a personal rivalry which was to develop between Brugha and Collins.

It was from this moment onwards that Collins, now 'on the run' though he made occasional appearances in public at political meetings,[10] began to assert a dominant control of the 'underground' organization of the movement, equal to that of de Valera and Griffith in the political field. The continuing strength of the organization in the country was manifested when, in spite of a proclamation at the beginning of July declaring Sinn Fein, the Irish Volunteers and even the Gaelic League dangerous organizations, Sinn Fein meetings continued to be held defiantly throughout the country. The police sometimes interfered and made arrests and sometimes took notes. When the military raided a Sinn Fein Hall at Charlestown, County Mayo, and removed a large tricolour flying from an upper storey, the newspaper report of the incident concluded: 'Shortly afterwards another flag was hoisted in the same position and remains there.'[11]

Arrests and sentences multiplied and with them the popular prestige of Sinn Fein and the Volunteers, now seen more and more generally, however imprecisely, as one movement. Crowds outside the courts invariably shouted 'Up the rebels!' or waved tricolour flags. A cinema was prevented from showing the film of Ashe's funeral or the scenes in Dublin when the rebel prisoners had returned from England the year before.[12] The proprietor of a concert party was sentenced to two years' imprisonment by a court-martial for singing 'seditious songs', which term was used indiscriminately to include 'Wrap the Green Flag round me, boys' (an exile's song of the American Civil War), 'God Save Ireland' and 'The Soldier's Song'. As a Sinn Fein spokesman declared to a group of journalists at the beginning of October 1918, there were by then five hundred people in Ireland imprisoned under the Defence of the Realm Regulations on charges ranging from singing a song written seventy years before to presenting their names in Irish when accosted by a policeman. But Sinn Fein's growing power was demonstrated most forcibly in a more effective field.

The success of the anti-conscription campaign had made the government temporarily abandon the idea of immediately implementing conscription for Ireland. But with the legal power to do so now in their possession they kept the threat of it permanently in the background, to Sinn Fein's continued advantage. The decision not to enforce it immediately had been conditioned perhaps less by sensitiveness to Irish susceptibilities than by a sudden change of fortunes in the war. For the Germans, who had been on the Marne at the end of May, were by the end of June being driven back in the retreat which was to bring them to sue for an armistice on their own frontiers a few months later. And, though the full scale of the allied success was not yet known, as an experiment a new voluntary recruiting campaign was instituted in Ireland, with the aim of raising fifty thousand new recruits there. The campaign got into full swing early in August with well-known Nationalist MPs in uniform, such as Arthur Lynch (once condemned to death for his part in raising a pro-Boer Irish Brigade in the South African war) and Stephen Gwynn, speaking to large meetings. Sinn Fein organized an efficient and systematic counter-campaign to reduce the meeting to chaos and prevent the speakers from being heard.

Historical hindsight now leads us to take the political success of Sinn Fein at this period so much for granted that it is instructive to note the difficulties with which it still had to contend in order to achieve that success. This last recruiting campaign is a case in point. The meetings were, more often than not, successfully broken up by small organized groups of articulate Sinn Feiners operating from strategic positions in the crowd.[13] But though the authorities got nowhere near their target of fifty thousand recruits, it is revealing to note the success they did have. Even during 1917 when disappointment with the Home Rule failure was so rapidly breathing life into the new movement the British Army, without any particular campaign at all, had managed to secure 14,013 voluntary recruits from Ireland.[14] Now, in the peculiarly unfavourable atmosphere produced by the conscription threat, the German plot and the arrests of the leaders in addition to the systematic campaign against recruiting so efficiently managed by Sinn Fein, it succeeded in getting more than eleven thousand recruits in eleven weeks.[15] The weight of nationalist opinion of the old Redmondite school was still by no means contemptible. And it now became the principal task of Sinn Fein to win over as much of it as possible in the General Election announced for December 1918.

The calling of this election in an immediate post-war atmosphere entailed many adverse conditions for Sinn Fein, including the arrest of consecutive Sinn Fein Election Directors and the censorship of part of the Sinn Fein manifesto. But in another respect the speed with which the election was called acted in Sinn Fein's favour. Very many soldiers on leave or otherwise separated from the units had not received their postal voting papers by the close of the poll, even though this was extended for soldiers for a further fortnight after the rest of the electorate had voted. In London, for instance, it was reckoned that by the end of that fortnight only about one-third of the soldiers' votes there had been cast and this was thought to have been typical of the rest of the country.[16] The figure for Ireland was often even lower. In North Wexford only one-sixth of the absent voters cast their votes; in south County Dublin one-fifth.[17] And it seems probable that many of the Irish soldiers' votes would have been for the old Nationalist Party rather than Sinn Fein, still often thought of as 'pro-German'. The torpedoing of the Holyhead mail boat in the last few weeks of the war by a German submarine with the loss of over four hundred Irish lives had not added to the popularity of being thought pro-German. Although on Armistice night itself in Dublin' there had been nothing worse than wordy discussions between those wearing orange, white and green colours and other celebrating crowds, two nights later the Sinn Fein headquarters in Harcourt Street, Liberty Hall and the Mansion House were attacked by hostile crowds, many of whom were Irish soldiers, and the rooms in Harcourt Street were totally wrecked, after which troops were temporarily confined to barracks. The premises had been wrecked, admitted Harry Boland, one of Collins's closest collaborators who had been inside the building at the time, but they had not wrecked Sinn Fein.[18] And the subsequent election campaign was to prove him right.

Sinn Fein was also much favoured in the election by the greatly enlarged new register which almost trebled the previous Irish electorate.* For the first time the vote had been extended to all males over twenty-one without other qualification and to women over thirty. A higher proportion both of young people and of poor people were voting than ever before – the numbers of young men being in any case swelled by the virtual suspension of emigration during the war.

Another telling factor was that in the course of the election campaign itself Sinn Fein was already revealed as the winning party. Not only did a number of prominent Nationalists of the old school publicly come down in its favour, such as William O'Brien and Colonel Maurice Moore of Red-mond's National Volunteers, but in no fewer than twenty-six constituencies the Nationalist Party failed to muster even sufficient enthusiasm to raise a candidate. And these twenty-six constituencies representing nearly a quarter of the total Irish electorate had thus gone to Sinn Fein even before polling day. The manifesto, for all the mutilations of the censor, made clear that Sinn Fein stood for an Irish Republic and that its elected candidates, refus-ing to attend at Westminster, would form a national assembly in Dublin, which would appeal to the Peace Conference. However, probably what most Sinn Fein voters were voting for was simply the greatest measure of inde-pendence, without partition of the country, which Ireland could get. If pressed, in the manner of modern opinion polls, as to what they thought they would actually be prepared to settle for, the majority would probably have replied: 'Dominion Home Rule', as a minimum. If asked the awkward question: 'How did they expect the British Government to concede this without the exclusion of six Ulster counties?' they would probably have given the Sinn Fein reply: 'By an appeal to the Peace Conference.' The one thing they were certainly not voting for was an attempt to win sovereign inde-pendence by force of arms or a campaign of terrorism. This was a goal

* The Irish electorate was now 1,931,588 compared with 698,098 on the old register. Some 800,000 of the new voters were reckoned to be women. (*Irish Independent*, 5 December 1918.)

← TO →

PUT HIM IN — GET HIM OUT

VOTE FOR **GRIFFITH**

The Man in Jail for Ireland.

President Wilson

May not hear from English Jails on his arrival in Europe, Dec. 10th, BUT he must listen to the demand of a United Irish Nation on Dec. 14th.

VOTE FOR INDEPENDENCE

WHY DID THEY DIE?

BRIAN BORU	1014	**NOT**	to give a colourable sanction to the slavery of Ireland,
EARL OF DESMOND	1467		
SHANE O'NEILL	1567		
HUGH ROE O'DONNELL	1605		
OWEN ROE	1649	**NOT**	to secure the Partition of Ireland,
BISHOP McMAHON	1650		
FATHER SHEEHY	1766		
ARCHBISHOP O'HURLEY	1798	**NOT**	to pledge to a foreign Government the troosers and the manhood of Ireland,
FR. JOHN MURPHY	1798		
LORD EDWARD FITZGERALD	1798		
WOLFE TONE	1798		
EMMET	1803	**NOT**	to enable out-of-date political hacks to bargain over Ireland.
O'NEILL CROWLEY	1867		
PEARSE	1916		
CONNOLLY	1916		
ASHE	1917		
COLEMAN	1918		

THEY DIED TO SECURE THE LIBERATION OF THE OLDEST POLITICAL PRISONER IN THE WORLD—

IRELAND!

RELEASE THE PRISONERS!
RELEASE IRELAND!

CZECHO-SLOVAKS **INDEPENDENCE**	X
Foreign (German) Domination	

THE VOTE OF THE CZECHO-SLOVAK PEOPLE IN 1918 WON THEM THEIR FREEDOM.

JUGO-SLAVS **INDEPENDENCE**	X
Foreign (Austrian) Domination	

THE JUGO-SLAVS DEMANDED, NOT HOME RULE WITHIN THE AUSTRIAN EMPIRE, BUT ABSOLUTE INDEPENDENCE. THEY ARE NOW ACKNOWLEDGED A NATION.

THE IRISH **INDEPENDENCE**	
Foreign (English) Domination	

IRELAND'S MARK IS NOT YET MADE. YOU CAN MAKE IT. WILL YOU HAVE THE COURAGE TO DEMAND WHAT RACES INFINITELY LESS HISTORIC HAVE DEMANDED? THE CZECHO-SLOVAKS AND THE JUGO-SLAVS ARE YOUNGER THAN THIS ANCIENT COUNTRY BY A THOUSAND YEARS. THEY HAVE VOTED FOR INDEPENDENCE, AND ARE NOW FREE.

WILL **YOU** VOTE FOR SINN FEIN AND THE INDEPENDENCE OF **YOUR** COUNTRY?

believed in only by a minority of Volunteer activists, who in the long run saw violence rather than democratic politics as the final arbiter, though they would have maintained that they were thereby expressing the national will. Publicly such thoughts remained tactfully unvoiced or even denied. De Valera who, like forty-seven of the other Sinn Fein candidates, was in gaol, had been conciliatory enough to all sections of nationalist opinion when he issued his opening election call from his cell in Lincoln gaol.

Every true son and every true daughter of Ireland is mindful of what the honour of the Motherland demands ... that individual opinions and individual interests, with a nobility befitting the occasion, will all be subordinated to the necessity of proclaiming unequivocally to an attending world that it is no slave status that Ireland's heroes have fought for, but the securing for their beloved country of her rightful place in the family of nations, a true sister among the free. It is thus with no uncertainty that we all place ourselves in your hands and it is not in accents of despair that we join in praying 'God save Ireland.'[19]

These stirringly vague sentiments would have seemed unexceptionable enough for any Irish nationalist in the past fifty years and were more than ever so in the heady climate of December 1918.

The results of the election were even more devastating to the party and triumphant for Sinn Fein than anyone had expected. The Nationalist Home Rule Party, which had maintained a dominant control over Irish politics for over thirty-five years and had held sixty-eight seats in the House of Commons at the dissolution of Parliament, was now reduced to six seats, four of which it held in Ulster only thanks to a local electoral pact with Sinn Fein. Elsewhere, the Party had been virtually obliterated, in terms of seats. For the first time in Irish history a party demanding total sovereign independence for Ireland dominated both the political scene and Irish public opinion. Symbolic of the whole victory was the triumph of de Valera personally in East Mayo where he defeated by a large majority John Dillon, the Party leader since Redmond's death, in a constituency Dillon had represented continually for thirty-three years. In Waterford alone, where the Nationalists won one of the only two remaining seats which they had fought against all-comers, there was a slight swing against Sinn Fein. For here Redmond's son was again returned with an almost identical majority to that of 1917. This, given the prevailing Sinn Fein climate and a much enlarged, younger electorate, was itself something of a triumph for the Nationalist Party against the overwhelming trend.

In the province of Ulster there was a Unionist majority on the popular vote in only four of the historic nine counties, and in only one of these (County Antrim) was it as high as two to one.* By the normal standards of

---

* In Counties Antrim, Armagh, Derry and Down, Unionists were in the majority on the popular vote; in Counties Tyrone, Fermanagh, Donegal, Cavan and Monaghan,

democracy this could hardly be said to justify such special treatment for six counties as would invalidate the nationalist principle for which the rest of the country had overwhelmingly voted. This seemed particularly so when such special treatment would itself create a much larger (Nationalist) minority within those six counties than the Unionists of those six counties represented within the whole of Ireland.

As to the overall result, suggestions made at the time and since that a low poll indicated considerable Nationalist abstentions and thus gave a misleading impression of Sinn Fein ascendancy cannot be upheld. The poll of seventy-three per cent in constituencies where there was a contest was around the average for Irish general elections in the past.[20] Thus, given the known low figure on the postal vote (which certainly did favour Sinn Fein) the percentage of ordinary voters may even be said to have been a little higher than usual. And though there was some disfranchisement owing to Sinn Fein candidates having been returned unopposed in 25 of the 105 constituencies, unopposed returns had long been a normal feature of Irish elections. There had been 63 of them in the last election in 1910, almost all returning members of the Nationalist Party. In short, Sinn Fein had taken over the party's place. There was, however, one important detail about the results that is often overlooked, but which held significance for the future. Though Sinn Fein, with a popular vote of 485,105, had won nearly all the Nationalist seats, 237,393 Nationalists, voting for the Nationalist Party, had still voted against Sinn Fein and an Irish Republic.[*21]

Nevertheless, the results were sensational. And when they became fully known one of those priests who had for the past two years been so active in the new movement, Father Michael O'Flanagan, a Vice-President of Sinn Fein, declared: 'The people have voted for Sinn Fein. What we have to do now is to explain to them what Sinn Fein is.'[22]

This would have been easier if Sinn Fein itself had known more precisely. The ambiguity of the movement, particularly where the role of Collins, Brugha and the other militant Volunteers was concerned, was largely concealed, and totally unresolved. Moreover, little thought seemed to have been given to the one aspect of the Irish situation which had hardly changed since the summer of 1914: namely, the British Government's refusal to include in any concept of Irish nationalism the six north-east counties of Ulster.

Meanwhile, Harry Boland, Collins's lieutenant, and an IRB man tried to

---

Nationalists (either Sinn Fein or the old Nationalist Party) were in the majority on the popular vote. In all these counties except Fermanagh the majority on the popular vote reflected the majority in terms of parliamentary seats. Fermanagh returned one Unionist and one Nationalist seat.

* The total anti-Republican vote, including Unionists, was 557,435 or a distinct majority over Sinn Fein. This latter figure, though, is not of great significance for the vast majority of Nationalist voters would almost certainly have voted Sinn Fein rather than Unionist.

persuade those who had voted Nationalist to accept Sinn Fein henceforth, saying that their differences were only in method and not in principle.[23] But the force of this depended rather on the extent to which Nationalists felt obliged to apply principles to methods.

5

Sinn Fein in a Vacuum
(January–May 1919)

The whole emphasis of the victorious Sinn Fein movement as the year 1919 opened was on the hope of securing Ireland's right to self-determination from the forthcoming Peace Conference. The American President, Woodrow Wilson, was expected to be the dominating figure at the Conference and he had long made clear his own special concern for the rights of small nations. Thus it was with a sense of righteousness and respectability that the majority of the Irish people now faced the future under the leadership of Sinn Fein. The paper *New Ireland* declared: 'If Irishmen today wish to prevent recourse to armed rebellion they should throw themselves whole-heartedly into the present Sinn Fein movement.'[1]

A sense of emotional inheritance from earlier historic attempts to assert Ireland's identity was fed by the presence in gaol of thirty-four or nearly half of her newly-elected representatives. And at one of the many meetings soon being held to protest against this fact, Harry Boland provided an answer to that question that might be in some supporters' minds as to what action could be taken if Ireland's case was not admitted to the Peace Conference after all. There were, he declared, twenty-five million Irishmen in America and they would insist on President Wilson's ideas being carried out.[2]

Meanwhile, the government disregarded all protests and the prisoners remained in gaol. Only Count Plunkett was immediately released and allowed to return to Ireland.

On the other hand, the authorities did stop the pursuit of those members of Sinn Fein who had escaped their net at the time of the 'German plot' the year before. Almost their last attempt was made on Collins himself on 6 January 1919 when he was addressing a prohibited protest meeting at Dunmanway in County Cork. Police and soldiers charged the crowds with batons and fixed bayonets but Collins escaped. He had, quite unknown to the authorities, just been helping to re-organize the very militant Cork Volunteers into three separate brigades.[3] The next day he appeared, with other Irish MPs who were still at large, in the Dublin Mansion House to make arrangements for the projected summoning of an Irish National Assembly or Dail Eireann. The authorities did not interfere and in fact released after three hours one of the wanted men they happened to have picked up in Cork that morning.⁴ In the Mansion House that day the representatives pledged themselves 'to accept nothing less than complete separation from England in settlement of Ireland's claims', and to abstain from Westminster.⁵

The tense but reserved atmosphere of the beginning of a long duel now settled over Ireland as people waited to see both what Sinn Fein and the British Government would do next. About Sinn Fein itself the correspondent of the sympathetic London *Daily News* reported from Sligo that the two distinct movements within it were drawing further and further apart. The 'physical force men', he said, were supremely contemptuous of the main body with its 'moral force' programme and still preached their secret doctrine of fifty years before. 'They are never in the ascendant except at times of extraordinary national emotion,' he wrote with historical accuracy. 'Such a time it is only too plain to see we are rapidly approaching now.'⁶ What this correspondent probably did not know, what no outsider had as yet fully realized, was the extent to which in Dublin itself the physical force men had inextricably entangled themselves in the main body.

All over the world international delegates were now being appointed to the Paris Peace Conference due to open on 20 January, but there was no official place for any from Ireland. In fact, though de Valera, Griffith and Plunkett were selected by Sinn Fein to represent Ireland there, the chances of the rest of the diplomatic world taking Sinn Fein as seriously as they took themselves were not bright. All the great powers at the Conference were specifically pledged against interference in each other's internal affairs, and by international law Ireland was unquestionably an internal affair of Britain's. It was with the minorities of the *defeated* powers that the Conference was prepared to concern itself.

The day after the Peace Conference opened, Dail Eireann, the first representative Irish political assembly since the demise of 'Grattan's Parliament' in 1800, met at the Dublin Mansion House. All other Irish MPs returned at the General Election, whether Sinn Fein or not, had been invited to attend, but only one took the trouble even to send a refusal.* Carson's name was actually called out on the roll call to some laughter. All observers commented favourably on the dignity and decorum with which the rather colourless proceedings were conducted. The London *Daily Mail* observed patronizingly of the brief speeches, which were almost entirely in Irish: 'Speaking in a difficult language, and one to which the orator is not born, is a great shortener of political proceedings.'⁷

The official Constitution of the Dail was announced. It provided itself

* A Unionist, Sir Robert Woods.

with full legislative and executive powers and a cabinet consisting of a Prime Minister, or President of the Dail, and other ministers to be nominated by him. These ministerial offices were soon to be filled – though the names were not immediately made public – by, among others, de Valera (Prime Minister or President), Arthur Griffith (Home Affairs), Count Plunkett (Foreign Affairs), John MacNeill (Industry), Cathal Brugha (Defence), Constance Markievicz (Labour), William Cosgrave (Local Government) and Michael Collins (Finance). The elevation of Brugha to the rank of Minister automatically promoted his former Deputy, Richard Mulcahy, an IRB man who had fought with Ashe at Ashbourne in Easter Week, to be the new Volunteer Chief of Staff.

It all sounded impressive enough, but it was not taken very seriously in London or, always, in Dublin. Even the normally sympathetic *Manchester Guardian* lapsed into sarcasm: 'One fancies that the Ministers of Finance, Home Affairs and all the other dignitaries will be hard put to it to find an outlet for any executive capacity they may possess.'[8]

The Dail also issued an Irish Declaration of Independence in which it linked the Irish Republic voted for by the electorate in December 1918 with that 'proclaimed in Dublin on Easter Monday, 1916, by the Irish Republican Army, acting on behalf of the Irish people'.[9] Further business included the unanimous adoption of a so-called Democratic Programme containing vaguely socialistic phrases which claimed to emanate from 'our first President, Padraic Pearse', but were more truly an acknowledgement to the memory of Connolly.[10] In addition there was a message to the free nations of the world asking for recognition of Ireland's national status, mentioning 'her last glorious resort to arms in 1916' and referring to an 'existing state of war between England and Ireland' which could only be ended when 'Ireland is definitely evacuated by the armed forces of England'.[11] It all reads rather hollow fifty years later, when the armed forces of England have still not evacuated Ireland; and it was hollow then.

At these first sessions of the Dail, Cathal Brugha presided in the absence of de Valera in gaol. He quoted Wolfe Tone to the effect that those wanting to save the country would have to do so 'without the help of those who looked to the foreigner',[12] thus ignoring the fact that looking to the foreigner in the form of the statesmen of the Peace Conference and the American electorate was the major part of Sinn Fein's official policy at that time. How in fact the Dail's noble-sounding declarations were to be made to bear any relation to reality was, as the *Freeman's Journal* reasonably pointed out, the question which dominated all other issues – that, and 'whether it is seriously proposed to take measures to give them practical effect'.[13] The real answer to the latter part of the question came that same week, though its full significance was as yet unappreciated.

On 19 January, two days before the Dail met, two RIC men who had discovered a party of Volunteers drilling on Three Rock Mountain, Rath-farnham, County Dublin, had been knocked down as they attempted to intervene and left bound and gagged while the Volunteers made off with their equipment. A few days later the constables were sitting as interested spectators of the Dail proceedings in the Mansion House.[14] They were more fortunate than two of their colleagues in County Tipperary, Constables McDonnell and O'Connell, who, escorting a cart carrying gelignite to a quarry at Soloheadbeg, were set upon by masked Volunteers and shot dead with revolvers at point-blank range. The Volunteers stripped the bodies of their rifles and ammunition and made off with these and the gelignite. The names of the chief participants in the attack were Dan Breen, Seumas Robinson, Sean Treacy and Sean Hogan, and they had taken the action entirely on their own initiative.[15]

The two Irish constables, both Catholics, one a widower with four children, were very popular locally and had never had any connection with political prosecutions. Their deaths aroused widespread indignation and horror, and there was a poignant moment at the inquest when one of McDonnell's sons asked if they had been given any time to surrender the explosives or had had a dog's chance.[16] The coroner's jury extended its sympathy to the relatives in their bereavement and a Tipperary priest immediately proclaimed in church that no good cause would be served by such crimes which would bring on their country disgrace and on themselves the curse of God.[17] Another said that no one would deplore the crime more than the leader of the Sinn Fein movement.[18] The action was condemned as a crime at masses throughout Tipperary the following Sunday and the Archbishop of Cashel in Thurles Cathedral proclaimed it an offence against the law of God. He added: 'We pray that we may be spared a recurrence of such a deed.' In St Michael's Church, Tipperary, another cleric, Monsignor Ryan, cried: 'God help poor Ireland if she follows this deed of blood!'[19]

Nevertheless, in spite of an offer of £1,000 reward, the killers were able to vanish without trace until an even more sensational appearance three months later.

The south riding of Tipperary was immediately declared a military area. Thus the precedent was set for a pattern of cause and effect that was soon to exercise a profound political influence. For military restrictions involving the closing of fairs and markets, personal searches, traffic delays and other frustrations inevitably diverted much of the original indignation at the out-rage itself into more conventional anti-government channels. The pattern was to repeat itself with cumulative effect throughout 1919, and to a large extent solve Sinn Fein's recurring political problem for it, of how to retain popular support in the absence of any positive political success. In fact, for those in Sinn Fein who had always secretly intended to try to obtain a republic by popular revolution, to create this pattern may well have been a deliberate tactic, although clear evidence of such Machiavellian design is limited.* Certainly their objects were often more successfully served by the British authorities' reaction to Volunteer exploits than by the military results of such exploits themselves.

Another act of violence took place a few days later in County Cork when an attempt was made to disarm some soldiers near their camp at Macroom. One soldier was seriously injured, a fact which caused much distress in the town, where relations between the military and civilians had always been good. The local RIC Inspector even rejected the suggestion that the Sinn Fein organization could have been responsible in any way for the raid and attributed it to 'persons whose evil instincts are apt to manifest themselves in times of marked political excitement'.[20] He was partly right: the raid had been carried out on the local initiative of one of the Cork Brigades, though it was one of those which Collins had just reorganized.†[21]

A pro-Sinn Fein priest had said of the Tipperary killings that 'the leaders of the popular movement were far too logical and God-fearing to countenance such crimes'.[22] This reflected a widespread belief among many moderate Sinn Fein supporters at the time, and even among observers generally unsympathetic to Sinn Fein. There was a particle of truth in it inasmuch as these particular actions had been the responsibility of local Volunteers. But the belief that the leaders were incapable of countenancing such actions was, as events were soon to show, sadly astray, however superficially plausible.

At all elections up to and including the General Election of 1918 it had been constantly repeated, even by former rebels of Easter Week, that further resort to rebellion was unnecessary. Only during the conscription crisis had it been held that the Volunteers would have a right, along MacNeillite lines, to defend themselves if attacked and to prevent conscription from being enforced. But the question of taking offensive action against police and soldiers in Ireland in order to establish an Irish Republic had never been before the Irish people and if it had been at the General Election of 1918 it would have been decisively rejected. The only specific methods proposed by Sinn Fein for establishing the Irish Republic had been an appeal to the Peace Conference combined with the passive resistance involved in abstention from Westminster and the creation of a National Assembly in Ireland. In 1917, when the Sinn Fein constitution had spoken of 'every available means' to make English power impotent, de Valera himself had defined these as being 'means justly available in the minds of all Irishmen' and, a little later, means 'in accordance with the moral law and the will of the Irish people'.‡ Now the will of the Irish people had never been sounded on the issue of shooting policemen and soldiers by surprise, and the highest

* For some evidence see below, p. 68.
† See above, p. 55.
‡ See above, pp. 36-7.

dignitaries of the Catholic Church were continually to proclaim it as contrary to the moral law.

At a later stage in the dramatic events which were now unfolding de Valera was to state that he had only to look into his own heart to know the will of the Irish people. He was as yet too circumspect to assume responsibility for the national will quite so unequivocally and his exact position at this time on the question of violence is therefore obscure, but many of his colleagues felt no such restraints. It is a recognized principle that a revolutionary may, with honour at least, assume responsibility for interpreting the national will even against apparent national wishes, provided he sincerely and selflessly believes it to be in the national interest to do so. Of the honour, sincerity, selflessness and patriotism of men like Brugha, Collins and others of this time who were about to lead the Irish people against their will, but with some spectacular results into the most effective rebellion in their history, there can never be the slightest doubt. And the same may be said of the vast majority of those who followed them. Such men, passionately conscious of the long injustice to Irish dignity in the past, must personally be granted a wholly moral motive. The more general moral validity of their actions can only be tested by the quality of the results they achieved and by consideration of whether or not better or as good results might not have been achieved another way. They were brave men, and to expose themselves to the risk of such a test more than physical courage was required. Many of them were devout Catholics, and, to them, it was a risk which might entail eternity.

Perhaps for some such reason there was at the time, and has been in retrospect, an attempt to give the whole operation the appearance of a democratic sanction from the start. Much of this was made possible by the cloak of ambiguity which shrouded the whole movement. Men like Collins and Brugha, and indeed a large proportion of Dail Eireann, were at the same time democratic representatives elected on one understanding, and also members of a clandestinely directed organization, the Volunteers, or even of a wholly secret organization within that organization, the IRB, operating on another understanding. The fact that the general public vaguely gave Sinn Fein, the Volunteers and Dail Eireann all one identity, made self-deception easier.

Brugha and Collins each had dual identities both as Dail Eireann ministers and as directors of the Volunteers. Since they were undoubtedly democratic representatives of the people on one count, it was possible to argue that being in fact only one man each, they were equally so on the other. Brugha's duality in this respect was particularly important at the very beginning because while de Valera, the Volunteers' nominal President and President of the Dail, was still in gaol, he, the Volunteers' far more active Chief of Staff, was the Dail's Acting President.

Thus in his role as Chief of Staff of the Volunteers Brugha sanctioned as early as 31 January 1919 a directive issued to all Volunteers by Piaras Beaslai, the editor of the Volunteers' secretly-distributed journal, *An t Oglach* ('The Soldier'). This told Volunteers throughout Ireland that the authority of the nation was behind them as the Army of Ireland, that Dail Eireann as the national authority claimed that right which every theologian recognized as belonging to every free national government to inflict death on the enemies of the State, and that enemies of the State were soldiers or policemen of the British Government whom every Volunteer was entitled 'morally and legally ... to slay ... if it is necessary to do so in order to overcome their resistance'.[23] No public statement to this effect was issued by Dail Eirean or any of the leaders of Sinn Fein.

Further sanction of the national authority, and thus, by implication, of the Irish people for such actions was alleged to be available in a phrase which Dail Eireann had used in its message to the free nations of the world. This, in drawing attention to the British Government's refusal of Ireland's national demands, had described the relations existing between the two countries as 'a state of war'. This was now interpreted by Beaslai and Brugha as meaning that a state of war had been declared. Beaslai also stated later that until January 1921 no Deputy of the Dail ever objected to the activity of the Volunteers.[24] But whatever Beaslai might say at the time or later, the theologians he invoked did not support him. There could be no shortage of them in Ireland, and throughout the so-called War of Independence from 1919 to 1921 Cardinal Logue himself, the three archbishops and the entire hierarchy, together with the vast majority of parish priests, condemned bloodshed by the Volunteers as crimes and offences against the law of God. Moreover, even if it could be argued that the Dail had, however tacitly, permitted such activity, it could not conceivably be argued that the war policy thus had the democratic sanction of the Irish people. If such a drastic change in policy were to be introduced by popular representatives without further consultation with the electorate, only a most exceptional change of the circumstances could, democratically, justify it. But the only change of circumstances that in fact took place between 14 December 1918 and 31 January 1919 was a relaxation of measures against those Sinn Fein MPs who were at large, permission for Dail Eireann to sit in public and the killing of two Irish policemen on routine duties by Volunteers in Tipperary.

Writing seven years later Beaslai tried to maintain that 'as far as the situation could be said to have been forced in the direction of bloodshed it was forced solely by the violence of the British Government.'[25] If by 'violence' in this context is meant physical brutality and bloodshed the statement cannot possibly be substantiated. Of the twelve civilian deaths at the hands of Crown forces that took place in Ireland between June 1916 and the end of

January 1920 only two could conceivably be described as evidence of brutality: one death from a bayonet wound in the search of a Sinn Fein hall and the other 'while trying to escape'. Three of the others resulted from failures to answer the challenge of military sentries, two from panicky misapprehension by police and soldiers that they were under attack (at a time when they were continually under attack) and three were those of Volunteers actually engaged in attacking the police or military with firearms at the time. One man was also killed in a party driving cattle off another man's land, after the police had given repeated warnings and even fired over the crowd's heads; another while committing a burglary. In the same period sixteen police or ex-policemen and soldiers were killed, almost all in cold blood.

If, however, by 'British Government violence' is meant the refusal to take any notice at all of the Irish people's political demand for self-determination as expressed democratically in the General Election of 1918, the refusal to make any alternative political offer by way of amends, the refusal at first even to release those representatives who had been in gaol when elected – then the classical case for terrorism by the weak against the strong can reasonably be made. But it still cannot be said that the policy of terrorism was the will of the Irish people. Throughout 1919 members of popularly-elected bodies, such as urban and rural district councils, often supporters of Sinn Fein, were to express condemnation or at least dislike of what was being done by the Volunteers. It was only when condemnation and dislike for what the British Government were to do by way of retaliation began far to exceed this, that popular acquiescence in what was in reality the open rebellion of a small minority materialized. What was enacted between 1919 and 1921 was a rebellion started in the Fenian tradition of 1916, but much more subtly conducted and gradually acquiring as it developed much of that active mass political support which had always eluded separatist movements in the past.

None of this was clear at the beginning of 1919. The grim niceties required for the rationalization of terrorism were conducted behind the scenes. The Volunteer paper *An t Oglach* was a secret publication and, as for the Dail itself, no word was heard from it one way or the other about the killings at Soloheadbeg or the attack at Macroom.

Apart from its hitherto apparently abortive attempts to get into the Peace Conference, the first official exercise of autonomous power which Sinn Fein displayed was a decree banning hunting in Ireland until the political prisoners were released. The 'decree' was, for obvious non-political reasons, not altogether popular in the Irish countryside, but it was treated seriously largely because of the ability of local bodies of Volunteers to enforce it. Some hunts respectfully asked Sinn Fein to rescind the decree but to no avail. Those hunts which did try to meet encountered bands of men armed with sticks and revolvers, and a horse of the Ward Hunt was actually grazed by a bullet.[25] By the end of January hunting had been brought to a standstill for the season.

Most of the prisoners, however, remained in prison. A few in poor health were released, for the death from influenza in Usk prison at the end of 1918 of the Volunteer Richard Coleman had alerted the government to the ever-present dangers of martyrdom. Of the rest, those who were free owed their liberty not to the government but either to their own ingenuity or to that of Michael Collins and Harry Boland. At the time of the Dail's first public session Collins and Boland had secretly gone over to England and at the beginning of February pulled off a spectacular coup by personally helping de Valera and two others to escape from Lincoln gaol with a duplicate key.*

The success did much to raise the morale of all supporters of Sinn Fein in the absence of positive political achievements. And the British Government, which might easily have diminished the impact by announcing the release of all prisoners anyway, delayed another month before doing so, thus, as so often in its dealings with Irish public opinion, getting the worst of all possible worlds.

Politically the escape of de Valera concentrated attention on Sinn Fein's future action. It was a matter with which de Valera had been much concerning himself while in prison. As the most sophisticated political mind in the movement he was well aware of the potential stalemate with which Sinn Fein was confronted and, being a politician rather than a revolutionary, he had come to a political conclusion. In the light of the total failure so far of the Peace Conference idea he would go to America to mobilize what was still Ireland's greatest single asset on the international scene: the vast wealth and influence of the twenty-five million or so men and women of Irish blood who lived there. His decision dismayed Collins and Boland and the other leaders of the Volunteers and it was only with some reluctance that he eventually agreed to go to Ireland for a period first.[27] There, at a secret hide-out, he gave an interview to an American correspondent in the form of a long written answer to a single question: 'Do you believe that the statesmen in Paris will force England to do justice to Ireland?' In his reply de Valera made it clear that he was pinning his hopes on the influence of President Wilson and the United States.[28]

A few days later he issued a St Patrick's Day message to the Irish people on what might have struck some as a distinct note of bathos. To save the Irish language, he said, was the special duty of that generation. The ultimate

* Collins's and Boland's names were answered to in the Dail on 21 January and their presence published in the newspapers, but this was a device to conceal their absence. The official Dail record was subsequently amended to accord with the truth. (Beaslai, *Collins*, vol. 1, p. 256.) The other prisoners to escape with de Valera were Sean McGarry and Sean Milroy.

winning of sovereign independence was not in doubt: '... should we fail, a future generation will succeed. But the language, that must be saved by us or it is lost for ever.'[29] And Joe McGrath, an IRB man and one of the internees who had contrived his own escape from prison in England, was hardly more inspiring when he told his audience in a St Patrick's Day speech: 'As to the future ... be patient for a little while.' Dail Eireann, he assured them, was working in committees day and night.[30]

Evidence of night work of a different sort had just appeared at an inquest on a monumental mason named Pearson, the father of a British soldier, who was shot dead in his house in Dublin for refusing to give up a couple of rifles and some ammunition he kept there. A woman in the house revealed how at least some Sinn Fein supporters were made in these times. Finding herself confronted by one of the masked raiders holding a revolver she had called out to him: 'Don't shoot! ... I am a Sinn Feiner, don't shoot for mercy's sake!'[31]

A more impressive raid for arms was carried out a few days later when about thirty men tied up the guard at Collinstown military aerodrome just outside Dublin and got away with no less than seventy-two rifles and bayonets without a shot being fired.[32] The raid had been organized by Collins whose vital role behind the scenes does not yet seem to have been suspected by the authorities, for he was moving uninhibitedly about Dublin until the end of March. When the body of another prisoner who had died of influenza in Gloucester gaol, just before the general amnesty, arrived in Dublin, Collins met it at the railway station with about five hundred other Volunteers, many in uniform, and personally helped to carry the coffin.[33]

A further boost to nationalist moral came at the end of March when, as a result of another skilfully planned operation by Collins, twenty prisoners including Beasli, the editor of the Volunteer paper *An t Oglach*, climbed over the wall of Mountjoy gaol with a rope ladder in broad daylight and escaped, to the delight of passers-by, through the Dublin streets. But, though such events might hearten or cause alarm, as the case might be, politically they did not bring an Irish Republic any nearer. It was to the political sphere that most Sinn Fein supporters still looked for success, and there none seemed forthcoming.

The political offensive of Sinn Fein proceeded on two fronts: in America, where Irish opinion was being mobilized both in Congress and outside, with the help of Patrick McCartan, Sean MacDermott's old IRB friend, who was now Sinn Fein's 'Ambassador' to the States; and in Paris, where Sean T. O'Kelly, also an IRB man from pre-war days, had set himself up at the Grand Hotel, Boulevard des Capucines, as Sinn Fein's man knocking on the door of the Peace Conference.* In Paris Kelly worked extremely hard, maintaining a wide range of press contacts and delivering, along with copies

* Sean T. O'Kelly became first President of the Republic of Ireland in 1949.

of the Dail's Declaration of Independence, letters to all the Conference delegates in which he asked for Ireland's case to be heard at the earliest possible moment. Very few even troubled to reply. The rules of the Conference also allowed the Secretariat to receive outside petitions, and such as were of political interest were to be summarized and distributed to all the delegates. This procedure was, of course, something of an anti-climax after Sinn Fein's confident election assurances that Ireland would be able to walk into the Conference by the front door, but it was only one of the many devices at the indomitable Kelly's command.

Most hope of all attached to President Wilson personally. But Wilson too failed to reply to Kelly's early attempts to see him, adjourning in any case to the States soon after Kelly arrived in Paris. There were, however, hopes of better treatment on his return, because while in the States Wilson was subjected to intensive pressure by the Irish lobby to get Ireland admitted to the Conference. On 22 February a great Irish Race Convention sitting in Philadelphia had demanded 'Irish Freedom' and the House of Representatives had passed a resolution urging the Peace Conference to consider Ireland's claim to self-determination favourably. As Griffith's paper *Nationality* put it: '... even if Wilson had simply been trying to avoid embarrassment in Paris he couldn't avoid the embarrassment which the question "What about Ireland?" would cause him in America.' Griffith announced that he was inclined to give Wilson 'a chance to make good'.[34] And Wilson himself seemed partially to encourage such thinking when he declared in Boston: 'It seems as if the settlements of this war affect directly or indirectly every small nation in the world. ... We set this nation up to make men free, and we did not confine our conception and purpose to America; and now we will make men free.'[35]

He returned to Paris where the persistence of Kelly – later joined by Gavan Duffy, grandson of the patriot of 1848 – in presenting the Irish case, was beginning to have some effect at least on the world's press and international opinion generally. Part of the weakness of the Irish position was that this was a conference of victors in a war in which many of the Sinn Fein leaders, including Kelly himself, had appeared at least neutral or even friendly to the losing side. The Republican Proclamation of 1916 had openly described the Germans as 'gallant allies in Europe'. Kelly clearly found this aspect of the situation awkward at times, and once replied quite inaccurately to a foreign correspondent that the only help given to Germany during the war came from Casement 'acting entirely on his own'.[*36] The old Redmondite supporters really had a far better right to argue the case for Irish admission, and indeed a memorial signed by 140 officers, including two Generals, had

* Casement's mission to Germany with, among other objects, that of raising an Irish Brigade, to fight against the allies, was a collective decision of both Clan-na-Gael and the IRB. (See *The Bold Fenian Men*, p. 224.)

petitioned King George V to have the claim of the Irish nation heard at the Conference. It is uncertain whether Kelly also judiciously applied this line of argument, but certainly he was soon reaping the benefit of it. The French newspaper *La Gazette* reminded its readers of the strength of Ireland's claim with the statement that 'the green flag of Erin' had floated above every major battlefield of the Great War and only yesterday her sons had been dying in the service of France and her allies.[37]

In the end, however, it was not to be any sort of eloquence nor even the claims of justice which were to be decisive at the Conference but the pragmatic demands of power politics. Lloyd George, at the head of his Unionist-dominated Coalition, had no intention of allowing Ireland to be considered as anything but an internal affair of the British Government. President Wilson, for all the embarrassing pressures of Irish-American influence, which were strengthened by the arrival in Paris of a special three-man American Commission for Irish Freedom to urge Ireland's case, had no intention of adding a major break with the British Government to his other international troubles. The furthest he was prepared to go when speaking to members of the American Commission was to express his own personal understanding of Ireland's claim while reserving the position of the President of the United States. And although this American Commission paid an important visit to Ireland in May to confer with de Valera on the whole question of securing international recognition at the Conference, de Valera himself was being forced to speak before long of 'our apparent defeat in Paris'.[38]

Sinn Fein, it seemed, would have to turn to other channels.

6

Michael Collins and Others
(April–December 1919)

Another in the series of systematic assassinations of Crown agents by the Volunteers, which was to mark the next two years in Ireland, had taken place in Westport on the night of 31 March. At a few minutes to eleven, a former Inspector of the RIC called Milling, now a Resident Magistrate, had just gone into his drawing-room to put his clock on to the new summer-time before retiring, when four revolver shots were fired at him in the old White-boy or Land League style through the window, shattering the glass and hitting him in the abdomen. He died next morning, murmuring to a RIC man who had been summoned to his death-bed: 'They have got me at last.' Milling had become particularly unpopular in the previous year when he had sent Volunteers to prison for unlawful assembly and drilling and had been under police protection ever since. A week before he had helped send two men to prison for cattle-driving.[1]

The deed seems to have been the work of local men acting without sanction from the Dublin executive headquarters, though it could conceivably have been ordered by the IRB. Many local activists were at this time afraid that inactivity would lead to a decay in the Volunteer organization and one of them has written: 'It was saved mainly because a minority of officers and men vigorously agitated the policy of action, argued its feasibility and more or less convinced or coerced General Headquarters into giving it a reluctant sanction.'[2] One of those at General Headquarters who almost certainly required very little persuasion along these lines was Michael Collins. He had made his own attitude towards future action clear in a revealing scene at the end of March.

On de Valera's return to Ireland, Collins, on his own and Harry Boland's initiative, had issued public notices to the effect that the President would make an official entrance into Dublin 'at the gates of the City' where he was to be received by the Lord Mayor and escorted to the Mansion House. The last person to be so received had been the British monarch Queen Victoria, nineteen years before. Understandably the authorities banned the proposed ceremony. But Collins insisted that it should go ahead and de

Valera prepared a fairly militant speech for the occasion.[3] Many Sinn Fein supporters were apprehensive of bloodshed and a meeting was called of the Sinn Fein executive, in whose name Collins had announced the ceremony. He had even attached the signature of the Honorary Secretary to the notice without consulting him. After some protest had been made at this high-handedness Collins rose and, admitting full responsibility, announced that the decision had been taken nominally by Sinn Fein but in reality by 'the proper body, the Irish Volunteers'. He said, according to one who was present, that

the sooner fighting was forced and a general state of disorder created through the country, the better it would be for the country. Ireland was likely to get more out of a state of general disorder than from a continuance of the situation as it then stood. The proper people to take decisions of that kind were ready to face the military, and were resolved to force the issue. And they were not to be deterred by weaklings and cowards.[*]

On this occasion he was over-ruled, but within the Volunteer organization itself he was not so easily hampered. Only a few weeks later he was to write to a Volunteer Brigade commander: 'When you ask me for ammunition for guns which have never fired a shot in this fight, my answer is a simple one. Fire shots at some useful target or get to hell out of it.'[4] The day before the shooting of Milling at Westport, a constable had been seriously wounded by a Volunteer with a revolver in Cork.

The Westport killing was received with horror and widespread indignation throughout Ireland. The jury at the inquest found that Milling had been 'foully murdered' and a public meeting held in Westport condemned the outrage unanimously as did the Westport Urban District Council. The Archbishop of Tuam described it as a dastardly crime and the perpetrator, if not insane, 'a criminal of the first order'. The *Irish Independent*, which had supported Sinn Fein at the General Election, wrote in a leader entitled 'Cowardly Crimes' that the killing had been 'indefensible' and 'morally

---

* This eye-witness account is that of Darrell Figgis, *Recollections of the Irish War* (London, 1927), p. 243. His book was written, according to the publisher, some two to three years after this incident and since Figgis says that Collins's 'words on this occasion are too well printed on my memory ever to be forgotten', they may reasonably be regarded as substantially correct. Figgis, who had played a part in the events leading up to the Howth gun-running (see *The Bold Fenian Men*, pp. 211–12) and in electioneering activities for Sinn Fein from 1917 until his arrest at the time of the 'German plot' in May 1918, was a self-opinionated and difficult man and, as his end was to show, to some extent personally unstable. His book has often been discredited by extremists partly because he was one of the first to oppose them. However, his analysis of the general trend within the Sinn Fein movement between 1919 and 1921 has much to recommend it and is substantiated by other evidence (see below, *passim*). Figgis committed suicide in Bloomsbury in 1925 after the death, following an abortion, of a London dancing teacher with whom he had been living for two years. His wife had shot herself in the Wicklow Mountains the year before. (*The Times*, 23, 28, 30 October 1925.)

wrong' and that it could 'only bring odium on the whole country and do irreparable harm to the national cause'.[5]

A week later a Constable O'Brien was shot dead in Limerick when a party of some twenty men rescued a Volunteer named Byrne in his pyjamas from a hospital where he was being treated under guard. In the mêlée, however, Byrne was himself shot by one of the police and died a few days later. In moving a resolution of sympathy with Byrne's mother and simultaneously paying a tribute to Constable O'Brien of the RIC, a speaker at the Limerick Board of Guardians repudiated 'English' statements that Sinn Fein had had knowledge of 'recent murders'. 'They would not tolerate,' he said, 'the murder of any man. They were prepared to meet their enemies by open day and would not hide themselves or act as assassins.'[6]

Even at this point in time, after the General Election, after all the sense of betrayal over Home Rule, after all earlier Irish history, the British Government, by some form of settlement which would have acknowledged the nationalist principle of a united Ireland, could almost certainly have driven a wedge between the vast majority of moderate Sinn Fein opinion and the extremists within the movement who were determined to force a bloody revolution at all costs. But the political realities of the time make such speculation irrelevant. Not only were the British Government and the British Parliament dominated by men with strong ties of loyalty to the anti-national minority in North-East Ulster, but Britain had just emerged triumphant and apparently unweakened from the greatest test of her strength in history and was as yet in no psychological mood drastically to re-think Irish policy. The government therefore took the only action it thought necessary: repression. This made it easier for Volunteer extremists to convince their moderate Sinn Fein supporters that the fight for nationalist principles was indeed as brutal and violent as Fenians had always said it must be.

The local sense of outrage at the Soloheadbeg killings in County Tipperary in January had been to some extent blunted by the subsequent imposition of military restrictions. The same thing now happened in Westport and in Limerick, which were both immediately proclaimed military districts. Whereas the funeral of Constable O'Brien had been sympathetically attended by some Sinn Fein supporters, that of the Volunteer Byrne took place down streets menacingly lined by British troops with fixed bayonets and armoured cars, and a military aircraft even flew overhead.[7] By the next day in addition to Tipperary, Westport and Limerick (both City and County), much of County Cork including the city, County Roscommon and County Kerry were under military rule. In Limerick, where the military restrictions on fairs, markets and social functions and the need of permits for movement caused much resentment, a particularly serious situation developed and a General Strike was called for a few days. On one occasion a thousand citizens who had left the town without permits to watch a football match were prevented from legally returning at night by the military. Most, however, had filtered back by their own devices the following morning, thus re-arousing all the traditional scorn for authority as well as resentment. Sympathetic farmers sent eggs, butter, milk and bread into the beleaguered city from the surrounding countryside.[8]

Such crude displays of British military strength disconcerted many otherwise moderate nationalists who had a more acute sense of Irish history than the British Government. The *Irish Independent* which, while pro-Sinn Fein, deplored the shootings, stressed that military measures were no way to deal with them.[9] Henry Harrison, the former Nationalist MP who had been an ardent supporter of Parnell's and had served with distinction and gallantry in the 16th Irish Division in France, wrote a significant letter to *The Times* on 23 April. Constitutionalism, he wrote – by which he meant the Home Rule movement – had achieved its success only to be robbed of its fruits by unconstitutional action on the part of the two great English political parties acting as accomplices. There would soon, he said, be nothing but counsels of despair. When he came to lay aside his uniform, his duty to Ireland would override all other loyalties, and if the betrayal of constitutionalism were finally consummated he would betake himself to 'such courses (if any) as may seem most expedient for helping Ireland's cause, whether or not the law allows or the Constitution warrants'.[10]

Robert Lynd, the correspondent of the *Daily News*, reported that 'even the soldiers who fought for the allies as they return home are becoming converted by the thousand into Sinn Feiners'.[11] One such was a young man of twenty-one from West Cork named Tom Barry, who had been in the British Army in Mesopotamia and who was soon to apply to join the Volunteers, or, as they were beginning to be called in the countryside, the Irish Republican Army. He had had no nationalist ideas at all before the war. Within two years he was to become one of the most skilled guerrilla commanders in Ireland.[12]

A feeling of separateness from Britain, which, up to now, the Fenians and Sinn Fein had had to argue and which Harrison and most Nationalists had always denied, was being created and visibly consolidated by the British Government with its refusal to offer Ireland anything but military force.

It was at this sensitive moment that the American Commission for Irish Freedom arrived in Ireland to see de Valera. They were to prove of considerably more value to the Irish republican cause in Ireland than they had been in Paris. For the week-long journeying of its three delegates about the country in the company of the Irish leaders, with many unabashed speeches calling for an Irish Republic on platforms where the tricolour waved with the Stars and Stripes, did much to convey the impression that the power of America was behind the cause, and to rally popular opinion when there was in fact little else with which to rally it. The Commission even managed to provoke a few incidents with the British authorities which rallied opinion still further.

On the afternoon of 12 May they attended in the Dublin Mansion House a private meeting of Dail Eirann which they addressed. Collins and Robert Barton – the latter had escaped from Mountjoy gaol some weeks before – were among the Dail representatives present, and though they withdrew up a long ladder into an adjoining building at the end of the proceedings, a large force of police and soldiers came raiding for them shortly afterwards.[13] To some extent at least the authorities were by now aware of Collins's importance. When, later that evening, guests began to arrive for an official public reception by the Lord Mayor for the American Commission, they found the building surrounded by troops in full field equipment with steel helmets and fixed bayonets and an armoured car pointing its machine-gun at the crowds. The delegates themselves, accompanied by de Valera and the Archbishop of Cashel and the Bishop of Killaloe, were actually prevented from entering for a time while the vain search continued. The reception was eventually allowed to take place, but as the London *Star* commented: 'A more maladroit exhibition could not well be conceived ... What a story they have got for American platforms...'

They had another from Westport, County Galway, where the military with fixed bayonets and an armoured car held the Commission up for one and a half hours outside the town and refused to allow them to enter. MacNeill, who was with them, was manhandled out of the way and moved off at the point of the bayonet. At the meetings which the Commission were allowed to hold in their progress through Galway, Mullingar, Athlone and other towns, Volunteers regulated the enthusiastic crowds.[14]

'Three weeks ago,' wrote the *Irish Times* when they left, 'none save fools and fanatics believed in the possibility of an Irish Republic. Today a large number of Irish Nationalists hope, and a still larger number fear, that in the near future an Irish Republic may come to birth from the grotesque union of British folly and American sentiment....'[15]

When the delegates called on Dr Walsh, the Archbishop of Dublin, to say farewell, he was able to say to them that they had had an experience of 'the kind of government under which we are living in Ireland'.[16]

In vain did the government's supporters as well as its opponents look to it for a policy. There was silence. 'Some solution must be found,' *The Times* had cried on 16 April, 'for the condition of Ireland is poisoning the broader currents of our Imperial and external policies.' And on 2 May the paper had sounded an eleventh-hour note of desperation in its plea that 'If there ever was a moment when it was vital that the Government should understand the situation in Ireland it is now. Most people agree that something should be done and done quickly.'

On May 22 came the first political pronouncement the government had made on the Irish question since the General Election. It came from Carson's old Galloper, Lord Birkenhead, now Lord Chancellor, hardly an auspicious source. He said that when the Peace Treaty was finally signed the government would consider what to do about the Home Rule Act. Meantime, he continued, the only proper policy for Ireland was any degree of force that might be necessary to maintain order there. For, he contended, with what was an absurd exaggeration, even if an exaggeration of a certain truth, the great majority of the Irish people were in a state of open rebellion.

The slow rebellion that the extremist Republicans were developing under the name of Sinn Fein was indeed gradually getting under way. And yet for all the rally of national sentiment in face of British activities, when, on 13 May 1919, two more RIC constables were shot dead in a daring rescue of a Volunteer prisoner from a train at Knocklong station, County Tipperary, many moderates felt dismayed, and the strongest condemnation was forth-coming from the Church at once. The parish priest of a locality in which the two constables had served declared that murder was murder, however much people might attempt to cloak it with a political motive. And Dr Harty, the Archbishop of Cashel who had been confronted with British bayonets outside the Mansion House in Dublin a few days before, denounced what he called 'the deplorable occurrence' at Knocklong as 'a crime against the law of God and a crime against Ireland'. He asked the young men of the country 'not to stain the fair name of their native land by deeds of bloodshed'. It was, he said, no use to appeal to the fact that the British Government had been committing outrages in Ireland: two wrongs did not make a right.[17] The inquest jury conveyed an ambivalence suggestive of the resentment which British military measures were creating. While expressing sympathy for the relatives of the dead policemen it added a rider that 'the Government should cease arresting respectable persons, thereby causing bitter exasperation among the people'.[18]

As far as the respectability of the arrested person in this instance was concerned, he was Sean Hogan, a Volunteer who had been present at the Soloheadbeg killings. He had been rescued by his former comrades in that venture, Dan Breen, Seumas Robinson and Sean Treacy with help from other local Volunteers. Breen later wrote that he had to fire at once on this occasion because otherwise the constables would have shot their prisoner as they had done in the Limerick hospital. Though Breen was himself severely wounded he again successfully disappeared with the others into the country-side, getting help from local people and being passed along the Volunteer network.[19] He and his comrades had again carried out the exploit on their own initiative.

The true attitude of the Dail representatives to these displays of Volunteer initiative cannot easily be discerned. Many Dail members, of course, being themselves Volunteers or even IRB men, had no scruples about such action for in their eyes all police and military could legitimately be treated as enemies. We have Beaslai's word that no voice was raised against such action in the Dail in 1919, and yet not all the representatives there can have felt at ease, particularly in view of the persistent condemnation of the Church. Eoin MacNeill clearly had to resort to self-deception in order to accept it. When asked about the shooting of policemen in an interview with the *Glasgow Herald* at the end of May he replied: 'As to the shooting of policemen, in all cases, as far as I know, these acts were committed in resistance to policemen engaged on purely repressive activities.'[20]

It is hard to see how the two local constables guarding a load of gelignite on its way to blasting operations at Soloheadbeg in January could have been regarded as engaged on repressive activities, or the two policemen caught at Knocklong guarding, in the normal course of duty, one of the Soloheadbeg killers. The raids for arms were easier to justify. MacNeill had been in favour of a defensive role for the Volunteers since before 1916. If they did not get arms now where they could, he told the *Glasgow Herald*, they would be 'overridden'.

But if such public utterances on the awkward subject were rare from the Dail 'Government' we do know what the attitude of the Sinn Fein executive was at this time. Collins castigated it in a letter on 17 May – five days after he had attended the Dail addressed by the American Commission. 'The position is intolerable,' he wrote, '– the policy now seems to be to squeeze out anyone who is tainted with strong fighting ideas or, should I say I suppose, ideas of the utility of fighting.' And the next day he wrote again: 'We have too many of the bargaining type already. I am not so sure that our movement or part of it at any rate is fully alive to the developing situation. It seems to me that official S. F. is inclined to be ever less militant and ever more political and theoretical. . . . It is rather pitiful and at times somewhat disheartening. At the moment I'm awfully fed up, yet 'tis in vain etc.'[21]

The last words were an evocation of the joking doggerel with which Wolfe Tone had often completed entries in his diary: 'Yet 'tis in vain for soldiers to complain!' Collins indeed embodied much of the dash and charm of Tone's fearless spirit, combining with these qualities considerably greater military effectiveness. From his own point of view he was soon to set the situation to rights.

Working from offices in Dublin, some secret, some not (one of the former in the first school started by Patrick Pearse, St Ita's) Collins not only supervised the organization of Volunteer brigades throughout the country, but built up a formidable active élite in the capital itself, ably assisted by the Volunteer Chief of Staff, Richard Mulcahy, together with a Chief Intelligence Officer, Liam Tobin, and what later came to be known as 'the Squad' of expert gunmen. At the same time Collins appeared openly at sessions of the Dail between January and September 1919, functioning in his other role of Minister of Finance, and relying on information from his increasingly subtle intelligence system to give him warning of raids on the Mansion House. During a Dail session in April, when his face appeared respectably in the newspapers,[22] he actually spent part of one of the nights inspecting British secret reports and documents inside the headquarters of the Dublin detective force, whither he had been conducted by a detective of the political section, working as a double agent in Collins's service. This man, Edward Broy, together with other double agents, James Kavanagh, Patrick Macnamara and David Neligan, Irishmen who had decided that loyalty to Ireland could no longer be identified with loyalty to the Crown they served, were to provide the heart of an intelligence system which was totally to reverse the traditional eighteenth- and nineteenth-century pattern by which the informers were on the government side. Collins was even at a later date to enrol the services of an English officer working for British Military Intelligence in Dublin Castle.[23]

A less easily determined force complementing Collins's underground revolutionary apparatus was what his British opponents called the Sinn Fein 'terror' in Ireland. The label 'Sinn Fein' in this context is confusing, but at a distance of fifty years the term 'terror' can be stripped of its pejorative content. Intimidation is an instrument of which the most high-minded nationalist revolutionaries have always made use as a means of ensuring that the often inert mass of the population should at least not hinder those operations conducted, according to the revolutionaries, on its own behalf. It was inevitably to figure prominently in these years in Ireland where it had historical roots going back to the agrarian secret societies of the eighteenth and nineteenth centuries, and had manifested itself most recently in the days of the Land League. Threatening letters, the infliction of cruel wounds, firing through windows of houses or at the person had intermittently been a feature of Irish rural life for agrarian purposes for two centuries. They became easily applied by individuals to new political objectives which also had to be pursued in secret.

So much history of what came to be known as the Irish War of Independence has been in terms of hagiography that the extent to which the intimidation of ordinary people – as opposed to the attacks on policemen, soldiers and officials – played a useful part is often omitted. The relative ease with which men like Breen or the killer of the magistrate Milling and Constable O'Brien of Limerick were able to remain undetected is evidence not only of reluctance to cooperate with the law for patriotic reasons but also of more self-interested motives. The fear of what might happen to a man who contravened the law of secret societies was a folk-tradition which rural Irishmen were inclined to respect, and of which they were not infrequently reminded.

A transgressor had his ears cut off with a pair of shears as late as January 1920 and a girl had the calf of her left leg shot off by two masked men the following month.[24] And though these punishments – probably for simple agrarian offences – would have been disapproved of by most Volunteers they created a climate from which they benefited. The Volunteers themselves usually preferred more direct methods, shooting the culprit cleanly and tying a label marked 'Spy – killed by IRA' to the corpse. Dozens of Irishmen were to die such deaths at the hands of their fellow-countrymen before the 'war of independence' was over.

Though physical violence against non-conforming individuals was not threatened in the name of the Volunteers or IRA on any scale until the second half of 1919, and did not assume significant proportions until the years 1920–21, some fear of intimidation at least played a part from the start. 'There is more terrorism.' wrote the Unionist *Daily Telegraph* at the end of May 1919, 'than in the worst days of the Land League. People are compelled to fall into line with the Sinn Feiners or they could neither trade nor buy the necessities of life.'[25] The paper may well have been exaggerating, but that a boycott was in force could not be disputed.

The boycott – that mildest but in some ways most effective of all agrarian weapons – had been decreed by no less a man than de Valera himself, when, in addressing the Dail in April, he described the RIC as 'spies in our midst' and went on, somewhat in the tradition of Charles Stewart Parnell:

... these men must not be tolerated socially as if they were clean healthy members of our organized life. They must be shown and made to feel how base are the functions they perform, and how vile is the position they occupy. To shun them, to refuse to talk to them, or have any social intercourse with them or to treat them as equals, will give them vividly to understand how utterly the people of Ireland loathe both themselves and their calling ...[26]

This was no incitement to violence in itself, but de Valera knew enough of rural Ireland, as Parnell had done, to know that there would be men in the countryside who saw to it that such a boycott was enforced. Later in the year a poster was to be found, placed close to where two policemen had been shot dead in County Clare, proclaiming: 'Shun all policemen and spies! Three cheers for the IRA!' and in the next two years apart from numerous executions of 'spies' there were to be many cases of women who had their heads shaved or were otherwise maltreated for consorting with Irish police or British soldiers.[27] Even though such action may often have been taken by local individuals independently of Collins and Headquarters, the atmosphere these actions produced certainly made conditions for more significant operations easier. From several counties in the south and west of Ireland the RIC were to report by the end of 1919 that degrees of Sinn Fein terrorism accounted for total lack of cooperation between the population and the police. '. . . Even persons upon whom outrages have been committed,' said the report from County Galway, 'are not disposed to give the police any information which might lead to the discovery of the perpetrators of the outrages, fearing that by so doing further outrages would be committed on themselves or their property . . .'[28]

But the most potent force of all operating in favour of Collins and the other militants was undoubtedly the British Government itself. The embittered Home Rulers and other moderates who had largely voted Sinn Fein into power had been offered nothing in response to their challenging demand for a radical new policy. The government had tacitly admitted they had none to give and, responding to the activity of the extremists, sent steel-helmeted troops and armoured cars, adding to the political injury the insulting presence of an unwanted military authority in the streets. Gradually, reluctantly, the moderates were brought to acknowledge the fact that in an extreme situation there was little place for moderation.

But the process in the middle of 1919 was only just beginning and Collins, confronted by the caution of the political forces of Sinn Fein, was sometimes in despair. His bitterness against the Sinn Fein executive in the middle of May had been partly caused by an inadvertent public revelation on its part that its secretary, Harry Boland, had left the country.[29] For, having refused to accept the deputy whom Boland left behind, they had insisted on electing a less belligerent figure in his place. Up to that point Collins had managed to keep Boland's departure a secret for five weeks. Boland had in fact left Ireland to prepare the way physically and politically for de Valera's clandestine departure for the United States. And early in June de Valera was successfully spirited out of the country by Collins and arrived in New York on 11 June. Collins may by now have been partly relieved to see him go.

De Valera's own view at this moment of the best methods by which to pursue the goal of the Republic was, as often when an issue was delicate, obscure. On the one hand he was still technically President of the Volunteers, as well as the President of the Dail: and he was ready enough publicly to proclaim that the men of the tiny minority of 1916 had been 'justified in regarding themselves as genuine representatives of the nation'.[30] His official position with the Volunteers could be said to have been effectively taken over by the Minister of Defence, Cathal Brugha, but he knew well enough the sort of extremism for which both Brugha and Collins stood. On the other hand, his very insistence on going to America at all made it clear that he was thinking primarily in terms of a political rather than a guerrilla solution. He was in fact to remain in America for eighteen months, from June 1919 until December 1920. During this time the situation in Ireland changed dramatically and irrevocably.

7

The Campaign of Killing
(1919–20)

A grim process, brilliantly master-minded by Collins, of systematic terror against Irish police and detectives began on 24 June 1919. An Inspector of the RIC named Hunt was shot dead in the back in the main square of Thurles in broad daylight. There was a large crowd passing through the square at the time on its way back from a race meeting, but it made no attempt to help the dying man and the assailant disappeared into it with ease. He was never caught. Hunt had recently been assiduous in directing the law against the Volunteers and on the two previous Sundays had broken up Sinn Fein meetings, seizing from one of them a Republican flag.

However, the jury at the inquest did not accept the view that such activities warranted a death sentence. They found a verdict of wilful murder and passed a vote of condolence to the Inspector's family.[1] The Archbishop of Tuam denounced 'this shocking crime' as 'a most grave violation of the law of God' and said that the man who committed it would one day 'also be called before the Judgement Seat of God, and will meet his victim face to face for his punishment through eternal life'.[2]

The very day of Hunt's death – though before it was known – the archbishop had been one of the signatories of a statement issued by the entire Irish hierarchy from Maynooth. This had castigated the irritations of military rule and the denial of political rights to the Irish people.* 'The existing method of Government cannot last,' this statement had run. '... We have the evils of military rule exhibited at our doors. In this ancient civilizing nation, the people are not permitted to rule themselves through men of their own choice.' The acts of violence which the hierarchy 'deplored' sprang, they said, 'from this cause and this cause alone'.[3]

Now too in the archbishop's condemnation of the deed at Thurles there was a note which for all his abhorrence made some justification of such things easier: 'For all this,' he said, 'there is only one solution: let the

---

* Piaras Beaslai MP, Lawrence Ginnell MP, J. J. Clancy MP and Constance Markievicz MP had all been arrested or given sentences that month.

military domination of Ireland cease at once. Let the people of Ireland choose for themselves the Government under which they are to live . . .'

At this time in the middle of 1919 there was an unresolved ambivalence in the minds of the Irish people. On the one hand they were being roused by government policy into a national political front such as had only been equalled in Irish history by O'Connell's movement for Repeal of the Union. Readers of the Nationalist Party paper, the *Freeman's Journal*, read headlines like 'Free Use of the Baton in Kilmallock'; 'Women Suffer'; 'Glen of Aherlow Aroused by Troops, Aeroplanes etc.'⁵ and reacted indistinguishably from those who had voted Sinn Fein rather than Nationalist at the election. The very appearance in the towns and villages of large numbers of soldiers with rifles and bayonets evoked associations of an ancient land war that went deeper than any political frustration. On the other hand the bloodshed caused by the actions of the Volunteers in provoking the government was disliked and deplored.

In the long run, in the light of history, there could be no doubt on whose side the Irish people would come down in a simple contest of brutality between the government and the Volunteers. In the absence of any realistic policy but repression from the government they were bound to come down, for all their early misgivings, on the side of the Volunteers. In this the policy of Collins and the other extremists in the Sinn Fein movement succeeded brilliantly. They won their battle against the moderates in Sinn Fein by making moderation irrelevant.

The Archbishop of Tuam had concluded his pronouncement on the killing of Inspector Hunt with the words: 'We humbly implore God to grant us soon that liberty for which we and our fathers before us have prayed and longed. We ask Him at long last to grant us peace – peace from the blighting rule of the stranger, and peace from that baneful influence of deeds of violence.'

The only answer came from Dublin Castle. It immediately banned the entire Sinn Fein organization in Tipperary and even the Gaelic League itself. From Lloyd George and the government, euphoric over the Peace Treaty which they had just formally concluded at Versailles, there came no vestige of a new policy for Ireland.

Unionists were now more than ever desperately aware that some attitude other than either repression or the old proposal for the exclusion of six Ulster counties was required. A group headed by Sir Horace Plunkett formed in June 1919 an Irish Dominion League demanding Dominion Home Rule for all Ireland. The minority in Ireland, they declared, had no right to deny the fundamental right of the Irish people to see the unity of their country preserved.⁶ English Conservatives. like Garvin of the London *Observer*. commented that it was 'no longer enough for the Ulster Covenanters to say "We won't have it." That pre-war formula is as dead as King

William.... Mere "won't have it" is what the vast majority of the United Kingdom won't have.[7] He recommended an Ulster government sub-autonomous to Dublin.

But for Irishmen the only Conservative voice that seemed relevant was that of Carson, and with some reason considering how many of his staunch supporters were in the government.* And what Carson now said was: 'We will have nothing to do with Dominion Home Rule, or any other Home Rule.... We avoid it as a thing unclean, we fling it back at them.'[8]

Carson knew well enough that the government would have to offer something eventually, but he was determined that the sacrosanct position he had built up for the exclusion of six counties of Ulster should not be tampered with. Bargaining from immense strength he actually called for a Repeal of the Home Rule Act and said that if there were an attempt to impose it he would summon his provisional government and call out the Ulster Volunteers.[9]

Talk like this made many moderates in Ireland feel that for all Sinn Fein's apparent shortcomings there was still nothing to support but Sinn Fein. After all, the respectable illusion that the Irish Republic might still somehow be implemented by moral pressure and by the abstentionist policy of self-reliance was still formally maintained. Announcements of the Dail 'Government's' establishment of Arbitration Courts for land disputes, of commissions of investigation into the country's economic resources and above all the launching of an ambitious Republican Loan of which £250,000 was to be raised with de Valera's help in the United States and another £250,000 in Ireland itself, had an impressive ring.

Collins himself, as Minister of Finance, was in charge of the loan. Many people thought at the time that the target was absurdly high for, having no idea of his extraordinary role behind the scenes, they were quite unaware of his exceptional administrative ability or organizing powers. Within a year he was able to announce the closing of the loan at a figure of more than £357,000 for Ireland itself.[10]

That pressure was sometimes used to help raise this money seems undeniable, for when lists of subscribers periodically fell into the hands of British Intelligence they even included the names of well-known Unionists.[11] But even though the IRB and Volunteer network which was Collins's principal concern made organization and collection easier, the technical business of successfully lodging the money in hiding-places and various bank accounts which would escape the scrutiny of persistent British attempts to locate it, at a time when Collins himself was continually on the run, was a masterly

---

* In addition to Bonar Law, Birkenhead and Walter Long, all the law officers of the Crown in Ireland were Ulster "Covenanters".

achievement. It seems all the more so given the extent and far-reaching impact of his other activities and responsibilities at the time.

The Volunteers were now coming more under the control of Collins and General Headquarters in Dublin, though it was in the nature of the situation that much flexibility had always to be left to individual initiative in the field. Through able organizers whom he himself appointed and sent out, like Ernie O'Malley, a young red-headed middle-class Catholic of literary tastes, or through dedicated young local commanders with whom he was in touch, like Liam Lynch from Cork, the energy and spirit of individual groups of Volunteers was slowly harnessed to a potential guerrilla force, with some counties, like Cork itself, active enough to provide as many as three brigades. In active areas like Cork such brigades contained at first about 3,500 Volunteers though their nominal strength at least was to grow greater.* The vast majority of these men, however, at all times through the next two years continued simultaneously to lead apparently normal everyday lives in the towns and countryside.

At this time, in the middle of 1919, their activities still had a desultory quality. 'We are still so to speak in the trenches,' the secret Volunteer paper *An t Oglach* had put it in May, 'but our "trench raids" and active operations against the enemy are growing more and more frequent, and are usually attended with brilliant success.' Though sometimes lethal, these operations also sometimes recalled the more ineffectual efforts of the Fenians. Thus in August a police hut in East Clare was besieged for over an hour by an unknown number of men with rifles and revolvers and successfully defended by six members of the RIC who had actually been in bed at the start of the attack.[12] Two days before, however, another barracks in Clare had been captured and two of the constables shot dead. The Bishop of Galway described their deaths as wilful murder and the ordinary citizens who composed the coroner's jury had no hesitation in confirming his judgement with a verdict to the same effect. There were sympathetic crowds at the constables' funeral.[13]

But again the pattern that had established itself at Westport and Limerick and in Tipperary was repeated. The whole of Clare was immediately proclaimed a military district and by the end of August 1919 some seven thousand troops were on the move throughout the county day and night. There was a ten o'clock curfew with lights out half an hour later. Significantly, when shots were fired at night through the window of a man who had been working for a relative under police protection, and the man's fifteen-year-old

---

* O'Donoghue, *No Other Law*, p. 36. By 1921 brigades were organized in divisions. The size of divisions varied greatly. The First Southern Divisions under Lynch numbered nominally 33,550, a quarter of the entire nominal strength of the IRA. The 3rd Southern Division numbered 6,000 which was much nearer the average size (ibid., p. 334).

son was killed, the coroner's jury, in a verdict that was treated with some scepticism, pinned the blame on the military.*

In Dublin Collins began systematically dealing out death to those Irishmen in the 'G' (detective) division of the Dublin Metropolitan Police whom his intelligence network told him were becoming well-informed about Volunteer activities.[14] He organized small units of skilled young gunmen who, filled with the highest patriotic motives, became proficient at liquidating both their fellow-countrymen and agents sent from England in the public streets. On 31 July 1919 an unarmed Irish detective sergeant named Smyth, a man with seven children, was shot in the back just outside his home in Dublin by one such group. 'You cowards,' he cried, understandably failing to appreciate the risks his assailants themselves incurred, and he turned and faced them. They fired again and continued to fire until he was within fifteen yards of his house, hitting him five times in all.[15] He was to die some weeks later.

A few days after the attack the Corporation of Dublin carried a motion condemning recent outrages and the Lord Mayor, Laurence O'Neill, who had done much to fight for better gaol treatment for Sinn Fein prisoners, strongly associated himself with the Bishop of Galway's use of the term 'murder'. 'There was,' he said, 'no justification for murder and outrage.'[16] It was a generally representative view at the time. The Westmeath County Council ten days later passed a resolution condemning 'in the strongest terms our language can afford the murders and outrages that are occurring in various parts of the country'. These were, it said, engineered by the dangerous parts of society. One of the speakers said that 'a storm of indignation should go forth from the elected representatives of the people. The instigators of those crimes are no acquisition to any political party or organization.'[17]

It did not yet seem to occur to the bulk of Sinn Fein supporters that it was precisely the elected representatives of the people – or an all-important element in them – who were applying the policy of 'murder and outrage' without popular sanction. On the very day of the Westmeath resolution, one such representative, who was still referred to in the newspapers as Mr M. Collins MP, gave a remarkable demonstration of his own extraordinary sangfroid as a revolutionary. For while Detective Sergeant Smyth lay dying in hospital Collins appeared at a Sinn Fein Congress at the Mansion House on 21 August, and, speaking as Minister of Finance, in a lucid detailed speech which was publicly reported, described the purpose and methods of

* The affair remains a mystery. The Army afterwards held an inquiry and found that the shots could not have been fired by any of the troops then stationed in the district. A year later such an inquiry would itself have been treated with scepticism. But at this stage it cannot be so easily dismissed. The Army had suffered no casualty here and the fact that the bullets by which the boy was killed were military is hardly conclusive evidence in the circumstances of the time. The connection with the man under police protection and the Land League style of the murder may, or may not, be significant. (*Clare Champion*, 30 August 1919.)

collection of the Republican Loan. On it, he said, the whole constructive policy of Dail Eireann depended. The money was to go to a Consular Service, to Irish fisheries, afforestation, the encouragement of industry, and the establishment of a national civil service and arbitration courts.

'Even if nothing comes of this moment', he said, '– which is impossible – the loan will be redeemed by the next Irish Government even as today we are redeeming the Fenian bonds.'[18]

Earlier in the summer when a search had been made for him at the Mansion House, Collins had escaped up a rope ladder, and this time he presumably took careful precautions when entering and leaving the building. Two days later he was writing to his sisters: 'For the moment . . . things are settled enough, but I am looking forward to the winter for significant happenings.'[19] On 12 September he had Detective Constable Daniel Hoey shot dead in the street outside police headquarters in the middle of Dublin. It had been a spectacular day, for only a few hours before the government had finally given an answer to the urgent question of what it was going to do about Ireland. It had suppressed and declared illegal Dail Eireann.

Hoey had taken part in the raid on the Mansion House that had followed the decision, but Collins had escaped through a skylight. A few hours later the detective's body slumped on to the pavement, hit by revolver bullets. He was unarmed and all that was found in his pocket was money and some religious emblems, for he was a devout Catholic.[20] His was the third death of a member of the Crown forces that week and the sixth in less than six weeks.

One of the other casualties had been a soldier killed in Fermoy, County Cork, in a daring assault on a party of troops marching to church on Sunday, 7 September. This raid had been formally authorized by Collins and the Volunteer GHQ in Dublin, although on condition that there should be no casualties.[21] It was brilliantly executed by Liam Lynch, revealing guerilla professionalism of which he was one of the earliest Volunteer exponents. The eighteen men of the King's Shropshire Light Infantry in the church party were swiftly overpowered and thirteen of their rifles loaded into waiting motor-cars which were immediately driven off. Military vehicles which took off in pursuit found roads blocked by fallen trees which had been sawn through during the night and held back by ropes until the escaping raiders were safely past. Only one detail of the operation had gone awry, for in the scuffle one of the soldiers had been shot dead and three others seriously wounded.

The jury at the subsequent inquest unanimously expressed horror and condemnation for 'this appalling outrage in the midst of a peaceable and civil community, between whom the most friendly feelings have always existed', but they did not find a verdict of murder because the raid's intention had clearly been to get the rifles and the killing had been unpremeditated.[22]

For this oversight, in spite of their additional expression of sympathy with the dead man's relatives, they were made to pay a heavy price. That night undisciplined troops broke out of barracks and did considerable damage in the town, smashing shop windows and particularly attacking the house of the foreman of the jury.[23] Just as Lynch's raid had indicated the sophisticated guerrilla technique which the Volunteers were eventually to develop in the countryside on a considerable scale, so this reprisal by the military foreshadowed a new pattern of violence that was to impress itself on Ireland with such profound long-term effects in the following year.

The official reaction to Lynch's Fermoy raid was predictable. Both Sinn Fein and the Volunteer organization were banned in the Cork district. Equally predictably, this decision had the opposite effect to that intended, for it emphasized an identification of the two elements in the new national movement at a time when a division could have been exploited. Thus, de Valera, commenting from New York a few days later, was able to say of the suppression of Sinn Fein in Cork that 'the English are ... seeking to goad the people into open rebellion in the field'.[24] What was really happening was that the Volunteers were goading the government into goading the people into rebellion – a process in which, much aided by the government itself, they were eventually to be successful.

For the time being, however, though Volunteer successes were enjoyed and applauded when they were achieved without bloodshed, those that caused casualties were still regarded by the Irish people with considerable reservation, if not dismay. Most of the victims after all were fellow Irishmen. A few days before the Fermoy raid a RIC Sergeant named Brady had been shot dead while on patrol duty in Tipperary. He left eight children and a widow, a simple Catholic Irishwoman who broke down pitifully at the funeral service, sobbing violently and calling out over and over again: 'Murdered by the roadside! Murdered by the roadside!'[25]

The following Sunday the local priest, with this and the recent systematic killings of Irish policemen in Dublin and elsewhere in mind, cried in an impassioned outburst:

'Who has authorized a small band of unknown, ignorant persons to meet in secret and decide that the life of a fellow human being may be taken lawfully.... The Irish people will not approve of bloodshed, and the freedom of martyred Ireland will not be achieved by midnight assassination.'[26]

A month later, on 19 October 1919, another Catholic Irishman of the RIC, Constable Downing, was shot in the stomach and killed in a Dublin street at 2 a.m. He was shot on Collins's orders and with the sanction of the 'Minister of Defence', Cathal Brugha, who, when Sinn Fein had been seeking democratic support, had declared that Ireland's freedom would never be won by assassination.* Three weeks later Brugha and Collins had a detective officer named Wharton shot in the back at night on the corner of

* See above, p. 36.

St Stephen's Green, Dublin, though his severe wounds did not prove fatal. Wharton had been prominent in a number of prosecutions of the Volunteers. On 1 December, again on the orders of Brugha and Collins, another detective of the political 'G' Division named Barton, an Irishman from County Kerry, was shot in the back and killed. The coroner's jury found a verdict of 'wilful murder' and added: 'We consider his death a loss to the citizens of Dublin and we condemn these outrages.' The Lord Mayor of Dublin, Larry O'Neill, a good nationalist, again publicly associated himself with the verdict, expressing his 'abhorrence of this terrible crime' and describing the dead detective as 'an asset to the city of Dublin'.[27]

When, dismayed by this slaughter of their best detectives, Dublin Castle sent for a particularly intelligent Inspector from Belfast named Redmond, Collins had him shot and killed in Dublin on 21 January 1920. Meanwhile, in his other capacity as a senior 'Minister' of the Dail, he had been issuing prospectuses for the Republican Loan, one of which ran: 'You can restore Ireland's Health, Her Beauty and Her Wealth: Subscribe today To the Irish National Loan.'[28]

In the countryside, too, the campaign against 'the enemy' continued bloodily. Another RIC constable had been killed when opening the door of a barracks to a Volunteer raiding party in County Meath at the end of October, an act which brought down the curse of God upon the perpetrator from the Bishop of Meath in Mullingar Cathedral.[29] The 'barracks' at Ballivor, County Meath, where this constable was shot, like very many of the six hundred or so 'barracks' in Ireland, was simply an ordinary two-storey house in the village street. It is understandable how such deeds, since sanctified into deeds of heroism, struck very many Irishmen at the time quite otherwise. This was long before any Irishman had been killed in a reprisal, and no Black and Tan had yet set foot in Ireland. When in December yet another RIC constable was shot dead by Volunteers in County Cork, in implementation of the doctrine long received from headquarters in *An t Oglach*, the Cork Corporation denounced the killing unanimously as a 'cowardly and disgraceful murder'.

That many Irishmen needed to be persuaded by the Volunteers to think differently about such things was as clear to the Volunteers now as it had been to them in the more rarefied atmosphere of 1916. Notices to 'Shun All Policemen as Spies and Traitors', signed 'A Soldier of the IRA (Irish Republican Army)' were appearing and were not to be taken lightly.[30] In Toomevara, County Tipperary, that autumn a notice naming for boycott a family 'which had done injury to three soldiers of the Irish Republic', and instructing that 'they must not be greeted or sat next to in Church', threatened punishment for non-compliance.[31] What punishment in the name of the Irish Republic meant in this sense was illustrated in Clare when an Irishman who had been in the British Army was appointed schoolmaster at

Knockjames. Notices were sent round to the parents of the local children reading: 'Keep your son from Knockjames, otherwise you will have reason to regret it. By Order of the Irish Republican Army.' The attendance was thus successfully reduced from forty-five children to sixteen, but one of the fathers who defied it received three hundred shot-gun pellets in both thighs, the groin and the lungs, in a manner that recalled the punishment of those who had always defied secret societies in Ireland.[32] The Judge who tried the case in which the victim applied for compensation voiced the common illusion of most Irishmen of the time. He said he was glad to believe that the perpetrators of such deeds got no sympathy whatsoever from 'any politician in this country. I would despair of my country,' he continued, 'if I thought the men elected to representative positions would or could for one moment sanction such outrages.'[33]

Elected representatives of the Irish people were sanctioning more lethal outrages than that against equally innocent people, but when in December Cardinal Logue, the Catholic Primate of All Ireland, was moved to speak out formally against the long sequence of killings in Dublin and elsewhere he, too, found it difficult to face the real truth:

Holy Ireland, the land of St Patrick, shall never be regenerated by deeds of blood or raised up by the hand of the midnight assassin .... It is hard to believe that the intelligent and reasonable members of any Christian political party could sanction or sympathize with crime. ... Among the body of the people those crimes inspire horror, contempt and reprobation. Their sympathies are with the unfortunate and innocent victims, not with the cowardly assassins.[34]

Even as the Cardinal was writing this address the men to whom he indirectly referred – Collins, Mulcahy and Brugha among others – had perfected plans on which they had long been working for a most daring assassination of no less a person than the Viceroy, Lord French, himself. His car was attacked at Ashtown, County Dublin, in broad daylight on 19 December 1919. The attack failed because those who lay in ambush for him, including Dan Breen, directed most of their fire against the wrong car in a small convoy of two and Collins was furious at the mistake.[35] The Archbishop of Dublin described the attack on French as 'an appalling attempt at murder'.[36]

The popular Dublin newspaper, the *Irish Independent*, concurred in the condemnation. Two days later a group of Collins's men armed with revolvers went to the editorial building where, after the editor had been informed of their disapproval of his comment and had been told that he would be shot if he stirred, the entire printing machinery of the paper was dismantled and destroyed.[37]

Patriotic motives must again be emphasized for Collins and others whom the Church, most responsible Irishmen and many ordinary Irishmen and women then regarded as murderers, though unaware of their identities. The

Volunteer leaders and their followers were acting in the pure Fenian tradition, setting out to redeem Ireland's past sufferings and redress her present wrongs by extreme methods because in their eyes these alone seemed appropriate to the extremity of the sufferings and the wrongs. There can be no doubt that their actions were immoral by the standards of the Church at the time, and were often by any standards vile. There can be no doubt that, like all revolutionaries, they had cynically exploited democratic processes to give the Irish people what they judged good for them rather than what the Irish people wanted. But for them these charges were irrelevant. For them the end alone would justify the means.

While de Valera's attitude to Collins's campaign of violence was further obscured by his long absence in America, the attitude of Arthur Griffith at this time, a man who believed in moral force and had disapproved of the 1916 rebellion, and whose moderating political influence on the movement Collins had feared two years before, must also remain something of a mystery. Griffith was now Acting President or Prime Minister of the underground 'Government' in de Valera's absence. We know that on at least one occasion, in 1919 when warned of an act of violence by Volunteers planned in Cork, Griffith intervened successfully with Collins to prevent it.[38] He must have known clearly enough who was having policemen shot down in the Dublin streets, or other Irishmen fatally ambushed on country roads or in their villages. It must still be guesswork to what extent he questioned the need for these things, or was worried by the condemnations of the Church and of secular organs of pro-Sinn Fein opinion. Perhaps, in spite of these, he justified such deeds by straightforward revolutionary logic. His own preoccupation was to establish a genuinely Sinn Fein or self-reliant Irish administration, with an independent national economy and judicial system. He was no pacifist. He had after all begun his nationalist career as a Fenian and had even remained a member of the IRB until 1906. His conversion to moral force had been more from consideration of the impracticability of physical force than from any moral conviction. He had the essential political gift of pragmatic adaptability. As 1919 proceeded it became clear that, with the activity of Collins and the country Volunteers, what had seemed foolishly impractical and therefore irrelevant before 1914, or even in 1916, might no longer be so. Since the total separation of Ireland from England in one form or another was his paramount concern, he may not have found it so difficult to adjust reservations about means to the consistency with which his one end could be kept in view.

That Griffith and others in the leadership felt some unease at the prevailing situation, however, and considered that it needed some form of regularization was indicated by the decision in August 1919 that the Volunteers should take an oath of allegiance to the Irish Republic and Dail Eireann. Reciprocally, members of the Dail, who surprisingly had not yet

made a formal undertaking of this sort, also took the oath. From then onwards, though the Volunteers still remained in fact under the control of
their own organization and were directed, in so far as they were directed from
the centre at all, by Collins rather than any cabinet decision, it was at least
easier to say legalistically that the Volunteers were now the official army of
the Irish Republic. Moderate men could regard what was being done as
'responsible'. The Irish Republican Brotherhood, of course, which Collins
also directed, remained responsible to no one but itself.

Collins was opposed to the Volunteers taking the Dail oath, maintaining
that the ordinary Volunteer oath to the Republic was sufficient. He eventually
agreed to the formality on the understanding that a separate Volunteer
executive should remain in being as an advisory body to the Ministry of
Defence.[39] But he seems to have been in no hurry to see the decision implemented in the Volunteer units up and down the country. Some of these
treated the oath to the Dail, as he must have guessed they would, with
extreme suspicion. Collins's organizer, O'Malley, who found himself swear-
ing in brigade officers to Dail allegiance as late as the middle of 1920, could
not take the whole thing too seriously when one of them pointed out that the
headquarters staff had had no authority from the Volunteers themselves to
hand over control of them to the Dail. 'The Dail might go wrong and accept
less than a Republic,' this Brigade Commander objected. '...I suppose the
Headquarters staff might go wrong also?' They both just laughed.[40]

There seems to have been nothing exceptional about O'Malley administer-
ing the Dail oath to the IRA so long after the formal decision had been
arrived at. It was not until nearly a year after that decision, on 16 July 1920,
that Collins officially notified brigade commandants that the oath was to be
taken, and it was a week later that the oath itself and the order to administer
it was issued as a general instruction from GHQ in Dublin.[41]

The truth is not only that Collins, with his special position of control over
the inner mechanism of the Volunteers, could be virtually a law unto himself
whatever he might undertake formally for the comfort of political elements
in the movement, but also that the Volunteers or IRA were by no means very
tightly even under his or GHQ's control.

Officers from active areas such as Cork would visit Dublin for conferences
with Collins at GHQ from time to time and good officers like Liam Lynch
would do their best to make the link a real one. It was in their interests to do
so for GHQ was a central source of arms, ammunition and information. But
the military situation did not permit easy contact and made it a necessity
to delegate much initiative to local areas. No senior GHQ officers from
Dublin visited Cork, the most heavily engaged county of all, after August
1919.[42] As to the political sanction that was supposed to lie behind GHQ,
Liam Lynch himself had once written revealingly that: 'The Army has to
hew the way for politics to follow.'[43]

The execution of civilian 'spies' and informers which was to become a feature of IRA activity in the following year was theoretically only to be carried out with sanction from Collins's GHQ. But as a leading guerrilla commander of the next year has pointed out, this was seldom sought although a certain local nicety was observed in ascertaining that the victim was the correct one." IRA commandants would often reply to GHQ directives that local conditions made them inadvisable or impossible to carry out. Even lower down the chain of command a spirited local independence was to be the keynote of much IRA activity. One Volunteer, on being told by a superior that the legitimacy of his raids on the post office mails was in doubt and that there would have to be an IRA inquiry, refused to attend it. When told he would be forcibly taken to it, he replied that he would shoot to kill if an escort was sent. He therefore asked his own battalion commander either explicitly to sanction or call off the next mail raid."

Such a state of affairs, an extension into politics of the whole Irish historical tradition of local secret societies, was to have significant political repercussions. The notion that the IRA was in anything but propagandist theory 'the constitutional army of Dail Eireann' was a myth.* For it, in the end, Ireland and Collins himself were to pay dearly.

At the latter end of 1919 the public attitude to the sporadic killings which, with the anti-police boycott, was still the chief activity of the Volunteers, continued ambivalent. On the one hand, there was a mounting dislike of the bloodshed on the part of the mass of moderate Nationalists who had voted Sinn Fein. On the other hand, there was also a mounting loathing of the military rule to which Volunteer activity gave rise, and this inevitably, given the whole background of Irish history, was directed not against the Volunteers who were the cause of these measures, but against the government which ordered them. The petty discomforts and insults of the military presence, to be read or heard about, if not experienced personally, acted as a continual goad to a sensitively conditioned Irish pride. Moreover, the enormity of the political insult which Ireland was experiencing in receiving, after the General Election and all the turmoil of the past few years, let alone the rest of Irish history, no further political acknowledgement of her national feelings at all, was something which festered daily in Irish minds. Not only

---

* For an example of the propaganda put out to this effect see the following passage from an interview given by de Valera to the *Neue Züricher Zeitung* on 3 May 1921:
  Question: 'What is the position of the Republican Government towards the Army?'
  De Valera: 'The Republican Army is the constitutional military arm of the Government of the Republic. It can be employed only where and in what manner this civil government prescribes. Its officers are under the control of and removable by the civil government. The Army is, therefore, a regular national defence force.' (Macardle, *Irish Republic*, p. 931.)

had many of her democratic representatives been arrested but the suppression at last of Dail Eireann itself in August 1919 had made the political impasse seem more hopeless than ever. Stories from Mountjoy gaol, where in October the Lord Mayor found thirty-nine Sinn Fein prisoners in handcuffs in solitary confinement, after refractory attempts to assert their political status, simply inflamed the national sense of political frustration, though most people probably shared the Lord Mayor's condemnation of Volunteer killings equally with his indignation at the prisoners' treatment.

The release of the Mountjoy prisoners later in the month after a successful hunger strike seemed like a national political victory in the absence of any other, particularly since only two days before, the government had prevented the annual convention of Sinn Fein from meeting with a display of armoured cars and lorry-loads of steel-helmeted troops in the Dublin streets. When, on 25 November 1919, the government suppressed Sinn Fein itself as a political organization throughout the country, Arthur Griffith was able to say with some substance to an interviewer: 'The English Government in Ireland has now proclaimed the Irish nation, as it formerly proclaimed the Catholic Church, an illegal assembly.' The old Nationalist Party newspaper, the *Freeman's Journal*, described the action as 'Nation-Baiting'.[16]

The confused popular attitude to the actions of the Volunteers was, however, well illustrated in a debate in the Clare County Council in December 1919. Tipperary North-East County Council had already passed a resolution placing on record horror at the outrages, saying they were acts of 'irresponsible persons with whom no responsible person could have the slightest sympathy'. It called on all public bodies 'to bring the perpetrators of such crimes to justice'. The Clare County Council met to decide whether or not to adopt this resolution itself. All the members were nationalists, either supporters of the old party or of Sinn Fein. One Nationalist Party supporter who wanted the resolution adopted said there was no man in the room who wanted to see an Irish Republic more than he did – 'If I saw an Irish Republic in the morning', he said, '– our own steamers leaving the Liffey, and being saluted by other Nationalities, I would die happy!' But outrages, he insisted, acted against Ireland's best interests. His chief Sinn Fein opponent who suggested that the resolution should simply be marked 'Read' argued that, if the government would grant Ireland self-determination, 'I have no doubt in saying it, in six months' time there will be no such thing as ... shooting at persons, or no such thing as outrages of any kind'. He spoke of the government as dealing out 'persecution and legalistic outrage' instead of justice and freedom. The Chairman summed-up by saying that nobody liked violence and the honest people of Clare did not like it, but the actual wording of the resolution played into the hands of Ireland's enemies. It was decided by a 9–5 vote simply to mark the resolution 'Read'.[17]

Just over a week later the government, speaking through no less a person than the Prime Minister, offered Ireland for the first time since the General Election something other than 'persecution and legalistic outrage' or simple enforcement of the *status quo*. Lloyd George had already announced at the beginning of the month that he hoped soon to make 'a real contribution towards settling this most baffling of all problems'.[48] Now, speaking on 22 December 1919 in the House of Commons, he outlined proposals for a new Home Rule Bill which he intended to introduce the following year.

It is possible now to see that in the context of the time this was at least an attempt to think up something new. What seems astonishing, if it is to be viewed at all as a genuine attempt to meet the wishes of the people of Ireland rather than simply an attempt to safeguard the wishes of the Protestants of North-East Ulster, is that its authors should not have realized that it would be the similarity of the proposal to what had already been rejected which would make the impact on popular opinion, rather than the new aspects.

In the first place, what was unchanged was the proposal to separate or partition North-East Ulster from the rest of Ireland. Instead, however, of excluding this area from Home Rule, it was to be given its own Home Rule legislature, subordinate to Westminster. Another innovation, important in the light of later events, was that the exact area of North-East Ulster to be partitioned from the rest of Ireland was to be determined by taking the six counties as a basis only and ironing out where practicable Catholic and Protestant communities one side or other of the border, thus producing 'an area as homogeneous as it is possible to achieve under these circumstances'.*[49] But it was the fact of partition that made the impression. This was particularly in the light of the bill's second major defect for nationalists, for the actual measure of Home Rule to be given both Parliaments of Ireland was virtually the same as in the 1912–14 period, as if nothing had happened in the interval to enlarge the concept of Irish national aspirations.

Some attempt to respect the concept of a united Ireland was met in a proposed Council of Ireland with twenty members from each Parliament which was to have the power, *without reference to Westminster,* to unite the two Parliaments. But all the minor virtues of the proposed bill were totally eclipsed by what seemed to all parties its major defects. The majority of the Irish people – whom after all it was intended to placate – did not want it because they regarded it doubly as an offence to their national feelings. The southern Irish Unionists did not want it, partly on patriotic principles, and partly because it isolated them from the rest of the Protestant community of Ireland and reduced their representation to insignificance. The Protestants of North-East Ulster did not want it, because they wished to

---

* This proposition, foreshadowing the later Boundary Commission, was dropped when the bill made its appearance.

remain bound by the closest ties with Westminster. Given the geographic compactness of their strength they could still refuse to acknowledge, unlike southern Unionists, that the majority of the Irish people had any right to determine their own future.* The *Irish Times* summed up Lloyd George's proposal as follows:

Its principle is hateful alike to Unionist and Nationalist. They know that national ideals and the ancestral spirit of a common patriotism cannot persist in a divided country. They know that the fantastic homogeneity which the Government proposes for the Ulster Unionists would be an excrescence on the map of Ireland, and would be ruinous to the trade and industry of the Northern Protestants. ... We yearn for peace, but in Mr Lloyd George's proposal we see not peace but a sword.[30]

This last forecast at least was soon proved accurate. Before the next year was out Ireland had become engulfed in horrors unsurpassed since the Rebellion of 1798.

* Though the proposal had no friends at all in Ireland, the northern Protestants eventually accepted it reluctantly as at least safeguarding what they regarded as the legitimate privacy of their interests. In 1920 it became the basis of the Government of Ireland Act (see p. 140) which, supplemented by the Free State Agreement Act and the Treaty, provides the constitutional basis for the present Government of Northern Ireland. The six-county state has in fact turned out far better for northern Protestants' private interests than its leaders of the day immediately visualized. It has suited a strong strain of local self-sufficiency and independence which has always been present in the Ulster Protestant character and which even manifested itself for a short time in identification with Unionism, and with leaders of a landed class who often became favour of Irish nationalism (see *The Most Distressful Country*). This strain's expedient more English than Ulster in their attitudes, has sometimes obscured its essentially independent character. This may be observed today in conflict with its own leadership. It is part of the southern Irish nationalists' argument that this strain would realize itself more fully in a wholly Irish context.

8

Enter Black and Tans (1920)

The last means of assessing with some reasonable accuracy the real attitude of popular opinion to the Volunteers' campaign of violence took place in the middle of January 1920, with the municipal elections of that month.* These were fought under a new system of proportional representation, recently introduced by the government to give full weight to the views of minorities in Ireland, and were therefore unusually accurate. In the overall picture Sinn Fein which, though banned, was represented by individual candidates, swept the polls. It won control of eleven out of the twelve cities and boroughs of Ireland. An analysis of the actual votes, however, shows a different picture of attitudes to the campaign of violence.

Even if it can be assumed that all Sinn Fein voters were in favour of the killings, which was by no means the case, they were in terms of actual seats in a minority of more than two to one in all Ireland. 550 seats were won by Sinn Fein, as opposed to 1,256 by Unionists, Nationalists (of the old Party), Labour, Municipal Reformers and Independents. If it is supposed that some Labour voters were in favour of violence at this stage they may be taken as cancelled out by those Sinn Fein voters who disapproved of it, though there was probably a greater number of the latter. Even omitting the four north-east counties of Ulster, where the Unionist vote was of course disproportionately high, there were in the twenty-eight counties of nationalist Ireland only 527 Sinn Fein seats as opposed to 872 seats won by other parties. On the simple issue of self-determination or even the Republic itself, both Labour and Nationalist could have been reckoned with Sinn Fein in an overwhelming majority over the other parties, but on the issue of violence they must be counted with the opposition, as the debate in the Clare County Council had indicated.

None of this, however, was of much concern to Collins and the other men who were conducting the campaign of violence. Like all revolutionaries they had a larger view of democracy than one governed by mere voting processes and were only interested in the latter inasmuch as they could

* The County Council Elections of May 1920, and the General Election of 1921, in which every one of the parliamentary seats in twenty-six counties were uncontested, can hardly be said to have been fought under representative democratic conditions.

be of use to them. On the day after the final municipal election results were announced, Collins had Assistant Commissioner Redmond of the Dublin police shot dead in the back about forty yards from the Russell Hotel in the centre of the city. In Thurles, County Tipperary, an unarmed constable named Finnegan, a native of Galway with twelve years' service in the RIC, was shot in the groin and killed a few yards from the house where he had lived with his wife and two small children. In both cases the coroner's jury brought in verdicts of wilful murder.[1] This brought the total number of Irish police killed since the General Election of 1918 to fourteen, while over twenty others had been wounded.

Perhaps the most remarkable feature of this campaign of killing to date, backed as it was by an intense social boycott of those who were spared, was that the police had so far not retaliated in any undisciplined form. In general, in fact, the police morale had held remarkably well. When, in the countryside, patrols or barracks were attacked the police almost always refused to surrender and fought bitterly, often driving off superior numbers of their fellow-countrymen after a fight of several hours – though the real numbers of the attackers were usually far fewer than the police in the elation of triumph or the humiliation of defeat tended to claim. But on the night in January on which Constable Finnegan was shot in Thurles, an incident took place which was to establish a sinister new pattern of events and add a whole extra dimension of hopelessness to the already desperate situation in Ireland.

About half an hour after Constable Finnegan had been brought into his house in great pain, the quiet of the town was shattered by the noise of breaking glass and the firing of volley after volley in the streets. The police had gone on the rampage. A scene was enacted that was soon to be repeated so often in most parts of Ireland that it would seem as if there had never been a time when such things did not happen. People barred their doors and windows in a state of terror as they listened to what sounded like a pitched battle being conducted in the streets. Certain houses were selected for special attention, in particular that of the President of the local Sinn Fein club, where every pane of glass in the porch was smashed and bullets were sent crashing into the upstairs bedrooms, riddling the walls and the furniture. By good luck no one in the house was hurt, and when a little later a dozen police arrived looking for the owner he, fortunately for him perhaps in the light of later events elsewhere, had made good his escape. The offices of the local newspaper, the *Tipperary Star*, had its windows smashed with rifle butts and hand-grenades were thrown in, one of which burst on the editor's desk. In Thurles Cathedral the following Sunday the Archbishop of Cashel and the officiating clergy at all other masses vigorously condemned both the killing of Constable Finnegan and the subsequent 'orgy of violence' by the police as 'most grave violations of the law of God'.[2]

Such clerical denunciations of violence which continued manfully were now to lose some of their force by increasingly having to be projected in two opposite directions. They expressed the grave deterioration in affairs graphically, but the moral guidance they bestowed seemed more and more remote from what was actually happening. Thus, writing soon after the killing by the military of a woman and child in Limerick, an event which itself followed the shooting in the face there of an RIC sergeant and the imposition of new military restrictions, Cardinal Logue addressed himself in a Lenten Pastoral Letter to his flock as follows:

Not within living memory can we find in Ireland such calamitous conditions as exist at present ... a military regime rivalling in severity even that of the most pitiless autocracy, vindictive sentences ... arbitrary arrests more frequent than in pre-revolutionary France, deportations such as raised a wild cry of reprobation against the Germans when in military occupation of Belgium; these and similar acts of power cannot fail to create exasperation, recklessness, despair and general disorder. On the other side ... lawlessness and crime, such as any man guided by God's law must regret and reprobate.

These crimes, he said, were the work of 'a few irresponsible desperate hot-heads, probably the emissaries or dupes of secret societies.... We should never forget that however oppressive and intolerable conditions may appear, they cannot justify crime.... Crime can never aid us in the assertion of our rights.' And the Archbishop of Dublin echoed the Cardinal when he said that 'the end, no matter how noble, does not justify immoral means'.[3]

As the hierarchy were thus pronouncing, news came in of the killing of a woman of sixty-one in Enniscorthy after a pathetically ineffectual raid for arms there by some young Volunteers in masks who had felt they ought to do something in that district to emulate what was being done elsewhere.[4]

From March 1920 routine killings of both Crown servants and – by one party or another – ordinary citizens began to appear in the newspapers with a monotony which was soon to dull the senses. While Dublin acclimatized itself to the routine of a curfew and night raids by soldiers searching for suspects and documents, while police were shot in the counties of Kilkenny, Limerick and Tipperary, it was in the city of Cork that the shooting of a District Inspector named MacDonagh sparked off events which confirmed the newest pattern of trouble in Ireland. Once again the police got out of hand.

That same night, 11–12 March 1920, they took to the streets, firing volleys at random, and smashed up the Sinn Fein and Thomas Ashe clubs, breaking furniture and crockery and wrenching patriotic pictures from the walls. They also raided and damaged the house of a Sinn Fein alderman and that of a number of other Sinn Fein supporters.

At the next meeting of the Cork Corporation the Sinn Fein Lord Mayor, Tomas MacCurtain, spoke out. He said that there had been an attempt to conceal the fact that it was police firing in the streets that night and to suggest that this had been done by civilians. It was policemen, he said, who fired the shots and the responsibility should be fixed on them for shooting at people's property and putting the lives of citizens in danger. 'When nobody was around policemen fired shots all over the place. There could not be anything like peace in the city if this thing went on.'[5]

Two nights later an attack took place in the streets of Cork on a local alderman, Professor Stockley. Superficially it looked like a standard attempt by one of the Volunteer assassination squads: two men in civilian clothes came up to the Professor and fired at him with revolvers at close range. But the curious thing was that Stockley was a Sinn Fein supporter.

Amazingly the bullets passed through his coat leaving him unharmed, and the next day, at a meeting appropriately of the Public Health Committee of the Cork Corporation, he was congratulated on his marvellous escape. MacCurtain, the Lord Mayor, said the time was approaching when they would have to take steps to defend their rights and the lives of the citizens and their property. He said that they would ask those in charge of the forces in Cork to withdraw altogether and let the Corporation take over control of the city, and he pointed out that the usual police patrol had been operating in the street in which Stockley was shot at.

The night of this speech, an authentic Volunteer assassination squad was at work. An Irish Constable named Murtagh, a man with twenty-four years' service in the RIC who had just returned from attending the funeral of another constable shot in Tipperary, was himself shot dead in the streets of Cork. Two hours later a party of men armed with rifles but with blackened faces and wearing civilian clothes arrived at the Lord Mayor's house and demanded entrance. The police had often searched the house in the past and were familiar with its layout. Two men rushed straight upstairs to MacCurtain's bedroom and shot him at point-blank range in his pyjamas. Members of the household who tried to cry for help from the upstairs windows were fired at from the streets. A short time later a party of soldiers which had heard nothing of this event arrived at the house with orders to arrest MacCurtain and found him dead. Though there was a police barracks, which would have heard the shooting, only a few hundred yards away from the house, no police from there came near the house for several hours.

Attempts were immediately made by the British authorities to say that MacCurtain had been murdered by IRB fanatics on his own side for being insufficiently enthusiastic about the campaign of violence. But this theory, though perhaps not quite so inherently impossible as Irish sources have sometimes suggested, cannot stand up to the evidence of the inquest, combined with a knowledge of the previous deliberations in the Cork

Corporation. Few people in Cork or Dublin were in a moment's doubt about the real authors of the crime and the coroner's jury, though indulging a certain poetic licence, was substantially correct in returning a verdict of wilful murder against David Lloyd George, Lord French (the Viceroy), Ian MacPherson (the Chief Secretary), District Inspector Swanzy of the RIC, and unknown members of the same force.

At MacCurtain's funeral, Irish Volunteers, who had stood guard over the body as it lay in state in the cathedral during the night, made all the practical arrangements and controlled the immense crowds with efficiency in the total absence of the police from the streets throughout the day. At the cemetery there was a roll of muffled drums, the Last Post was sounded and three volleys were fired by Volunteers over the grave, sending, in the words of the *Freeman's Journal*, 'their message of defiance in ringing echoes through the Glen of Glasheen. The echoes,' continued the paper, 'came from the hillside where stands the birthplace of the brothers Sheares.'[*6]

When Professor Stockley had so narrowly escaped the same fate as Mac-Curtain a few days before he had noticed one significant thing about his would-be assassins. They had talked, he said, 'like strangers'.[7]

For some time now the campaign against the police had begun to show results that were even more important than the number of dead and maimed. Individual members of the RIC had begun to prefer discretion to valour and to resign from the force. With them went an indeterminable number of others who felt a conflict of Irish loyalties in the present situation. This last factor may well have been exaggerated in propaganda both at the time and since, but for whatever reason a substantial number of resignations were taking place. The Recorder of a Crown court in February 1920 commented on the fact that they appeared to be going on 'to an extraordinary degree'.[†8]

The important consequence was that to fill the gap the authorities started recruiting for the RIC in England as well as Ireland. This had been going on since December 1919 and by 15 April 1920 some four hundred English recruits had been obtained in this way.[9] There was a shortage of the traditional dark bottle-green uniforms of the RIC – a fact which indicates that the force was being expanded as well as filled up – and at an inquest in April on a young man shot dead by the police it was noticed that 'Constables Grey and Hardwicke had khaki trousers'.[10] Thus there came into being the first consignment of what were soon to be known all over Ireland and go down to history as the Black and Tans.

The term seems first to have been applied to a group of RIC operating from a police station near Upperchurch, County Tipperary, and was adapted from the name of a local pack of hounds.[11] It began to come into regular popular usage in the late summer of 1920, although there were at that time

* For the Sheares brothers see *The Most Distressful Country*, pp. 100 and 46.
† Even so, only about ten per cent of the RIC had resigned by August 1920.

only some 1,200 such new recruits in the force. There were eventually to be about 7,000 of them altogether, the greater part recruited after 1 November 1920.[12]

The Black and Tans were supplemented by a new specially-raised Auxiliary Division of the RIC which was brought into being on 27 July 1920. The Auxiliaries were eventually to reach 1,500 in numbers, though only just over 500 of them had arrived in Ireland by the end of September 1920.[13] In some ways this Auxiliary Division, which permitted its members to wear either the traditional dark RIC uniform or army officers' service dress without badges of rank, with dark Glengarry caps, and which was to hunt rebels in motorized packs across the Irish countryside, qualified even more aptly for the term Black and Tans.[14] All the new forces were often referred to in tones equally expressive of hatred, contempt and healthy respect as 'the Tans'. And as such they have gone into Irish myth.

It has so often been stated that the Black and Tans were the sweepings of English gaols that it is necessary to re-state some facts about them and the conditions under which they were recruited. Appeals for recruits to the regular RIC were originally addressed to men who had been demobilized from the British Army and they had to supply, together with the name of their regiment, their army discharge and 'character'. No man was eligible with less than a 'good' character.[15] Their pay was to be £3 10s a week, rising to £4 15s. Only about 4,400 of them were recruited in England, Scotland and Wales which means that perhaps as many as a third were recruited in Ireland, mainly presumably from North-East Ulster.[16] The majority were not active in Ireland for more than eight months.

The members of the Auxiliary Division of the RIC, or 'Cadets' as they were officially called, had to be ex-officers of the army and also supply full particulars of their service. They were paid £1 a day plus allowances and had a month's leave a year. They were, as things turned out, to fight in Ireland for slightly under a year, most of them for not more than nine months.

In both cases the period was to be quite long enough. The Black and Tans left an indelible imprint on Anglo-Irish relations. Yet the new members of the old RIC and the members of the new Auxiliary Division were probably neither better nor worse than most battle-conditioned young men at the end of a long war. The large contingent of Englishmen among them, who were to prove the most callous, knew and cared little about Ireland, where they found themselves immediately not only unpopular and the object of an intense social and economic boycott but also in extreme physical danger, liable to be shot at as individuals or in groups at any hour of the day or night by civilians indistinguishable from other civilians who did not shoot at them. Whereas in 1919 thirteen policemen and one soldier had been killed by the Volunteers, in 1920 Crown casualties were to be much more than ten times that number – 182 police and 50 soldiers killed and 387 wounded altogether.

The anxiety and resentment which such conditions inevitably provoked in individuals strained even the traditional discipline of the British Army beyond breaking-point on occasions. It is not surprising that temporarily recruited men, subject to the less rigid discipline of a police force whose traditions they hardly shared, should increasingly take the law into their own hands, and when they saw the dead or mutilated bodies of their comrades brought into police stations and heard their cries of pain, want to wreak their vengeance on the locality, in their frustration at being unable to get at the real culprits. The vengeance they took as the year 1920 pursued its brutalizing course was increasingly savage.

Historically, what was to be important was that this vengeance, usually exacted from people quite innocent of the act that had provoked it, further consolidated national feeling in Ireland. It made the Irish people feel more and more in sympathy with fighting men of their own who were engaging a force actually composed increasingly of Englishmen. But so much emotive propaganda has been made, both at the time and since, out of reprisals, that it is necessary to remember that they were reprisals for things that had been done to the police, and that the majority of the personnel of the RIC remained, to the end, Irish. The increasingly brutal behaviour of the police, and the very rough Black and Tan reprisal campaign which was soon to develop, grew out of a situation in which an Irishman could have a shotgun discharged into his knee simply for joining the RIC or be killed while sitting drinking in uniform in a bar, or, having been shot in the back while on routine patrol, be finished off while lying on the ground asking for mercy.[17] These things all happened before any Black and Tan campaign had started in Ireland and at a time when all attacks on the police were abhorred and vigorously denounced both by local priests and also by bishops of the Church that represented the vast majority of the people of Ireland.

'Who are the police?' asked the national-minded Bishop of Cork, Dr Cohalan, in March 1920. 'They are Irishmen doing their duty,' and added with a confidence that was sadly misplaced: 'I am satisfied that the National Organization which the country has accepted and which it supports has no responsibility for these outrages.'[18] He pronounced their perpetrators to be outside the moral law.

The police at Thurles in County Tipperary who included some of the first constables in dark tunics and khaki trousers and who had suffered a number of casualties in March were already dealing out sterner medicine. In the last two days of the month a group of about six of them with blackened faces visited the houses of two young men from families of well-known national sympathies and shot them dead.[19] Apart from MacCurtain, the Lord Mayor of Cork, these were the first civilians to be murdered in retaliation. It was fifteen months since the campaign of killing had been begun against the police.

While the RIC which was already developing along these dangerous lines was being expanded by an influx of newly demobilized Englishmen, the government announced new public appointments for Dublin. The post of Chief Secretary was given to Sir Hamar Greenwood, a Canadian and a Coalition Liberal, who came to Ireland, in his own words, 'a life-long Home Ruler ... full of sympathy with Home Rule aspirations'. He seemed almost unaware of the deteriorating situation he was facing. The day on which he made this well-meaning statement, which time was so swiftly to render fatuous, was a typical one. The body of an Irishman named Foley, a former soldier in the Irish Guards who had later joined the RIC, was found in a yard in Kerry with hands tied and eyes bandaged, struck by twenty-six bullets – one of the 'spies' executed by the IRA to discourage the others.[20] A man who had been interned for a time after 1916 as a rebel was shot dead by the police in Dundalk with less ceremony. In Milltown-Mallbay, County Clare, the funeral took place of three men who had been shot dead the day before when restless police and military had fired into a crowd. The crowd had been celebrating the release from Mountjoy gaol of seventy prisoners who had beaten the authorities with a ten-day hunger strike. This seemed an unmistakable national victory in which all Irishmen could join without reservation, some evidence at last that the government could be made to give in to moral pressure.

In the fortnight before Greenwood actually took up office the pace of events quickened horribly. Two Irish RIC constables were shot down as they walked out of Mass on Sunday in County Clare; a detective was shot by Collins's men in Dublin, bullets being fired into his stomach as he lay on the ground; two police were shot by masked men in County Cork; a man was shot by the military in Arklow, a police barracks in Tipperary was captured and its armoury ransacked, while another in County Dublin successfully beat off an attack. Two new nation-rallying hunger-strikes took place; one of 160 prisoners who had been deported to Wormwood Scrubs in London, and another of seventy-four prisoners in Belfast gaol.

For all this Lloyd George and the British Government had nothing to offer but the new team in Dublin and the 'Partition' or Government of Ireland Bill which was winding its way, unwanted and irrelevant, through the House of Commons. Those selected to assist Home Ruler Sir Hamar

---

* Collins had already had a number of such spies executed, including, in Cork, a man named Quinlisk, a former member of Casement's Irish Brigade, who had unquestionably been trying to betray Collins to the authorities for money. Others such as J. C. Byrne, alias Jameson, and Fergus Molloy, an RASC pay clerk, seem to have been professional agents of the British Government. (See Beaslai, *Collins*, vol. i, pp. 329–410.)

Greenwood included General Sir Nevile Macready who was made Commander-in-Chief of the Army in Ireland, and another regular army officer. General H. H. Tudor, who was put in charge of the RIC.

Macready, a son of the great Irish actor ('I have never considered myself in any way an Irishman,' he said), had taken part in the last battle in which the British Army had fought in red coats, at Tel-El-Kebir, and had a meritorious professional army career which, while it did not dispose him to think well of natives generally or indeed of any sort of people who gave trouble, had inculcated certain standards of decent behaviour. When he had been officially in Dublin and Belfast during the pre-war Home Rule crisis he had despised and disliked Birrell, as he did most politicians, but had scrupulously maintained the view that it was the British Army's duty to fight Carson and the Ulster Volunteers if called upon to do so.[21] Like many professional soldiers of the period he took an exaggeratedly straightforward view of complex problems and now as C.-in-C. of some fifty thousand troops in a country where many districts were to be under military rule, he hardly exercised an influence for enlightenment where subtler minds than his found themselves at a loss for policy.

A few months later the military hierarchy in Dublin was joined by a brash and fanatical adherent of the old imperialist school, the forty-year-old Brigadier-General Crozier, who was given command of the Auxiliary Division of the RIC. Brought up in Ireland in a classically Unionist tradition, Crozier had fought in a British square against the Hausa in West Africa, believed that military executions should be carried out by machine-gun fire, as being 'easier, more humane, less exacting and more accurate than a firing squad', and, having at one time been excessively addicted to alcohol, had taken the pledge eight years before. The eccentric violence of his irascible personality within its conventional framework led to clashes with Macready and Tudor over attempts of his to discipline his often undisciplinable Auxiliaries and he was to resign before the year was out and end up curiously, smarting under his experiences, an advocate of justice to Ireland.[22]

This, then, was the face the British Government presented in 1920 to the IRA and to the Irish people between whom it increasingly made no distinction, thus rendering them indeed increasingly indistinguishable. One young Irishman of this time was to write later: 'What probably drove a peacefully-inclined man like myself into rebellion was the British attitude towards us: the assumption that the whole lot of us were a pack of murdering corner boys.'[23]

Not only the RIC but the IRA too was developing its organization and extending its operations.

Collins in Dublin, taking great personal risks and cycling about the city without disguise on the principle that the absence of disguise was the best disguise for a 'wanted' man, had further perfected his intelligence system and was usually aware of most moves the authorities intended to make before they made them. Through his contacts not only in the police but in the post office and other services he kept a continuous check on official correspondence, even seizing on one occasion with the aid of armed men the entire Viceregal and Dublin Castle mailbag. Nor was his systematic liquidation of troublesome government agents confined to detectives and spies.

A Resident Magistrate of some experience, named Alan Bell, an Irishman of sixty-two from King's County, who as a young man in the RIC had helped investigate the hidden workings of the Land League, was appointed to try to locate the growing Republican Loan in the labyrinth of 'cover' bank accounts in which Collins had concealed it. Travelling to his office just after 9 a.m. on a Dublin tram, reading his newspaper, Bell suddenly found two young men standing beside him as the tram stopped at a routine halt. 'Come on, Mr Bell,' said one of them. 'Your time has come.' He was so aghast that he appeared unable to do or say anything. There was a moment of terrible suspense and anxiety in the crowded tram as everyone looked at each other in bewilderment. Nobody said a word. Then one of the young men spoke again: 'Ah, come on,' he said, and he and his companion with the aid of some other young men who came down from upstairs forced Bell out of the tram and along the pavement to where, while he stood erect and apparently unperturbed, they shot him dead. His killers, who were undisguised and were described as 'respectable young men', walked calmly away in a group and dispersed after a hundred yards or so. Of two passengers who came forward to try to do something for Bell, one had the use of only one arm. They called out, 'Is there nobody then to help us?' But nobody dared come forward.[24] The Irish half of the Republican Loan was successfully closed later that year at £357,000.

In the countryside the Volunteers, or IRA, began to move towards more ambitious operational methods. *An t Oglach* had announced at the beginning of 1920 that the period in the trenches was over and that a continuous policy of guerrilla war was now to be applied: 'Surprises, ambushes, raids on their fortified positions, sniping at their stragglers, capturing of their arms and equipment, interruptions of their communications.'[25] This sort of thing often sounded more impressive in theory than in practice. Sniping at stragglers, for instance, meant in reality shooting Irishmen emerging from Mass or cycling absent-mindedly along a country road. When two policemen (both Irishmen) were shot dead from their bicycles in this fashion in April, their comrades from Nenagh set fire to two creameries in the locality and the Volunteers, for all their military talk, were unable to do anything to prevent or even harass the reprisal. The Bishop of Ardagh and Clonmacnoise, speaking of what the Volunteers were doing, said that in fact it was nonsense for them to talk of being at war with the enemy;[26] and this was true in more than just the moral sense in which he meant it. Nothing like a coherent fought-out action between two bodies of troops had yet taken place, or was really ever to do so, and the continual assaults with rifle and bomb against local police stations, though occasionally successful, were still continually beaten off. Nearly two-thirds of the raids made on occupied police barracks during the year were unsuccessful.[27]

Such attacks had, however, at least led to garrisons being withdrawn from a considerable number of small isolated outposts and, in an action in many ways more impressive than some of the attacks themselves, on the night of 3–4 April 1920 over 150 of such posts were simultaneously burned all over Ireland together with income tax offices in sixteen different counties. Such action showed at least a remarkable ability to coordinate a plan on a national level where serious opposition was not a factor. There were to be repeat performances on a smaller scale in the following month and by the end of the year 510 unoccupied 'barracks' in Ireland had been destroyed altogether.[28] Also, evidence of something more than mere bravado was the capture in June and successful concealment for over a month of the British Commander of the forces in the South, Brigadier-General Lucas.

Lucas was surprised by Liam Lynch and some of his men while fishing with other British officers on the River Blackwater. A nation-wide search in which all means, including aircraft, were deployed failed to reveal the General, and he only emerged again after loosening a bar over the window of a room in which he was being held. He had spent the month 'on the run' like his captors. He was reported as calling them 'delightful people', saying he had been treated as a gentleman by gentlemen.[29] This was handsome of him since he had a slight wound on his forehead as he faced the press, caused when the military lorry which had picked him up wandering along a road had later run into an ambush and, in the firing in which he participated, a bullet had grazed his head. Two soldiers in the lorry were killed.

One of the few army reprisals of the time had taken place after Lucas's capture. Many shops in the town of Fermoy were attacked; plate-glass windows were smashed; the local Sinn Fein hall was wrecked and damage done to the town was generally estimated at several thousand pounds. No one, however, was killed. This, in the grim daily balance sheet of the time, was a gain compared with what was then happening, for instance, in Bantry. For the police there were conducting what the *Freeman's Journal* described as 'a reign of terror', beating up citizens with little concern for the niceties of questioning procedure and incidentally shooting dead a crippled Sinn Fein supporter named Cornelius Cowley.

The Bantry RIC had themselves just been through a particularly unpleasant time. On 12 June one of their number, Constable King, a native of County Galway, had been cycling unarmed and in civilian clothes along the road to Glengariff when he had been attacked and wounded by masked men with revolvers. He managed to escape to a neighbouring house where he hid in a cupboard, but on being discovered was dragged out, and had his head blown off by his captors. His body was thrown on to a dungheap in the yard outside. Just over a week later another member of the Bantry force, Constable Brett, a Waterford man with thirty years' service in the RIC, had been shot and killed three miles outside the town.

Similar patterns of outrage and reprisal were establishing themselves as a routine feature of Irish life. In County Limerick where, after a five-hour siege, the RIC barracks at Kilmallock – last attacked by the Fenians in 1867 – was utterly destroyed and a sergeant and a constable were killed and six other constables wounded, hundreds of townspeople fled from their homes immediately in anticipation of reprisals, because a fortnight before, after the shooting of two constables in Limerick City itself, the RIC had run amok in the streets, felling people with rifle butts, breaking ribs, firing into houses, and shooting one man dead.[30] Those policemen who killed civilians in reprisals in this way were hardly ever brought to justice, any more than were those civilians who killed the police.

As well as the more spectacular outrages and reprisals dozens of smaller but equally painful examples interrupted everyday life over the greater part of Ireland, each one exacerbating the state of bitterness and apprehension in which people on both sides anticipated the next. Either soldiers or police might be involved. The burning of creameries on which the livelihoods of so many ordinary people in the Irish countryside depended could follow a small incident. Hugh Martin, the correspondent of the English liberal *Daily News*, reported that summer how on the afternoon of 22 July 1920 a number of young Volunteers attacked a girl of eighteen who was milking her father's cows, cut off her hair with a pair of shears and left her bound hand and foot in a field because she had been walking out with English soldiers. A few hours later the nearby cooperative creamery – one of the finest in Ireland – was burned to the ground. 'It is not difficult to understand the point of view of the soldiery,' wrote Martin. 'Here was a cowardly assault upon a woman, intended to insult the King's uniform. As usual, no official redress was possible.... Let it be known that a group of creameries will be wiped out for every outrage that occurs, and the community may be induced to stop the outrages.'[31] But, as he pointed out, the flaw in this argument was that the community could not stop the outrages even if it wanted to.

The frustration of knowing that there was no way of getting at the guilty was often responsible for the disproportionate scale of many reprisals. Thus when a few weeks later two Black and Tans were set upon in a Limerick park, robbed of their arms and tied humiliatingly to a tree, some thirty or forty of their comrades wrecked a number of streets in the city in a desperate attempt to obtain retribution of some sort.[32] In such an atmosphere the frontiersman's law of a life for a life soon came to seem like a natural right.* The real responsibility lay with a government which had let the political atmosphere deteriorate to such a pitch.

Politically indeed the most striking feature of the whole summer of 1920 lay less in the growing daily series of deaths and acts of violence, to which Ireland was becoming sickeningly accustomed, than in the extent to which king's writ was not only failing to run over large tracts of the country but was actually being replaced by the writ of the underground Dail Eireann. In this, of course, the IRA played a major part by asserting the Dail's writ where necessary by force.

Between 15 April and 8 June it had been possible to introduce the Sinn Fein courts of Arthur Griffith's concept together with Volunteer police patrols in twenty-one of the thirty-two counties of Ireland. The *Irish Bulletin*, a Sinn Fein propaganda sheet of considerable journalistic ability, run by two Volunteers, Desmond Fitzgerald and Frank Gallagher, with assistance from the former Home Rule gun-runner Erskine Childers, now an ardent Republican, made the most of this astonishing fact, so much more palatable for international and British home consumption than the killings of policemen which made it possible. By the middle of June the *Irish Bulletin* was able to report that eighty-four arrests of criminals in twenty-four counties had been made by Republican police in the past thirteen days. Both Republican Arbitration Courts and Criminal Courts met and performed their functions quite openly under Volunteer guard in those parts of the South and West of Ireland where Crown authority had temporarily vanished.

Perhaps the most spectacular feat of all had been to bring to Republican justice three men who had carried out a highly successful bank robbery at Millstreet in County Cork the year before. They had got away with some £20,000 and it had been assumed by many at the time that this raid by masked men had been simply one more example of the way in which the Volunteers were prepared to exploit patriotic motives for lawless ends. But Liam Lynch, the zealously ascetic Commandant of Cork No. 2 Brigade, in whose area the robbery had been carried out, had been determined to track them down as inexorably as he tracked the RIC or the British Army. He and his men eventually recovered almost all the money, which he faithfully returned to the banks concerned and, having arrested the thieves, brought them before a Republican court. They were sentenced to terms of fifteen, ten and eight years' deportation from Ireland, a sentence increased in the case of the first

---

* A curious echo of this summer's events in Ireland took place in June in India where some two hundred men of the Connaught Rangers mutinied at Jullundur in the Punjab. They had their own grievances and seized on the disturbing reports in letters from home to make a national protest and to refuse to soldier any more for England. The mutiny did not become very serious, the ring-leader was eventually shot by firing squad and several other mutineers were sentenced to long terms of imprisonment. See T. P. Kilfeather, *The Connaught Rangers* (Tralee, 1969).

man to twenty years when it was found that he had returned soon afterwards with a list of names for 'execution' in his pocket. This time he was escorted across the Irish Sea by a Republican armed guard.[33]

Other work of the Republican police at this time involved the enforcement of licensing laws, the suppression of illicit stills, arrests for house-breaking, cattle-stealing, drunkenness, 'riotious behaviour' and even on one occasion the apprehension of a bookmaker caught absconding with £67 12s from Barrastown Races in County Tipperary.[34] Methods of interrogation were sometimes rough and ready and at least once included flogging. Punishment was always a difficult problem for the Volunteer police because they had to contend with the anomaly that a rival system of justice was continually trying to arrest them and release their prisoners. Nevertheless, sentences of imprisonment were sometimes imposed – for instance, for breach of a Sinn Fein Land Court finding in County Galway. The guilty were described as being removed 'to an unknown destination'. When some prisoners serving a three-week term on an island off the west coast were rescued by the RIC they refused to accept their release on the grounds that they were loyal citizens of the Irish Republic.[35] Fear of still direr Republican punishment if they accepted their freedom at the hands of the police may have had something to do with it. In other cases sentences included fines – for example, twice the amount stolen from an old-age pensioner – banishment from the province, or, in the case of some land-hungry men who had levelled the walls of a Galway land-owner, the rebuilding of the walls.

There had been an understandable tendency on the part of the agrarian poor and the landless to try to take advantage of the prevailing chaos to improve their position, and a good part of the Sinn Fein court activity was concerned with such operations or disputes over land. The courts respected the rights of property and a Unionist peer, Lord Monteagle, went so far as to praise in the House of Lords the high standards of justice and equity that were dispensed there. Simultaneously, a Sinn Fein Land Commission held inquiries in many parts of the country to determine what might legitimately be done by proper authority to assist genuine cases of land hunger and hardship.

One special activity of Volunteer or Republican police had been to patrol polling stations and protect ballot boxes when Local County Council Elections took place at the beginning of June 1920. The results were, as expected, an overwhelming victory for Sinn Fein. County Council after County Council now declared their allegiance to Dail Eireann, withholding payments of rates and taxes from the Local Government Board wherever practically possible. The Meath County Council carried a resolution thanking the Volunteers for their efficiency in the elections and allowing them expenses, and also resolved that the Republican tricolour should be hoisted above the Council Chamber in place of the old green flag. In Sligo prayers invoking success for the Republic were recited in Irish and a speaker advised the new local Scholarship Committee to see that no policemen's children were allowed to compete. Roscommon County Council extended congratulations to the Irish Republican Army on its success in the field 'and the many fortresses it had captured'. Copies of the resolution were ordered to be sent to 'the Commander-in-Chief of the IRA'.[36]

When, in July and again in August 1920, sessions of the underground Dail were held in Dublin and most members were able to participate, in spite of the incessant military raids and searches which made day and night so irksome to ordinary citizens, the claim that there was an alternative government in Ireland with real authority was able to look quite plausible and impressive. The Dail laid down limitations on rent, declared religious tests for employment illegal, announced an Economic Commission for Ireland and made emigration from Ireland without special sanction illegal. Within the country, the important British rail communications system was severely hampered by an edict ordering train-drivers, guards and firemen not to work trains carrying troops or police. Some complied with straightforward patriotic enthusiasm. For others perhaps, as in the days of agrarian secret societies, faced by two rival systems of authoritarian law, it was a question of acquiescing most easily with the one which claimed to be on your side. There were, however, also those who had to be persuaded and there were a number of cases of engine-drivers and guards who were stripped and tarred by the IRA as a punishment for defying the edict or seized and frightened into signing a document that they would never do so again.[37]

On the whole, what might so easily have been just a pretentious illusion – the notion of a genuine 'Ourselves Alone' or Sinn Fein government operating simultaneously and in many ways more effectively than the king's writ – was by the late summer of 1920 something of a reality. That this was possible was due to the violent campaign against authority conducted by the Volunteers, or IRA. It was a fact which inevitably blurred still further such reservation as Griffith and other moderates may have had about the campaign of violence itself. Their own policies had been brought to fruition because of violence; it was difficult any longer to dissociate the one from the other. And it became easy for Sinn Fein moderates to forget the extent to which their political activity took place on sufferance from the IRA.

In another important respect, too, the members of the Dail were living in an illusion. They claimed, of course, to be a Parliament for All Ireland, but considerable areas of North-East Ulster were not represented in the Dail at all and regarded the claim with abhorrence. Tne fact was unpleasantly emphasized in the summer on a number of occasions when members of Carson's Ulster Volunteers in the North, inflamed and exasperated by accounts of events in the South, took the law into their own hands and exacted vengeance from the minority of Sinn Fein Irishmen who lived among them.

In June there had been appalling scenes of anarchy in Derry when at least nine people were killed in two days. The Dail in its partial success found itself glossing too easily over the fact that the really important obstacles to realization of an All-Ireland nationalism not only remained as intractable as ever but was actually being made more intractable still by events. In the wake of this illusion came a semi-parochial view of nationalism concentrating too easily on twenty-six counties of Ireland instead of thirty-two.

The Dail's confidence of that summer was reflected at an important conference which took place in Dublin between senior IRA officers from the country and Collins and Brugha. Some of the officers pressed for a campaign in England of counter-reprisal for reprisals in Ireland. The final directive issued was that the guerrilla campaign should be slowed down so that the civil administration could be allowed to develop.[38] But the pace of the guerrilla war was determined not by directives from Dublin but by what was actually happening in the countryside. And with the inauguration of the Auxiliary Division of the RIC at the end of July, and a continuing influx of Englishmen into the RIC, the war was to be speeded up rather than slowed down. There had been 556 more Irish resignations from the RIC between 1 May and 31 July 1920 and their places had been taken by over eight hundred more Black and Tan recruits. The British Government was not prepared to see the royal writ in Ireland superseded so easily.

9

Murder by the Throat (1920)

In the summer of 1920 the situation, from the British Government's point of view, looked bad on every count. Politically there was no longer even an attempt to make progress; the discredited Government of Ireland Bill had to continue to serve as a panacea. But militarily, too, the position was humiliating. The least that might have been expected of a government that had decided not to compromise with political demands was that its authority should be effective. But the government's authority was plainly not effective. The royal writ no longer ran in many parts of Ireland. The RIC, for all its numerical strengthening over the 10,000 mark by the Black and Tan element, was increasingly confined to barracks and depots, unable, in face of the campaign of slaughter, to continue usefully that steady day-by-day patrolling by small groups or individuals which is the essence of effective police work. General Macready had some 50,000 troops, mostly of British regiments, at his disposal, but troops are notoriously bad at police work, a fact which was demonstrated all too plainly in Cork at the beginning of August. For there, at a meeting in the Town Hall, troops captured not only five senior officers of Cork No. 1 Brigade IRA, but also Liam Lynch himself, apparently without realizing the importance of their find. Lynch gave a false name, but some of the other IRA men did not even do that. Four days later all were released with the exception of Terence MacSwiney who was held, presumably for prestige reasons, in his capacity as Lord Mayor. The troops were unaware that he was also OC Cork No. 1 Brigade, thinking that what they had surprised was a Republican court in session.

But if the government could no longer effectively police the country, they also could not hope to keep it effectively under military control with only 50,000 troops and without the benefit of martial law. Although military restrictions were in force in the disturbed areas and courts-martial had taken over the work of the normal courts, the penalties they applied were often in the circumstances amazingly light. At a time when any policeman was liable to be shot dead by any civilian at any time, sentences for illegal possession of a revolver and ammunition had hitherto never been more than two years' imprisonment, even when the prisoner proudly proclaimed himself 'a soldier of the Irish Republic'. Often they were as little as six months. Similarly, large numbers of Volunteers were readily identifiable and might easily have been interned even though no individual charge could be preferred against them. But though the government had powers to intern without trial under the Restoration of Order in Ireland Act 1920 it had not yet taken them and no internment camp had yet been opened. In fact, if the authorities had simply arrested in a body the chief mourners at the funeral of Tomas Mac-Curtain in March they would have apprehended some of the important men engaged in Collins's headquarters operations in Dublin: Richard McKee, Peader Clancy, Gearoid O'Sullivan and Frank Thornton were all there openly and even photographed in the procession.[1]

What in fact was happening was that the government was earning all the political opprobrium of a tough policy with very few of its attendant military benefits. Sir Henry Wilson, Chief of the Imperial Staff, was exasperated by the illogicality of the situation. 'I don't see any determination or driving power in the Cabinet,' he wrote in his diary on 28 June. 'I really believe that we shall be kicked out.'[2] Slowly, cumbrously, over the next few months and particularly after the arrival of the first companies of the Auxiliary Division of the RIC, the government was in fact to grow effectively tougher and re-establish at least some of its lost control. But the price was to be a still bloodier contest and a proportionate further deterioration in the general Irish situation. Meanwhile, humiliated like the government they represented and in considerably greater physical danger, the RIC and particularly the Black and Tan element increasingly exercised a tough and vindictive initiative of its own.

On the night of 20 July a motor-car bringing four Irish constables of the RIC back from Galway Assizes was brought to a halt by trees felled across the road three miles outside Tuam. A volley of shots was fired into it from behind a hedge and a Constable Burke of Birr, and a Constable Carey of Skibbereen were shot dead, the other two being overpowered, blindfolded, disarmed and told to return to Tuam. At about three o'clock in the morning the patrols which had been out looking for the ambushers returned to the police barracks and, after viewing the bodies of their dead comrades, marched fully armed into the streets of Tuam and started firing into windows, wrecking shops, rushing into houses and dragging the occupants from their beds with threats to shoot them. No one in fact was killed. 'We are going to give you more mercy than you or some of your chums showed to my comrades,' a constable said to a young electrician named Neville whom he dragged out into the street. But Neville, a Sinn Fein supporter, hardly felt reassured when he saw ten to fifteen police there with their rifles raised and heard one of them say, 'Have you made an Act of Contrition? If not, make it.' They contented themselves with marching him to the barracks for questioning and firing shots over his head. Meanwhile, terrified inhabitants, confined to their houses by cries of 'Get back or you'll be shot', and huddled on the stairs or in the backs of houses, recited the Rosary and listened to the smashing of glass, the firing of shots and the dull thuds of hand-grenades in the streets outside. The Town Hall, the most prominent shops and some houses were set ablaze by the police with cans of petrol.

There seem to have been no Black and Tans among the police on this occasion. So much efficient propaganda about reprisals was made on behalf of the Sinn Fein cause that it can now be too easily forgotten that a strong element of civil war was involved in the events of 1920–21; it accounted for much of the peculiar savagery. The effect of reprisals, however, was much the same whoever committed them and was simply further heightened as English Black and Tans increasingly came to carry them out. As the *Galway Express* put it after these first reprisals at Tuam: 'When they throw petrol on a Sinn Feiner's house, they are merely pouring paraffin on the flames of Irish nationality.'³

From a Sinn Fein point of view this was in itself a strong argument in favour of ambushes. From the government point of view it was an equally strong argument in favour of the need to keep reprisals in check. But although the police were, admittedly, technically more difficult to discipline than the Army, the government seems to have awoken slowly to the political consequences of reprisals, concentrating at first on the wholly irrelevant point that while deplorable they were understandable. They did not seem understandable to the innocent people who usually suffered from them. And the vile incident that often provoked them quickly got lost sight of in the subsequent much more spectacular outburst. Though the Archbishop of Tuam castigated equally the 'murder' of the constables and the wrecking of the town as crimes, there could be little doubt how the inhabitants of Tuam and every other nationalist Irishman who read of the events would weigh the two crimes in the political balance. And when a few days later in Thurles a Sergeant Mulhern of the RIC was shot dead going in to Mass by two men who had been waiting for him with revolvers inside the porch, it was the subsequent reprisal which in the national situation easily became the greater event. The atmosphere round Thurles became tenser still when a few days after Mulhern's death an ambush took place near the village of Upperchurch a few miles away and two Black and Tans were badly wounded. A family of four in Upperchurch then experienced what was soon to become the standard type of Black and Tan raid.

Roused from their beds at two o'clock in the morning by a battering of rifle butts on the door, they opened it to be faced by a group of police, some wearing ordinary dark uniforms and others khaki, several of them also with blackened faces or wearing masks in imitation of similar raiding parties of the IRA. The family was ordered out of the house clutching their clothes while the roof was set ablaze. They moved towards the stable, but the police fired at them and the young man of the family received two flesh wounds.

'After this,' he recounted later, 'we dashed for the stable. We prayed for God's protection. The house was blazing, but we could do nothing. There were a few minutes silence that appeared to be ages and we thought our assailants had withdrawn. I made a move to put on my clothes when suddenly a man wearing police uniform rushed in. He flashed a light upon me, put it out again and then fired at point blank range.' The young man fell over backwards but had not been hit. The policeman, apparently thinking him dead, went out again, and a few minutes later there was the sound of a motor lorry driving away with a firing of shots and 'loud yells like the whoops of savages'.[4]

In Limerick innocent people were less lucky. A small boy was shot dead by reckless firing in the streets, and a young man who was an epileptic was killed while having tea. Limerick suffered again at the end of August when Collins had a District Inspector Wilson shot in Templemore, County Limerick. Wilson was particularly popular with his men and an area of the city was badly wrecked when the police ran amok there the next day. A young Sinn Fein supporter named Patrick Lynch was taken from his house by police and shot dead. It was the beginning of an appalling fortnight. At the weekend no fewer than seven policemen and one army officer were killed in ambushes in different parts of Ireland, one of them being the District Inspector Swanzy whom the Cork jury had indicted for the murder of MacCurtain. Swanzy was shot dead in his home town of Lisburn, County Antrim. It was an Orange town and forty houses of Catholics were burned down in revenge. During this same week, in riots in Belfast triggered off by events in the South, twenty people were killed and eighty-seven wounded.[5]

Even in nationalist Ireland there was still strong disapproval of the attacks on the police which provoked these reprisals. The IRA made it a dangerous sentiment to express. But there were brave men who spoke out what was on their consciences. Thus, in County Kildare the foreman of a jury at an inquest on a RIC constable killed near Naas, tactfully directed by the Coroner to give an innocuous verdict of 'slugs fired by person or persons unknown', said he could not agree to that. It was murder, he said, and not less so because it had a political motive. He would rather go down in his coffin than have the taint of murder on his soul.[6] Braver still were a coroner's jury in County Carlow the following month, who in their verdict on two RIC sergeants named Delaney and Gaughan killed near Tullow, actually dissociated themselves from a policy of attacking the police.[7] It was safer for the Church to say such things. At Mass in Longford at the beginning of September the Most Reverend Dr Hoare, referring to the killing of two more police, indignantly denied the excuse that all this was part of a war. 'We are not at war,' he cried. 'If we are, it should be declared or waged by the public and competent authority and not by a few individuals.'[8]

But increasingly it was horror at the reprisals and the special moral indignation aroused by acts of lawlessness committed by the forces of law themselves which dominated public opinion not only in Ireland but in liberal England too. It became easier to think of the ambushes and even the individual killings as acts of revenge for the ruthlessness which the authorities let loose with the Black and Tans. By September 1920 reprisals were already routine. In fact, in that month more than twenty police of the RIC were shot dead in singles or in groups, in ambushes on country roads or in the towns in which they were stationed, bringing the total of RIC deaths for 1920 alone to over a hundred, with 170 wounded. Only a few of those killed were English Black and Tans, the majority being Catholic Irishmen like Constables Keefe and Downey, shot leaving a pub where they had been having a drink in County Clare, both men who were well-liked locally. Constable Downey had already sent in his resignation from the force.[9] But it was the chain of reprisals, in which civilians were killed and creameries burned down that affected opinion and were effectively publicized by the *Irish Bulletin*.

At Balbriggan (County Dublin) on 21 September a Head Constable Burke was shot down in daylight in the streets. Burke had been popular as an instructor at the nearby Black and Tan recruits' depot at Gormanstown and lorry-loads of Black and Tans arrived in Balbriggan during the night, and again during the following day, setting fire to shops and houses, firing rifles and throwing hand-grenades indiscriminately, generally terrorizing the inhabitants under cover of a search for the culprits and shooting and bayoneting two citizens to death in their nightshirts. Their corpses, declared an eye-witness, looked 'as if they had been killed not by human beings but by animals'.[10] A sight hitherto associated with the flight of Belgian and French refugees before the German invaders was thus seen within twenty miles of the Irish capital as women and children fled from the blackened ruin of their homes with belongings on perambulators and hand-carts in anticipation of another visit from the Black and Tans during the night.

A phenomenon not seen in Ireland since the terrible summer of 1798 now made its appearance, as a regular sunset exodus took place from small towns and villages which were anticipating reprisals, and people slept out at night in hedgerows and beside haystacks and in old barns just as Thomas Cloney had described them as doing in County Wexford over a century before.* When as many as four police were killed at once in one ambush at Dineen in County Clare,† the towns of Miltown Malbay, Lahinch and Ennistymon experienced the full force of RIC and Black and Tan fury. The wife of the local Secretary of the Irish Transport and General Workers' Union was driven from her house in the middle of the night with her baby in her arms,

---

* See *The Most Distressful Country*, p. 100.
† Only one of those killed was an Englishman; the others came from Counties Cork, Roscommon and Sligo.

while her husband was kept behind and shot and then cremated in the blazing ruins of his own house. Another civilian was killed for trying to help a neighbour whose house had just been set fire to. An eye-witness wrote:

You never saw anything so sad as the sight in the sandhills that morning. Groups of men and women, some of them over seventy years, practically naked, cold, wet, worn-looking and terrified, huddled in groups on the wet grass. I met two mothers with babies not three weeks old, little boys, partly naked, leading horses that had gone mad in their stables with the heat, and then when we got near the village a group of men standing round the unrecognizable corpse of Salmon [the civilian who had tried to put out his neighbour's blaze], distracted people running in all directions looking for their friends with the awful thought haunting them that the burned corpse might be some relative of their own. Oh, it was awful! Every evening since then there is a sorrowful procession out of the village. The people too terrified to stay in their houses sleep out in the fields.[11]

Similar scenes followed a few days later the wrecking and burning of houses in Trim, County Meath, by Black and Tans after the RIC barracks there had been captured in an IRA attack and destroyed. This time some refugees spent the night in a Protestant churchyard. The next day the army itself took reprisals in Mallow, County Cork, after the death of a sergeant in a raid on the barracks there. The attack had been carried out with much resource by Lynch and O'Malley who smuggled themselves and their men unobserved into the town in the course of the night, and hid in the Town Hall until daybreak. While they waited O'Malley told his men the story of the wooden horse of Troy.[12] They captured thirty rifles and two Hotchkiss machine-guns in the raid and the subsequent wrecking and firing of the town, which they witnessed impotently from the hills around, and which involved the destruction of property belonging to Unionists and Sinn Feiners alike, lasted for three and a half hours.

By the end of September 1920 there were still only just over five hundred members of the new Auxiliary Division of the RIC in Ireland, but they had quickly made an effective impact.[13] Their role was envisaged from the start as more mobile than that of the regular RIC and Black and Tans with whom, because of the similar mixture of uniforms, they tended to be indiscriminately labelled. Divided into companies of about a hundred men each they were distributed as independent units to different bases in particularly disturbed areas, and from these they emerged periodically in their Crossley tenders or motor lorries, asserting their presence by a liberal discharge of ammunition in a search for trouble. By the spring of 1921 there were to be fifteen such companies altogether, three in County Cork, three in Dublin itself and one each in Counties Kerry, Clare, Tipperary, Kilkenny, Meath, Roscommon, Sligo and Longford – an indication of the areas of Ireland where the IRA operated as an effective force.[14] The first mobile company to be thus installed took up residence in Macroom Castle which was commandeered for them in October 1920.[15]

The introduction of the Auxiliaries matched a new development in the style of operation of the IRA. At the end of May two senior officers of the Limerick IRA, who had themselves just successfully crossed about thirty miles of open country, armed, in broad daylight, by judicious selection of resting-places and avoidance of the towns, came to the conclusion that there was no reason why a larger body of armed men should not be able to move about the countryside in a similar fashion.[16] This notion of an active service unit, or flying column, was then put into practice in East Limerick and the principle enthusiastically adopted and advocated to other IRA brigade areas by Collins at GHQ in Dublin. The flying column, a nucleus of about thirty-five men on full-time active service for specific periods, supplemented where necessary by part-time IRA men who otherwise continued with their normal civilian lives, now became the chief offensive weapon of the IRA. Probably no more than about three thousand men took part in such flying columns altogether, though the full nominal strength of the IRA in 1921 was 112.650.[17] But with the RIC Auxiliary garrisons increasing simultaneously and new Black and Tan recruitment for the regular RIC force being stepped up dramatically, the 'war' was to take on a new ferocity, with, as usual, the ordinary Irish population suffering in the middle.

The illusory calm in some districts in which it had appeared that the royal writ had been successfully replaced by that of Dail Eireann was shattered as the Auxiliaries and other Black and Tans asserted their presence more and more aggressively. Republican courts were raided and broken up and had to retreat to the shadows. Places which had seen no police other than those of the IRA for weeks were suddenly jolted back to the reality of a more regular authoritarian government as a lorry-load of Auxiliaries came to a halt in the main street: Englishmen who regarded the Irish as hostile natives, firing off their rifles at random to show it. Thus at Moycullen in County Galway a Crossley tender full of Auxiliaries, trailing a Republican flag behind it in the dust, arrived one Sunday just as the congregation was leaving Mass. The men were herded into a field at revolver point and told that an unpopular land agent was being reinstated in his house and that if anyone touched him, six Republicans would be killed. At Athenry in the middle of the night a lorry-load arrived firing shots and forced a number of people in their night clothes to call off their boycott of the police. These abrupt reminders of the realities of power began to have their effect and a number of IRA officers wrote to GHQ in Dublin in October saying that they were hard pressed in their localities. The police boycott had to be called off in Ballaghdareen, Dungarvan, Arklow and many other places. One IRA man wrote of 'a great falling-off and loss of confidence, as if a kind of terror were slowly creeping in'.[18]

Members of the government began themselves to feel a new and fatal confidence. 'We are going to break up this murder gang,' declared Winston Churchill at Dundee on 16 October. 'That it will be broken up utterly and absolutely is as sure as that the sun will rise tomorrow morning.... Assassination has never changed the history of the world and the Government are going to take good care it does not change the history of the British Empire.'[19]

But assassination continued. Whenever an ambush took place families now automatically fled from their homes in anticipation of the inevitable reprisals, and further to complete the analogy with 1798 the Black and Tans started stripping civilians and flogging them with straps and whips to obtain information about the IRA. Twenty civilians were so dealt with on one day in County Clare in October.[20] They took, too, to the cropping of the heads of known women Sinn Fein supporters in retaliation for the same treatment which the IRA had long been inflicting on Irish girls rash enough to fall for policemen. And a sixteen-year-old boy was reported to have been half-hanged at a farmhouse near Angharan.[21]

Feelings grew more and more savage on both sides. Attempts on the part of decent RIC officers to exercise discipline over their men grew more and more ineffectual. 'I have never seen men in such anger,' declared one, describing how he had been totally unable to restrain his own men as the body of an Irish Detective Inspector shot in an ambush at Tobercurry, County Sligo, was brought into their barracks. A constable who had been in the ambush with him was wandering about with shotgun pellets in his face while in an adjoining room another constable was moaning with pain as he lay there with the calf of his leg blown off. That night four heavy lorries entered Tobercurry crowded with men who loosed-off volleys of rifle fire and, smashing their way with sledge-hammers into groceries and other stores, looted and wrecked them and later destroyed two local creameries.[22]

Again, however valiantly the Roman Catholic clergy might continue to maintain that the ambushes were as wrong as the reprisals – the Bishop of Kildare categorically insisted that they were worse[23] – it was the reprisals that seemed to ordinary people the wrong that mattered. Even the Bishop of Achonry, writing to the parish priest of Tobercurry to sympathize with the people in their ordeal, while conventionally condemning the ambush as 'a shocking atrocity' clearly found his sympathies torn by the situation.

That bad government is primarily responsible is only too true [he wrote]. But ... for myself and for my priests who know our young men so well and admire them for their sobriety, for their virtue and for their sensitiveness to honour's reproach, the bitterest ingredient in the cup of sorrow which is ours is the thought that these fine fellows, so stainless and pure in most ways, will, under the delusion that they are doing a service to their country, imbrue their hands in the blood of a brother, and speed the bullet that leaves wife without husband, the child without the father.... These boys allege that they must obey orders. What does that mean? It must mean that they are in the grip of some secret organization which arrogates the authority to impose its will, no matter whether the thing proposed is right or wrong.[26]

A few days later one of these 'boys', Sean Treacy, who had been with Breen at Soloheadbeg and Knocklong and had since been OC of No. 3 Tipperary Brigade, was cornered and shot down in a daylight gun battle in Dublin. He easily became a hero as legendary as Cuchulain and an ancient Irish lament was adapted to commemorate his death: '... Our lovely Sean is dead and gone, Shot down in Talbot Street.'*

Not only in Ireland but in England, too, it was the horror of the reprisals that increasingly counted. And it could be convincingly argued that it was right and proper that it should. The violence was after all the product of the government's failure to solve the political problem in a manner acceptable to the majority of the Irish people. Having chosen instead simply to assert its authority, it was intolerable by any recognized standards of civilized government that that authority should itself be asserted by lawless methods. This was the point on which the government's critics seized to the exclusion of all others, however much they might also deplore the methods of the IRA.

Excessively heartened perhaps by premature hopes of success with the 'murder gang' the government continued to be slow to appreciate the political threat thus developing on its own flank. Lloyd George after all was a Liberal Prime Minister and he led a coalition partly dependent on Liberal support in the country. But he concentrated at first simply on the point that the police had been 'unendurably provoked'. 'There is no doubt,' he said at Caernarvon in October, 'that at last their patience has given way, and there has been some severe hitting back. But take the conditions ...'[26] He argued that civilians in Ireland shot at the police without warning so that it was no wonder the police shot fast.

Though a perfectly fair point, it was not the one that was relevant politically. Aside from the moral issue that no civilized government should exercise its authority by uncivilized methods, what mattered politically was that in Ireland the conflict was being daily regarded more and more in the purely nationalistic terms in which the extremists had always painted it. Every day aggravated still further the original difficulty of achieving a political solution.

By 1921 the authorities were fully alive to the dangers of lawlessness by the Crown forces and were to make considerable efforts to impose discipline. These were at least partly succcessful. There were no more of the large-scale undisciplined reprisals of the sort that had caught the headlines in the summer and autumn of 1920 and reached their climax in December 1920 with the burning down by a company of Auxiliaries of a large part of the

---

* He had shot his way out to safety a few weeks earlier when trapped in a raid on a Dublin house together with Dan Breen.

centre of Cork.* Reprisal killings by Crown forces on the other hand continued ruthlessly, either by men with blackened faces dragging individuals from their beds in the middle of the night or in the traditional form of men shot 'trying to escape'. Yet considering the very sharp intensification of the conflict which took place in 1921 the government attempt at least to impose discipline cannot be ignored.

In the first three months of 1921, some 208 Black and Tan RIC and 59 Auxiliaries were dismissed as unsuitable; a further 28 RIC and 15 Auxiliaries were removed from the force as a result of prosecutions and in addition a total of 24 more RIC and Auxiliaries were sentenced by court-martial.[26] Some of the sentences awarded were even quite severe and included five years' imprisonment for assault, stealing a bottle of whisky and demanding two bottles of whisky and a bottle of stout with intent to steal, or three years for stealing clothes and a piece of jewellery to the total value of £10.[27] Only one successful prosecution for murder was, however, instituted against an Auxiliary for the deliberate killing by the side of the road of a priest, Canon Magner, and a civilian, which was witnessed by an Army officer. The Auxiliary was found guilty but insane. In another court-martial of three Auxiliaries for the murder of two men in the Dublin suburb of Drumcondra, the accused were found not guilty in a verdict that seemed seriously at variance with the disclosed facts.†[28] But even so, such measures revealed a change of attitude from the latter part of 1920 when General Macready had on one occasion said to an interviewer that it was only human that the police should act on their own initiative, adding: 'Punishment for such acts is a delicate matter, inasmuch as it might be interpreted as setting at naught the hoped-for effect of the training the officers have given the men.'[29] Sir Hamar Greenwood had made the unfortunate statement in the House of Commons about the same time that he had yet to find one authenticated case of members of the Auxiliary Division being accused of anything but the highest conduct.[30]

One means by which more discipline was eventually achieved was the substitution of a policy of 'official' for unofficial reprisals – the destruction by the military of houses near the scenes of ambushes when it was thought that their owners could have given the authorities warning of what was being planned. This, however, was a double-edged device. In the first place it appeared to add to the reprisal policy since unofficial reprisals by no means

* The results of an official inquiry into the burning of Cork by General Strickland were never published – in itself a conclusive enough indictment of the Crown forces. Though making some injudicious statements at the time about the fire being caused by accident, Sir Hamar Greenwood virtually conceded later in the House of Commons that the Crown forces were responsible.

† One of the Auxiliary officers found not guilty was a captain who had beaten and tortured Ernie O'Malley when he was captured for a time under the false name of Stewart. He eventually escaped. (O'Malley, *On Another Man's Wound*, pp. 246–8.)

ceased and all thereby tended to seem official. Second, though official reprisals may have made some of the Crown forces feel better, they hardly
diminished the sense of indignation on the part of the house-owners who
were thus presented with the alternative of the destruction of their house or
their own 'execution' by the IRA as spies if they gave information to the
authorities. And although General Strickland, Commander of the Forces in
the South, maintained that this factor was taken into account, the probability
of being given much benefit of doubt by the forces on the spot in the circumstances of the time must have been remote.[31] The owners' sense of indignation was echoed by all who read about or saw pictures of such things in the
newspapers.

This was the all-important effect of all reprisals, however caused. They
consolidated a real sense of national struggle, confirming the point separatists
had always tried to make but which had never before seemed much more
than interpretative fantasy, that it was the Irish people on one side and the
forces of England on the other. Blackened houses, wrecked creameries, the
corpses of innocent civilians were constant visible symbols of the total bank-
ruptcy of British Government policy in Ireland. And to fight against such
things seemed now, more and more, the only policy Ireland herself required.

Encouraged by the undoubted superficial success of the autumn campaign Lloyd George tended to lean on it heavily for comfort. Like any good
politician he kept open such other options as there seemed to be, but these
were few. This was not entirely his own fault. His whole political nature was
of the sort that was happiest with as many options open as possible. But as
Liberal leader of a Coalition Government in which the Conservative, pro-
Ulster and anti-Irish Nationalist element was the dominating one, he was a
prisoner of the political situation into which his own skill and ambition had
manoeuvred him. Nor was this his only problem. The curiosity of the Union
had always been that it maintained its own subordinate miniature government in Dublin Castle and the men in charge there now, with certain excep-
tions among the civil servants, were simple militarists of the old school with
whom the Chief Secretary Greenwood was happy to identify himself.

When the first tentative suggestion of a peace move from a private Irish
source close to Griffith reached Lloyd George in October 1920, his natural
political instinct to explore it had to be tempered by consideration not only
for the Unionists in his own cabinet but also for the die-hard element in the
Castle on which he was, with his present policy, so dependent.

The peace move came through a businessman named Moylett who before
one of his private business journeys to London had been to see Griffith to
ask if he could help. Griffith had said that the first necessity was to get the
British Government to recognize Dail Eireann. Moylett, stressing that he was
acting solely on his own initiative, had consultations in London with one of
Lloyd George's civil service secretaries and with H. A. L. Fisher, the

Minister who headed the Cabinet Committee on Ireland. He returned to say that Lloyd George might be prepared to meet three or four men nominated by the Dail in a conference in which both the Republic and the Union would be 'left outside the door', like coats to be assumed again by the two parties if necessary as they left. As this implied partial recognition of the Dail Griffith was much moved.[32] Collins was notified of the tentative moves and approved, though an event that was about to occur suggests that he did not attach great importance to them. Moylett returned to discuss the possible calling of a truce between the two armed sides.

Meanwhile, Lloyd George in public made the most of the government's new-found confidence. On 9 November he delivered himself of the momentous announcement that he had 'murder by the throat'. Within a fortnight Collins had given him a terrible answer.

Just after nine o'clock on the morning of 21 November 1920 in a well-planned operation he sent his 'execution' squads to different parts of the city of Dublin, including the Gresham Hotel in O'Connell Street, and had twelve British officers, all but one of them members of a counter-terrorist network, shot dead in bedrooms and on landings, some of them in front of their wives. Only one 'mistake' seems to have been made, on a harmless veterinary officer sitting up in bed reading his newspaper in the Gresham. All the gunmen except one escaped.* Two Auxiliaries who had happened to be passing one of the houses where the bloodshed was in progress and had stopped to investigate were also seized and shot out of hand – the first casualties the Division had suffered. It was only the beginning of a day that was to be known as Bloody Sunday.[33]

A Gaelic football match was to be played that afternoon at the Dublin ground of Croke Park between Dublin and Tipperary. In the circumstances of the time, it was not unreasonable of the authorities to have surrounded the ground, intending a search for IRA gunmen in the growd. The move had indeed been planned anyway some days before.[34] On the other hand, in the emotional climate of that day it was a fatal move. Nothing could illustrate better the futility of substituting firmness for a political policy; for in such a situation even the right moves made by authority were inevitably wrong. Whether or not shots at Croke Park were first fired from the crowd cannot now be ascertained with certainty, but in the light of contemporary evidence it seems unlikely. It seems more likely that some of the RIC may have thought they were. They were in any case in an ugly mood after the events of the morning. What is certain is that Auxiliaries and RIC opened fire on the crowd, killing twelve civilians including a woman, a child and a Tipperary forward. The same night two of Collins's most valued Dublin Brigade IRA men, Richard McKee and Peadar Clancy, who had been picked up in a raid

*The captured IRA man, Frank Teeling, who had been wounded by Auxiliaries, was tried and sentenced to death but escaped from prison.

twenty-four hours before, were killed by Auxiliaries in the guard room at Dublin Castle. With them and also killed was a harmless Gaelic Leaguer from the West of Ireland named Clune, a man quite unconnected with the IRA who had happened to be in Vaughan's Hotel, a known nationalist rendezvous which was raided the same night.

Whether the deaths of the three men were acts of vengeance for what had happened that morning or were really, as Dublin Castle put out, the result of an attempt to escape cannot now be stated with absolute certainty. General Sir Ormonde Winter, Chief of British Intelligence, maintains that they were indeed attempting an escape and claims that he convinced a sceptical Sir John Anderson, then one of the Under-Secretaries at the Castle, that this was so.[35] But Winter was a notorious 'hard-liner' at the time and the fact that writing over thirty years later he had still not discovered that Clune was not an IRA man makes him seem at best a cursory assessor of evidence. All that can be said for certain is that it seems improbable that the innocent Clune at least would have inculpated himself so easily and that if an attempt to escape did take place something may have happened to make the prospects of the three men seem desperate indeed. Though their bodies were riddled with bullets their faces did not bear marks of torture and brutality as popular myth has often asserted.* Collins, in a typical gesture, took an appalling risk of capture when he was one of those who went to view them in the Pro-Cathedral after they had been given up by the authorities, and even helped carry a coffin at the Requiem Mass next day.[36]

The loss of the fourteen officers in Dublin was a severe blow to the authorities' new-found confidence. Although Lloyd George tried to keep a line open to Griffith through Moylett even after 21 November,[37] the events of that day temporarily put an end to further discussion of a truce. The only terms that would have been politically acceptable at such a moment required the exception of Collins from any amnesty and such an exception was unthinkable to Griffith or anyone on the Irish side. The deadlock was made all the more grim and complete when a week later the authorities received from a different quarter another shattering blow to their prestige. Two lorry-loads of the company of Auxiliaries stationed at Macroom Castle ran into a well-laid ambush position prepared by Tom Barry and the West Cork Flying Column on a lonely site of bogland and rocks near Kilmichael. It was the Auxiliaries' first major engagement and a terrible one.

After a savage fight at close quarters in which three IRA were killed and,

---

* Edward MacLysaght, *Master of None* (private MS. shown to the author in 1954). 'I am bound to say,' writes MacLysaght, 'that the statement which was afterwards made to the effect that their faces were so battered as to be almost unrecognizable and horrible to look at is untrue ... I remember those pale dead faces as if I had looked at them yesterday. They were not disfigured.' The MS. was written in 1951. Clune had been an employee of the MacLysaght family.

according to Barry, the Auxiliaries made use of notorious 'false surrender' tactics, the entire convoy was wiped out, and seventeen of the eighteen Auxiliaries were killed. The eighteenth was so severely wounded that he was in hospital for long afterwards.* Some of the Auxiliaries' bodies were afterwards found to have wounds inflicted after death and the first British officer on the scene after the fight said that although he had seen thousands of men lying dead in the course of the war, he had never before seen such an appalling sight as met his eyes there. The doctor at the inquest, an Irishman, said that there was no doubt that some of the injuries had been inflicted after death.[38]

The government made full propaganda use of the injuries, even going so far as to state that the corpses of the 'Cadets' had been mutilated 'by axes'. Bayonets were certainly used in the fight and, since moments before and after death are not immediately ascertainable in hand-to-hand fighting, they may well have accounted for some of the 'mutilation' on both counts.† That some bayoneting may even have taken place deliberately after death is not impossible, since irregulars in action often have to make up with primitive emotion for the steadier nerve acquired by professionals in long training. Barry concedes that the morale of the column was so disturbed by the fight that to reassert discipline he had to drill them in the road for five minutes afterwards among the corpses and blazing lorries.[39] In any case the matter is irrelevant, given the other horrors of guerrilla warfare and reprisal in which Ireland was then engulfed‡ The fact that the government still thought that effective points could be scored against the IRA by propaganda was what was revealing, disclosing further its total failure to come to grips with the Irish situation in any meaningful way.

In any case, as far as the propaganda war was concerned the government had long been left far behind by Sinn Fein. Two other events of that autumn had already been turned into symbolic evocations of Ireland's martyrdom and her spirit of defiance. One had been the first British execution of an

---

* Barry, *Guerilla Days in Ireland*, pp. 34–46. Barry states that the only survivor never recovered consciousness, but he can be seen sitting up in bed with a bandage round his head in the *Freeman's Journal*, 17 January 1921.

† Survivors of an ambush in County Clare two months later said that the wounded had been bayoneted in the road by the IRA. (*Irish Times*, 25 January 1921.)

‡ The victory was celebrated in a cynical rhyme which perhaps conveys more of the true atmosphere of the period than a heroic bowdlerized version beginning 'Hurrah for the boys of Kilmichael' which also exists. The former runs:

'On the 28th day of November
Outside of the town of Macroom,
The Tans in their big Crossley tenders
Were hurtling away to their doom.
For the lads of the column were waiting
With hand-grenades primed on the spot
And the Irish Republican Army
Made sh—t of the whole f—ing lot.'

Irishman in the post-war period, that of Kevin Barry, an eighteen-year-old medical student caught with a revolver beneath an army bread lorry in Dublin after a raid on its armed escort. One of the soldiers had been shot dead. Barry was found guilty of murder by court-martial, and executed by the common hangman in Dublin, in spite of pleas for mercy from all sides on account of his youth. An affidavit of his to the effect that he had been beaten by British officers in the course of interrogation made a considerable impact on public opinion. By contrast the fact that the soldier he had shot was as young as himself made virtually none.

The other event also concerned a courageous individual, but in a manner which uniquely concentrated attention from all over the world on the spirit and determination of Irish militants. Terence MacSwiney, the Lord Mayor of Cork, arrested in August in Cork Town Hall at the IRA conference which his military captors had mistakenly supposed to be a Republican court, had displayed a spirit as brazen as it was courageous by immediately going on hunger-strike in protest against the British Government's interference with elected civic functionaries. He had been deported to Brixton prison in London where his hunger-strike continued.

In previous hunger-strikes of the period, in Mountjoy gaol earlier in the year and in 1919, and in Wormwood Scrubs also in 1920, the government had given in after ten days or so when the hunger-strikers had appeared close to death, being naturally unwilling to create martyrs. In the case of MacSwiney the government had announced early, with a certain amount of courage of its own, that it did not intend to surrender to moral blackmail. What it had underestimated, however, was both the physical courage of MacSwiney and the length of time it took a resting man to die of hunger. After a fortnight of MacSwiney's hunger-strike it was assumed that he was on the point of death and public opinion not only in Ireland, but in Britain and much of the rest of the world, focused on the lonely suffering figure of this defiant Irishman in his British cell. He became an easily graspable symbol of the entire political situation in his country. And so he remained for a further fifty-nine days.

The British Government, unnerved by MacSwiney's stand, gave some credence to the story that he was being brought secret supplies of nourishment. The prison authorities even sent the contents of the hand basin in which he had cleaned his teeth to a laboratory for analysis.[40] There was a rumour that the priest who visited him brought food concealed in his beard. On 24 October 1920, after a seventy-three-day hunger-strike, MacSwiney died. Another IRA hunger-striker died in Cork gaol a few hours later, while yet another had died there the week before.

These deaths, and MacSwiney's moving funeral attended by vast crowds in Cork, made a profound impression on all observers of the Irish scene. Of all the many individual incidents that had made the year 1920 so extraordinary in the history of Ireland, none seemed to convey so solemnly the message that whatever resources of civilization the British Government might continue to summon to its aid in the form of police or military reinforcements, there was at last a force in Ireland which could not be deflected from its notion of Irish freedom and which would never give in.

It was against this background of hardened attitudes that the last phase of the struggle was to take place.

10

War and Truce (1921)

The so-called 'Anglo-Irish war' or 'War of independence' can be divided into three phases.

The first, which had run from January 1919 to the beginning of March 1920, had consisted largely of cold-blooded attacks by Volunteers on individual Irish policemen carrying out their duties as unprovocatively as was consistent with their carrying out their duty at all. During this time more than twenty serving or former members of the RIC were killed and over forty wounded. Perhaps the most remarkable feature of this whole phase had been the way in which the RIC morale held firm. Only towards the end had the strain begun to tell. Resignations took place, though not yet numbering more than five per cent of the original force.* More important: among the new English recruits in particular the urge for undisciplined vengeance had begun to assert itself.

This was the phase in which the extreme Fenian element in the new Sinn Fein movement, personified by Collins, gained domination over the political non-revolutionary element for which the country had voted. By the spring of 1920 the country found itself committed to a violent rebellion against British rule for which it had given no sanction. In the nature of the situation, as Collins had foreseen, the country was left with little option but to support the rebellion.

The second phase of the 'war' had run from March 1920 to October 1920. In it a strange two-faced anarchy had established itself in Ireland. As the government's law and order broke down under the continuing pressure of the Volunteers, a rebel law and order grew up as an alternative. Reciprocally, the conventional forces of law and order had increasingly resorted to lawlessness to assert themselves, a process further accelerated by the arrival of Black and Tan recruits and the Auxiliaries. However, by October 1920 there were still only approximately 1,500 Black and Tans in Ireland and a little over 500 Auxiliaries.

It was from October 1920 onwards that the really considerable reinforcement of the RIC by the Black and Tan element took place, averaging nearly a thousand recruits each month from November 1920 to March 1921, by

* They were never more than about thirty per cent altogether.

which time the Auxiliary Division had reached its full strength of 1,500.[1] And with the increase in government forces not only was the alternative rebel administration forced underground again but, with a corresponding development in IRA techniques principally by the flying columns, the 'war' entered its third and harshest phase.

Crown casualties – soldiers and police – for the first nine months of 1920 had been 125 killed and 235 wounded. For the next nine months, to 11 July 1921, there were some 400 killed and 700 wounded.[2] By late 1920 the government had stopped trying to give full official civilian casualties as there was little possibility of making them realistic. The number of IRA casualties – technically 'civilian' – was for obvious reasons unobtainable. It was almost equally impossible to keep track of those civilians shot either accidentally or intentionally by Crown forces, or of the so-called 'spies' and other non-cooperators with the Irish Republic shot by the IRA. But one of the last sets of figures on specific casualties which the government did release in 1920 carried an emotive patriotic note: ex-servicemen killed by the IRA during the year (all serving members of the police) had been forty.[3] The government were also able to reveal the number of civilians killed in 1920 when failing to halt in response to a military challenge: 41 killed and 43 wounded.[4]

Civilian casualties for the six and a half months' conflict in 1921 were higher to an appalling extent. The *Freeman's Journal*, simply by going through its files, reckoned that there were 707 civilians killed from all causes between 1 January and 11 July 1921, and 756 wounded.[5] It would almost certainly be no exaggeration to say that well over a hundred of these dead were 'spies' shot by the IRA: seventy-three were shot between 1 January and 1 April alone.[6] Perhaps an even larger number were deliberately killed by Crown forces in cold blood. Many civilian casualties, particularly in Dublin, were also caused accidentally in the course of fusillades between the Crown forces and the IRA.

'The long drawn out struggle is reaching its final stages and Ireland is winning,' Dail Eireann had proclaimed when setting its ban on emigration in 1920. 'All that is needed is a little more patience and then a bracing up for a final tussle.' In 1921 the final tussle began in earnest.[7] The form the fighting took during the last phase was similar in kind to that in the earlier phases, only considerably intensified. Sometimes the IRA were winning and sometimes not. Limerick provided an example of its fluctuating fortunes. A Limerick flying column had carried out a successful ambush of twenty men of the Lincolnshire regiment at Glencurrane just before Christmas, killing four of them and depriving the rest of their arms and equipment after they had surrendered. But at Christmas, when a number of Limerick IRA men rashly attended a dance at Caherguillamore House, the place was surrounded by Black and Tans and Auxiliaries, and five IRA were killed and over forty others arrested. A month later the flying column destroyed a convoy of Black and Tans at Dromkeen, killing nine of them.[8]

An equally successful ambush had taken place at Ballinalee in County Longford two days earlier when the IRA commandant, a blacksmith named Sean MacEoin, forced eighteen RIC and Auxiliaries to surrender after a three-quarters of an hour fight in which three police were killed. In County Clare at Sixmilebridge six police were killed.

On the other hand, the IRA suffered severe reverses early in the year in County Cork where, on 28 January at Peake, on 15 February at Mourne Abbey, and again on 20 February at Clonmult, parties were surprised and surrounded, with the total loss of seventeen dead and twenty captured, the high ratio of dead to captured leading some to surmise that prisoners had been shot after surrender.[9] By contrast, although it was maintained by survivors of the Sixmilebridge ambush that the IRA had bayoneted wounded men in the road, the behaviour of MacEoin at Ballinalee had been chivalrous. He had delayed his withdrawal after the ambush to care for the wounded police and had himself whispered an Act of Contrition to a dying District Inspector.[10] Chivalry on the part of either side in this conflict was rare enough to be worthy of note. In June Sean Moylan of the Cork IRA was revealed at his court-martial as having saved the lives of wounded after an ambush when some of the men in his column had wanted to shoot them. Discipline was often difficult to enforce in the brigades, partly because of the lack of regulation punishment.[11] 'If you shoot them, then I'll shoot you,' Moylan had cried to his men. The President of the Court said that in something like five thousand cases he had tried in Ireland this was one of the few instances of chivalry by the IRA.[12] But there were others apart from MacEoin's, and two army officers released after being held for five minutes by the South Mayo Flying Column were treated 'with every courtesy and consideration', being told that they were lucky they were regulars and not Black and Tans, in which case they would have had 'other treatment'.[13]

Many senior IRA officers were in fact anxious to behave as correctly as possible as belligerents, partly perhaps to ease nagging doubts about the morality of what they were doing. Doubts were not even always unconscious. One man who had been out in what he called 'a good stand-up fight' in Easter Week had written to GHQ the year before saying that quite candidly ambushes seemed to him too much like murder.[14] And the Catholic Church continued to give no mercy. 'The misguided criminals,' declared the Bishop of Tuam after an ambush at Headford, County Galway, in January, expressing sentiments which must have been echoed by many of his flock, 'the misguided criminals who fired a few shots from behind a wall and then decamped are guilty of a triple crime ... knowing as they must know the nature of the reprisals that are likely to follow an ambush, they came from outside to do a foul and craven deed, and then having fired these few cowardly shots, they beat a hasty retreat, leaving an unprotected and innocent people at the mercy of uniformed forces.'[15] And in his Lenten Pastoral for 1921 the Bishop of Cork stated categorically that Dail Eireann could not be held to constitute a sovereign state. What, he asked, in words which before long were not to seem nearly so ridiculous as they were now intended to be, what if Connaught or Munster suddenly declared itself a Republic, did that give it the solemn right to be so regarded and to declare war?[16]

Yet nothing perhaps conveys more clearly the profound and rapid change brought about by the intensified conflict of these months than the fact that only a short time after this pronouncement by a prominent member of the hierarchy, other members, including Cardinal Logue, Dr Walsh, the Archbishop of Dublin, and Dr Gilmartin, the Archbishop of Tuam, were prepared to associate themselves with an appeal for an Irish White Cross relief fund in a General Committee on which stood the names not only of prominent Unionists but that of Michael Collins himself.[17] 'The Irish White Cross,' concluded the appeal, 'believes that the names of those who have associated themselves with it will justify and give confidence in the appeal for funds.' In answering a question in the House of Commons some time before, Sir Hamar Greenwood had already given Collins's name as that of the Commander-in-Chief of the IRA.

As both the number and size of ambushes increased, so for all their horror did their status. The idea that there was a sort of war going on in Ireland took root with all sides. Birkenhead, the Lord Chancellor, was to refer to it as 'a small war'. And the acknowledgement was itself a victory for the IRA of some political significance. For it automatically implied that there was a nation fighting this war in a sense in which no Englishman had ever quite acknowledged the Irish nation before. Thus the very scale of the IRA activity, whether militarily successful or not, won preliminary ground for that negotiation which would one day surely have to come.

In detail it was a vile and squalid war. As the *Irish Times* wrote in February, for those whose sense of horror recent events had not blunted, the daily newspaper had become a nightmare. An item such as the killing of an RIC Inspector and his wife outside Mallow station and the subsequent shooting by Black and Tans and Auxiliaries of three railwaymen when searching the station had become routine. Women were now killed frequently, not just through careless firing on the part of the Crown forces but increasingly as the result of IRA operations. A woman passenger on a train was killed along with five other civilians when the IRA ambushed the Cork–Bantry train at Upton in February. On two consecutive days in May women were killed in ambushes in County Galway and County Tipperary: a Mrs Blake, the wife of a District Inspector with whom she was travelling, and a Miss Barrington, the friend of another on her way back with him and others from a game of tennis.

Many more martial occasions were, of course, also recorded in these months of 1921: at Glasdrummon in County Leitrim where six soldiers of the Beds. and Herts. Light Infantry were killed and one captured; at Clonbanin in County Cork where (under Sean Moylan) a British colonel and three other soldiers were killed; in County Kerry where another train was ambushed, this time killing an officer and six other ranks; at Crossbarry where not only did Tom Barry and his flying column successfully ambush a convoy of nine military lorries but fought their way out of a massive attempt to encircle them afterwards; at Tourmakeady in County Mayo where another column after killing four also escaped subsequent encirclement. One of the hottest fights for a police barracks in the whole war resulted in March in the capture of the building at Rosscarbery in County Cork by Barry's column; the RIC garrison were specially commended by Dublin Castle for their defence. At Rathmore in County Kerry in May, nine RIC were ambushed and killed when going out to bring in the body of an eighty-year-old Irishman shot by the IRA as a spy and left on the road. At Clonmore, County Kerry, in June, four RIC were killed, and at Carrowkennedy in County Mayo, six more were killed the next day. These last two bloody victories were won by the IRA without loss to themselves though seven out of the ten men they killed on those two days were Irishmen.

But it was less the regular police and military casualties inflicted in these operations and in the many smaller ambushes that took place continually during the same period, than the endless daily series of individual killings on both sides, that emphasized the horror from which there seemed no escape. The bodies of 'spies' bearing some cautionary message such as 'Tried by court martial and found guilty – All others beware – IRA' were found littered throughout the four fields of Ireland. Sometimes they would actually be British officers. A Captain Thomson of the Manchester Regiment had already been found blindfolded and shot near Bishopstown in November 1920.[18] In County Galway in February 1921, the above message was found attached to the bodies of three unarmed privates of the Oxford and Bucks. Light Infantry. More often they would be ordinary Irishmen, labourers or farmers of all ages, though one boy on the day in March when two such 'spies' were shot at Thurles was simply left tied up with the label 'Too Young To Be Shot. Keep Your Mouth Shut' attached to him.

Callousness and brutality on one side was being continually duplicated by the other. A single day in February which saw a man shot dead by civilians in the streets of Enniscorthy – one of many shot in these times for little other reason than that he was an ex-British soldier – a labourer named Fabray shot dead by the IRA for filling up a trench dug by them in the road near his home, and the body of the managing director of a catering company, a JP for twenty-three years, found with an envelope pinned to him reading 'Beware of the IRA', also saw two nationalists taken from their homes in

Drogheda and shot by Black and Tans, and two young Dublin men who had previously been taken to the Castle for questioning found fatally shot with badly beaten faces behind a wall in the suburb of Drumcondra.[19]

Young Irishmen seized by Crown forces in vengeance seem often to have been selected almost at random. Similarly, the IRA definition of a spy was often a most general one. 'Convicted Spy. The penalty for all who associate with Auxiliary Cadets, Black and Tans and RIC – IRA Beware' was the notice found on the body of a well-known Cork business man.[20] There was no discrimination of class among the victims by either side. A Galway councillor was taken from his bed by Black and Tans and shot after an ambush; the body of the Postmaster of Navan who had been unfortunate enough to catch some Black and Tans looting was discovered some time later floating down a river; a Cork JP of seventy, a member of Plunkett's Dominion Home Rule League, was taken from his house and shot dead by Black and Tans for making an affidavit in favour of IRA men captured in Cork.[21] Sir Arthur Vicars, a prominent Unionist of Listowel, was taken from his house by the IRA after breakfast and shot in his dressing-gown.[22]

The *Manchester Guardian*, a paper friendly to the Irish cause, described Vicars's death as one of the most horrible in the black recent records of crime and counter-crimes in Ireland, though it was difficult to see why it was any worse than most of the others except that the victim was a member of the upper classes.[23] The Black and Tans were reputed to have killed an Irishman in East Limerick by trailing him along the road from the back of a Crossley tender.[24] On one occasion the IRA actually seized from Cork South Infirmary the unconscious figure of a former recruiting-sergeant whose execution they had already bungled and shot him again outside.[25]

On another they were to stop a car carrying an officer of the Worcester Regiment and three ladies near Dublin, take the officer out, shoot him, and then when they found they had not done the job properly, make one of the ladies drive him and them up into the Dublin mountains where they shot him again.*[26]

An eighty-year-old Protestant clergyman, Dean Finlay, was shot by the IRA apparently for no other reason than that his house was about to be commandeered by the Auxiliaries,[27] but for good measure the house was subsequently burned as well. A man who had been on the jury which found the RIC guilty of MacCurtain's murder was taken and shot dead by Black and Tans to help him prove his point still further. 'The whole country runs with blood,' the *Irish Times* had written. 'Unless it is stopped and stopped soon every prospect of political settlement and material prosperity will perish and our children will inherit a wilderness.'[28]

Only in North-East Ulster and particularly Belfast did the bloodshed assume a serious sectarian character and this had been aggravated by the

* See below, p. 141.

creation towards the end of 1920 of a new special police force, the Ulster Special Constabulary, with its 'A' (full-time) members some 2,000 strong and 'B' (one night a week reserve) 'Specials' recruited from among Carson's old Ulster Volunteer Force. The hope was to control the murderous rioting that had tended to break out in the North so easily in reaction to events in the South. But even such martinets as Sir Nevile Macready and Sir Henry Wilson took alarm at the thought of giving such men armed authority at such a time. 'Simply inviting trouble,' Wilson called it, '. . . to arm a lot of "Black North" on the chance of their keeping order is childish and worse.' And Macready replying to him said that it had been suggested that such constables should accompany the military to act as guides as to who was bad and who was good. 'This just shows what you and I know, what they are driving at,' he commented. He said he would on no account allow the military to go with special constables, 'unless the latter are under full control of the police'.[29]

The anti-Catholic nature of much of the violence that followed in the North, thus justifying Wilson's and Macready's worst fears, led in turn to retaliation against individuals particularly in the Catholic areas of Ulster, and in the second quarter of 1921 there was a noticeable increase in the number of spies and other undesirables shot dead who were also Protestants. But it was officially declared by IRA headquarters in Dublin, for what such a declaration might be worth, that no one was to be attacked just because he was a Protestant.

Similarly, for what it might be worth, Erskine Childers's Sinn Fein Publicity Department made an announcement to counter a rumour that the IRA would prevent Trinity College Sports Week from being held that summer. 'We desire to state expressly that the IRA do not send threatening letters,' this announcement ran. 'Any person receiving such a thing might safely rest assured that whether they emanate from an anti-Irish body or from private individuals they do not come from the source from which they purport to come.'[30] 'Safely' was the operative word. What, for instance, were the citizens of Waterford to make of a communication signed by the 'Brigade Commandant and Brigade Quartermaster IRA Brigade Head-quarters Waterford' which ran: 'A levy is being made throughout the area, with the sanction of the proper authorities, to help in the work of arming and equipping the IRA. You will be expected to contribute a fair amount.'[31] Was this to be regarded as not being a genuine communication from the IRA? Or, alternatively, at a time when bodies were found daily with 'Beware the IRA' pinned to them, was this not a threat? In either case few Waterford citizens would have felt that they could safely disregard it.

Moreover, the apprehensions about Trinity Sports Week had some foundation in fact. A girl of twenty-one had been killed ten days before when shots were fired from the street at a cricket match being played in Trinity College

Park between the Gentlemen of Ireland and the Military.[32] The *Irish Times*, which now subordinated its traditional dogmatic Unionism to a personal sense of horror at what it had to record daily, commented: 'The increasing callousness with which these things are read is hardly less dreadful than the growing helplessness with which they are watched.'[33] In the previous three days twenty police and soldiers had been killed in four incidents in different parts of the country, two of the soldiers being boys of the Hampshire Regiment's band who died when a land-mine was exploded in the road beneath them near Youghal.[34]

Dublin itself had increasingly become a scene of violent action, and by the summer of 1921 street ambushes of the Auxiliaries and the military, with bombs and hand-grenades thrown at passing lorries, had become everyday occurrences. Collins had formed an Active Service Unit for the city itself headed by a special élite known as 'The Squad'. Casualties among civilians in the street including many women and children were frequent. Between 1 January and 4 June 1921 there were 147 street attacks on Crown forces in Dublin, as a result of which 46 civilians were killed and 163 wounded. These figures included known IRA casualties, but the majority were ordinary Dublin citizens, several of them women and children.[35]

Sometimes a pitched battle would take place in the street, as on the morning of 14 March when a company of Auxiliaries surrounded 144 Brunswick Street in the supposition that Dail Eireann was in session there. They were briskly engaged by the IRA from neighbouring houses – a fact which seemed to confirm the supposition – and there were casualties on both sides and among passing civilians.[36]

Twice the IRA in Dublin attempted something more ambitious than executions and ambushes. On the first occasion, on an evening in February, an attempt was made by a bogus telephone call to lure Crown forces into a trap at Amiens Street railway station around which 165 IRA armed men were waiting for them. The telephone call was, however, suspected by the Auxiliaries who merely arrived warily to probe the railway line and surrounding streets with searchlights. The IRA eventually withdrew.[37]

On the second occasion, on 25 May, a large party of over a hundred IRA entered by day the celebrated eighteenth-century Dublin Customs House which was the headquarters of the Local Government Board and thus virtually of the British civil administration in Ireland, and successfully set fire to it. They were, however, surrounded by troops and Auxiliaries before they could escape and five were killed and seventy taken prisoner. One of those who watched the Customs House burn from O'Connell Street was the old parliamentarian, John Dillon. His thoughts were bitter and very different from the triumphant note immediately struck by Childers in the *Irish Bulletin*. But perhaps his description catches the true flavour of the time more exactly.

The whole scene [wrote Dillon the next day] was one of the most ... tragic I
have ever witnessed. A *lovely* summer afternoon, the crowds of *silent* people,
afraid to express any opinion, and the appalling sight of the most beautiful
[building] of Ireland [of] our period of greatness, wantonly and deliberately
destroyed by the youth of Ireland as the latest and highest expression of idealism
and patriotism.[38]

But compared with other expressions of idealism and patriotism that had
taken place in recent months in Ireland it was an almost noble event.

Corresponding with the increase in fighting there had gone undoubtedly a
vicious increase in the callousness with which both sides fought. On the
government side the callousness was partly official. It was at the beginning
of the year that official reprisals were first carried out by the Army: the
burning of six houses at Midleton, County Cork, after an ambush there. It
was also announced then that henceforth civilian hostages would be carried
in convoys liable to ambush. Martial law had been decreed for the Cork
area in December and extended on 5 January 1921 to Counties Clare, Kilkenny, Roscommon and Waterford. The power to intern without trial
throughout the country had also been taken at last and by the end of January
1921 there were 1,463 civilians interned in camps at Ballykinlar and elsewhere.[39] The Chief Secretary, Sir Hamar Greenwood, was careful to
announce that they would be given prisoner-of-war treatment without
prisoner-of-war *status*.

The distinction was important. The IRA, while breaking – for what it was
worth – the first rule of war by fighting in civilian clothes, claimed to be
belligerents and, if captured in arms, entitled to honourable treatment as
prisoners of war. The British Government, on the other hand, under their
new martial law regulations, were preparing to execute all rebels taken in
arms.

In February the first executions since the hanging of Kevin Barry in
November took place by firing squad in Cork. Seven IRA men were shot in
Cork Barracks that month. A priest who was present to the last with a group
of six of them, shot in batches of two at quarter of an hour intervals, described
them as going to their deaths like schoolboys.[40]

The old Parliamentary Nationalist T. P. O'Connor, who still sat for Liverpool in the House of Commons, made the obvious point that at this stage in
Irish history the judicial shooting by the British Government of six young
Irishmen, the youngest of whom was nineteen and the eldest twenty-three,
could hardly lead to an improvement in the situation. In fact, the bitterness in Ireland was already so great that the executions did not, as in
1916, stir new emotions, but rather simply hardened those that already held
sway.

The executions provoked IRA retaliation. An elderly lady, a Mrs Lindsay
of Coachford, County Cork, a Unionist Irishwoman, had given warning to

the authorities of an ambush being prepared in her locality. It was her information which led to the arrest of those IRA men who were shot in Cork barracks. She had meanwhile been kidnapped by the IRA as a hostage and when the sentences were carried out in Cork barracks she was herself shot dead. Her execution as 'a spy' did not prevent further reprisals being taken by the IRA the next day on six unarmed soldiers who were shot dead in the streets of Cork.[41]

Collins at headquarters in Dublin had not been informed of the Cork No. 1 Brigade's initiative in shooting Mrs Lindsay, and indeed, nearly two months later, Erskine Childers was in a state of some embarrassment on the subject. Another Irishwoman of a different class, Kitty Carrol, had also been shot by the IRA apparently because she had disobeyed a Republican police injunction to stop distilling illicit whisky.[42] 'Shall we,' wrote Childers to Collins on 2 May 1921, 'say (a) the execution of women spies is forbidden, and that Kitty Carrol was not killed by the IRA? Or (b) Kitty Carrol was killed in contravention of orders by the IRA, and that (c) Mrs Lindsay is now in prison for giving information to the enemy?' Mrs Lindsay, unknown to Childers, had then been dead for seventy-nine days.[43]

Another of the very many 'executions' of which headquarters was not informed was that of a British officer, Captain Compton-Smith, captured as a hostage, again by Cork No. 1 Brigade, and shot when four more IRA prisoners were executed by firing squad in Cork at the end of March. Compton-Smith had been a popular officer in his locality and was liked even by his captors; Collins wrote afterwards that he would have tried to prevent his death if he had known what was happening.[44]

On these occasions certain prescribed conventions were correctly complied with by the IRA, such as the returning of rings and money and the delivery of a last letter to the next of kin. In fact, in the case of another hostage executed by the IRA, District Inspector Potter of the RIC, the receipt of such things was his wife's first notification of what had become of him since he was taken prisoner in an ambush. There could be no clearer evidence of the brutalizing atmosphere of the time than the fact that even the sensitive O'Malley, by now Officer Commanding the 2nd Southern Division IRA, seems to have felt relatively resigned to what he regarded as his duty to shoot three British officers whom he captured while out for a country walk in June. As with similar ceremonies in Cork barracks, compliance with the niceties of procedure protected those involved from serious doubts.

One of the officers remarked to O'Malley that some banks they saw on the way down to the churchyard wall in the dawn would make stiff banks for hunting. 'There's not much hunting now,' said O'Malley, who was then just twenty-four. 'None of us want to do it,' he told them, 'but I must think of our men.' He tied handkerchiefs round their eyes and shook hands with them and his Quarter-Master, Dan Breen, finished them off with a revolver as they lay twitching on the grass beside the road after the volley.[45]

The scene was in its macabre and wistful way a small indication of how much things in Ireland had changed since Breen and Treacy had shot the unfortunate Constables McDonnell and O'Connell at Soloheadbeg in January 1919. Something very like a formal state of war had by now indeed come about and was accepted as such by both sides and by the Irish people. In this acceptance the old fantasy proclaimed since the days of Strongbow that the Irish were fighting England for their freedom at last became a sort of reality. The Republicans had drawn the Irish people into their view of history. Whether all this should have been started was one thing; but after this there could be no going back.

A quite genial young Black and Tan looking back later on his service in Ireland was to write: 'It has been said that no one can serve two masters, yet the common folk of Ireland were forced to do so.'[46] In one way this was true. The ordinary small farmer might at any moment be called out from his house by revolver-carrying IRA to dig trenches across roads for the sabotage of police and military transport, and a day later be forced out at bayonet point by the police and military to fill them in again. But the small Irish farmer had been in that sort of situation off and on since the days of the earliest agrarian secret societies. It was the continuity of Irish history that was being enforced with its emphasis on some sort of Irish 'freedom'.

Thus, while there was for the Irish people that year much suffering and personal hardship as they tried to pursue their daily round, there was also sometimes a certain fateful elation in the air, a whiff of ancient legend.

IRA men found themselves becoming folk-lore in their own lifetime. It was not only the dead Sean Treacy who was sung about. O'Malley heard his own name in song at dances he attended.[47] In the countryside people could see in the flying columns the ghosts of the Fenians or those of the old Celtic warriors of legend, made suddenly flesh and blood. And inconvenient as they might often be, they were in a tradition they had been brought up to revere. Ancient emotions about land and the depredations of 'the stranger' going back beyond the famine and the penal laws, beyond even the great O'Neill and the battle of Kinsale, emotions that had lain so deep so long that they had lost coherence in all but poetry, found what seemed plausible everyday expression in the leather-gaitered, trench-coated, rifle and bandolier-slung figures of the flying columns. And the lorry-loads of Glengarry-capped Auxiliaries, firing their rifles and revolvers and yelling in their English accents as they jumped down into the road, were the 'English enemy', who were always supposed to have been there, and were now made flesh and blood too. Even the old homely enemy, the police, had become invading Black and Tans. In a curious way these grim and horrible times were for some also a fairy tale come true. 'Many of us,' wrote O'Malley, 'could hardly see ourselves for the legends built up around us.'[48]

In the towns, too, among the middle classes, thanks partly to the rhetorical nationalism which the old Parliamentary Party had always kept alive and even more to the Irish revival of the early part of the century which had given it substance, there was a quite well-formed reserve of national consciousness to draw on as the times grew harder. So that what as late as 1919 had often seemed mere rhodomontade or plain murder on the part of the Volunteers, acquired under the pressure of events something of the heroic aura they awarded themselves. It increasingly escaped people's attention that the change from a political impasse into a national struggle had been manipulated without their own consent. 'We were becoming almost popular,' wrote O'Malley. 'Respectable people were beginning to crawl in to us, neutrals and those who thought they had best come over were changing from indifference or hostility to a painful acceptance with the knowledge that some kind of a peace settlement would be made.'[49] In the circumstances, for all the routine denunciation of the Church it was now easily forgotten that much of what was being done by the 'National Army' was as vile as what was being done by the small murder gangs of Black and Tans.

Often in fact it was a problem to tell their work apart. When the Lord Mayor and ex-Lord Mayor of Limerick, George Clancy and Michael O'Callaghan, were murdered by masked men bursting into their houses on the same night in March 1921, Collins himself had an inquiry initiated to make sure that the deed had not been done by IRA extremists critical of Clancy's and O'Callaghan's rather unagressive attitude to the struggle.* In this case it was the king's men who fired the bullets. But their work was no more squalid than that of some of the IRA men who dealt with spies and traitors. Among the latter might be people as relatively innocuous as process-servers who continued to try to earn their livings by serving writs issued by the royal courts, or simply, as at Tormanbarry in July, a young man who refused to help dig an IRA trench. His body was found riddled with bullets.[50]

Paradoxically, throughout this final bitter stage of the conflict between the Crown forces and the IRA there had run a continuing undercurrent of talk of peace. It was not just that in the horrific circumstances of the time a longing for peace on the part of ordinary people could hardly be ignored. Real tentative possibilities for negotiation existed in the background throughout these months and even accounted for much of the ferocity of the struggle as both sides manoeuvred up to the very last moment for a better negotiating position.

* The British also held an inquiry which unlike Collins's absolved the forces of the Crown. There seems little doubt, however, that the murderers were Black and Tans or Auxiliaries or both. Mrs O'Callaghan, who herself struggled with the raiders, certainly believed this to be so. (See Dail Eireann Official Report on the Treaty between Great Britain and Ireland, Dublin, 1922, p. 60.)

In this manoeuvring the advantage was really with the IRA. Anything short of their total annihilation by the Crown forces was going to leave them in a position of advantage. For the government to negotiate with them at all was to undermine much of the attitude it had adopted towards them throughout, to recognize at least some substance in what they stood for and acknowledge them as representatives of the Irish nation. To this extent, though Sir Hamar Greenwood might talk manfully as late as May 1921 about fighting on 'until the last revolver had been plucked from the hand of the last assassin', the government were engaged in a losing battle.

Militarily, the British Army, by a series of large sweeps and the use of flexible columns of their own, were proving increasingly troublesome to the IRA's flying columns, who were also short of arms and ammunition. It is not true, as was later alleged, that Lynch came up to Dublin in July to tell Collins the Southern Brigades could not continue the fight; but Barry was certainly in Dublin that summer making clear the shortage of ammunition to Collins and others, and there is no doubt that life for the IRA was becoming more difficult and unpleasant.[51] Collins himself was later reported to have said privately that the IRA that summer were within three weeks of defeat. If he did so it was in the middle of a night charged with emotion when he would personally have wished to convince himself of the impossibility of facing renewed fighting.[52] The essential truth of the time, militarily, is that though the IRA did not have the same control of parts of Ireland they had had in the middle of 1920, they were now more experienced and better organized, and to have beaten them would have required a far greater British military effort than any yet seen in Ireland.

Subsequent experience of regular forces with guerrilla movements enjoying support from their own people – in Palestine, Cyprus and Algeria – suggests that a military victory is never possible in such circumstances. Once such guerrillas have been able to establish themselves effectively at all there can only be a political solution. British public opinion in 1921, deeply disturbed about the violence in Ireland and the apparently inevitable lawlessness of Crown forces in the prevailing conditions, would have been most reluctant to see further repression on the inevitably gigantic scale required. In this sense the IRA won a victory by forcing political negotiation. The question was: what sort of political solution could there be?

De Valera had returned from America at the end of 1920. Though he had made much effective propaganda for the Republican cause and had raised over £1 million for the Republican Loan, his eighteen months in the States had not been an unqualified success. Thinking only of Ireland, he had become uncomfortably entangled in the always essentially American character of Irish-American politics and there had been unfortunate quarrels and recriminations involving himself and John Devoy and Irish-American politicians.

He had failed to secure the recognition of the Irish Republic, which had been one of his ultimate aims. But he returned to Ireland at an opportune moment.

The political side of the movement had necessarily been eclipsed by the military, as military activity intensified. But military activity was, after all, for political ends. The time was approaching when the effectiveness of the IRA would have to be translated back into political terms and some political leadership, now admittedly carried far beyond the official moderation of 1918, would have to reassert itself.

Only de Valera, Griffith and Eoin MacNeill had so far seemed to have public political stature in the Republican movement. And both Griffith, who had been Acting President while de Valera was away, and MacNeill, had been arrested by the Castle authorities in a rather futile gesture after Bloody Sunday in November. Apart from the need for some political figure of stature who was physically free, nothing indicated more clearly the need for de Valera's return than the extent to which on arrival he revealed himself as partly out of touch with the situation in Ireland. When he met the Dail in January he argued for a certain cooling-off in IRA activity, a holding action rather than continued aggressiveness, in order not only to quieten some of the doubts international opinion might have about guerrilla methods but also to ease the burden on the people of Ireland. Clearly he had little understanding of the practical situation in the countryside where the IRA could hardly have disengaged even if they had wanted to. Nor did he appreciate the extent to which political considerations within the movement had long had to cede place to military. He did something to bridge the gap between the two spheres when in a press interview in March he was the first political leader openly to accept responsibility for the IRA's activity in public, insisting that it was not 'a praetorian guard' but 'the national army of defence'.[53] The very fact that there had been no such statement before showed the need for political leadership to assert itself. Above all, political leadership was necessary to handle the inevitably delicate nature of preliminary overtures for peace.

These had continued simultaneously with the intensification of the conflict, even after Bloody Sunday and the Kilmichael ambush of November 1920. At Dublin Castle the Under-Secretary, Sir John Anderson, and the Assistant Under-Secretary, Sir Alfred ('Andy') Cope, were both favourably disposed to the idea of a settlement and encouraged any serious intermediaries who presented themselves. In December an Australian cleric, the Archbishop of Perth, had acted as go-between for Anderson with Griffith in prison and there had seemed a momentary likelihood of official negotiations starting. Griffith, with Collin's approval, made his only conditions a mutual cessation of armed activity, a moratorium on arrests and permission for the Dail to meet. The proposal broke down on Lloyd George's last-minute insistence that there must first be a surrender of arms by the IRA. Both Griffith and Collins firmly asserted that while they were for peace on honourable terms there could be no question of capitulation.[54]

But Cope in particular persisted in his optimism and on de Valera's secret return to Ireland the British Cabinet took an important step. Though they had in fact wished to prevent his return to Ireland if possible, once he was there they decided not to arrest him unless some definite criminal charge could be proved against him. In other words, a line to those behind the IRA was to be kept open.[55]

In April 1921 a further independent effort to get peace moves going was undertaken by Lord Derby, who had just completed a two-year term as British Ambassador in Paris. He visited Dublin, staying at the Shelbourne Hotel under the name of 'Edwards' in what he imagined to be a disguise afforded by unaccustomed horn-rimmed glasses. He was taken to see de Valera. He had previously seen James Craig, who had now taken over leadership of the Ulster Unionists in the North on Carson's retirement. But Derby had disappointingly little to offer beyond goodwill, and de Valera played the whole move down. Determined not to give away negotiating points before negotiation started, he stuck to the position assumed by Griffith and Collins at the time of the visit of the Archbishop of Perth: an equal truce and no preliminary conditions. Lloyd George defined the British Government's attitude in the House of Commons on 21 April. The government, he said, was ready to meet representatives of the Irish people 'for the purpose of discussing any proposals which offer the prospect of reconciliation and settlement, subject only to the reservations that the strategic unity of the Empire must be safeguarded, and that Ulster must not be coerced. Every facility of safe conduct for a meeting of members of the Dail would be granted' with the exception of three or four members accused of serious crime. (Among them obviously men like Collins and Mulcahy.) Pressed, Lloyd George stated that if such three or four were found to have been guilty of serious crime they would be subjected to the law of the land.[56] It was not clarified whether or not there would be a truce in the fighting while such negotiations took place.

The exception of men like Collins from an amnesty was obviously unthinkable to the Dail as Lloyd George knew already from his contacts with the businessman Moylett and the Archbishop of Perth. But if there were to be negotiations he had after all to condition his predominantly Conservative supporters to the idea by easy stages. Besides, he was himself in a personally embarrassing position. He had continually referred to the people he would have to negotiate with as murderers and needed time in which to shift his ground at least with some show of political dignity. It was a difficulty in which he was not alone. 'Surrender to a miserable gang of cowardly assassins, like the human leopards of West Africa,' Winston

Churchill had said at Dundee in October 1920, 'would be followed by a passionate repentance and a fearful atonement.'[57] A clear indication, however, that the personal position of Collins and others was not the important point lies in a message which he transmitted to de Valera via Lord Derby just before he delivered his speech in the House of Commons. Was it so, Derby asked, that those controlling the Irish movement would not consent to meet the Prime Minister unless the principle of complete independence was first conceded? To which de Valera replied, again through Derby, most typically and significantly with another question. Was it so, de Valera asked, that Lloyd George would not consent to negotiate unless the principle of complete independence was first surrendered?

Thus months before these two gifted practitioners of the political arts were to meet, the first issue between them was clearly defined: were negotiations to take place without commitment on either side or must at least the integrity of the British Empire be first proclaimed as non-negotiable? If, of course, it were not to be so proclaimed as non-negotiable, then it could be said that it was theoretically negotiable. And in that case the Irish would have won a major victory right at the start.

The end, when it came, came almost suddenly. It took place in the aftermath of a major political change in Ireland which the IRA for all its effectiveness elsewhere had been quite powerless to prevent.

Under the Government of Ireland Act 1920 elections were held in May 1921 for the first time for the two new Parliaments thereby created: those for Northern and Southern Ireland. The Dail decided to accept the electoral machinery for the Southern Parliament as its own. There were 128 constituencies in the new twenty-six-county area, four of which were Trinity College seats to which four Unionists were returned unopposed. These four members actually met as the Parliament of Southern Ireland and then adjourned. In the other 124 constituencies Sinn Fein candidates were returned unopposed and constituted themselves the Second Dail. In the six counties of the new Northern Ireland a more normal election was held for the Northern Parliament – though there was intimidation against the united Sinn Fein–Nationalist coalition.* The result was that forty Unionists and twelve Nationalists were returned to the Northern Parliament.

The partition of Ireland – the very issue over which Sinn Fein had deprived the old Nationalist Party of its mass support in the first place – was now, after two and a half years of bloodshed which the Church condemned as murder, the loss of some fifteen hundred lives and much material destruction throughout Ireland, a more unalterable fact than it had ever been in the whole previous nine years it had been under consideration. The area thus apparently lost to Irish nationalism was larger than that involved in the final

---

* In the South, Dillon, the leader of the old Nationalist Party, though still strongly opposed to Sinn Fein, had decided not to oppose it in any constituency.

offer to Redmond at the time of the Buckingham Palace Conference in 1914.*

De Valera, the Dail and the IRA were at the time so deeply involved in maintaining their own Republican integrity both in face of the authorities' ruthless physical pressure and Lloyd George's peace manoeuvres that the full force of what was really a major defeat, questioning the validity of the entire policy of the past two and a half years, does not seem to have struck them. But it must have been a factor at some level of consciousness impelling them to bring Irish nationalism back once again from the field of battle to that of political negotiation. For whatever the IRA might prove capable of in the South it was clearly never going to achieve the All-Ireland nationalism which had been the Sinn Fein party's original *raison d'être*.

In fact there were at this stage – though this is often forgotten today – two unusual indications that the leaders of the Ulster Unionists in the North were not wholly indifferent to aspirations for a united Ireland. These can be taken to have been based on self-interest rather than ideology, for at this time it was by no means a foregone conclusion in Ulster Unionist minds that the Six-County State which they had not wanted would be a viable political and economic entity. The Government of Ireland Act in accordance with Lloyd George's original proposals provided for a Council of Ireland to consist of twenty representatives each from the Northern and Southern Parliaments and with the right by agreement to unite the functions of the two Parliaments on any matters within their powers, even including the union of the two Parliaments' powers altogether without further reference to Westminster.

Carson himself, just after announcing on 25 January 1921 that for reasons of health he would be unable to assume the Ulster leadership in the new Parliament, had made a significant statement at Torquay on the 30th.

'There is no one in the world,' he said, 'who would be more pleased to see an absolute unity in Ireland than I would, and it could be purchased tomorrow, at what does not seem to me a very big price. If the South and West of Ireland came forward tomorrow to Ulster and said – "Look here, we have to run our old island, and we have to run her together, and we will give up all this everlasting teaching of hatred of England, and we will shake hands with you, and you and we together, within the Empire, doing our best for ourselves and the United Kingdom, and for all His Majesty's Dominions will join together", I will undertake that we would accept the handshake.'[58]

It was the spirit of this statement that Craig, Carson's successor, took up in an election speech at the beginning of May. Pointing out that the Council of Ireland provided automatic machinery for a meeting with de Valera, he said it would be the first duty of his colleagues and himself 'to select a band of men to go down or wait here for the others to come up, to meet in council under the Council of Ireland'.[59] Three days later he proved with some personal courage that this was not mere electioneering. He went to Dublin and, strongly encouraged by Cope to believe that good could come of the venture, entrusted himself to an IRA escort which brought him to de Valera at a secret meeting-place in Dublin. In fact both de Valera and Craig had been led to believe by Cope that the other wanted the meeting and nothing came of it. As a result de Valera now felt more convinced than ever that it must be the British Government's responsibility to solve the Ulster problem.[60] Perhaps he did not sufficiently appreciate that by reciprocating something of the Ulster Unionists' tentative gestures he could have made it easier for the British Government to do so.

Instead, in conformity with previously declared policy, when the Northern Parliament came into being after the election at the end of May the Dail declared an economic boycott of Ulster goods. The slight predisposition in the new circumstances on the part of Ulster Unionists to show at least some awareness of their political weakness where the South was concerned was thus further blighted; and the daily bloodshed made traditional sectarian embitterment between Protestants and Catholics a more formidable factor than ever.

But Cope's efforts to secure peace negotiations continued assiduously. On 22 June a party of the Worcestershire Regiment, acting on a tip-off, surrounded the villa in the Dublin suburb of Blackrock in which de Valera was hiding. The soldiers were clearly unaware of any higher political directive that de Valera was not to be arrested, and were proud of their capture. However, after three or four hours in a prison cell he was, on the intervention of Cope, suddenly transferred to the relative splendour of an officer's room in Portobello barracks whence he was released in some bewilderment the next day.

Just before his release de Valera witnessed from his window what his official biographers describe as 'the funeral of a British officer killed in an ambush in the Dublin mountains'. In fact this was the officer who had been taken from a car by the IRA and clumsily shot in front of three lady companions, one of whom had been made to drive him further up into the Wicklow mountains for the *coup de grâce*.* Remonstrated with by his captors, de Valera replied that ambush techniques were permissible to a nation which only had stone walls and hedges to protect it against tanks.†[61] That a kindly, civilized politician could use such an argument in the circumstances, and that it could be simultaneously both relevant and irrelevant,

---

* See above, p. 129.
† The dead officer was from the same regiment – the 2nd Worcestershire – as the soldiers who had effected de Valera's capture.

was an indication of the terrible pass to which the political situation in Ireland had degenerated.

The very day of de Valera's arrest King George V made a speech at the formal opening of the Northern Parliament. It reflected plain human dismay at the situation in a tone far transcending the stately occasion at which it was delivered:

> I appeal to all Irishmen to pause, to stretch out the hand of forbearance and conciliation, to forgive and forget, and to join in making for the land they love a new era of peace, contentment and goodwill. ... May this historic gathering be the prelude of the day in which the Irish people, North and South, under one Parliament or two ... shall work together in common love for Ireland ...

The speech had been prepared on the advice of General Smuts – then in London for the Imperial Conference – and with Lloyd George's approval, by Sir Edward Grigg, the Prime Minister's Private Secretary. It was a good deal more conciliatory than the draft which the Irish Office in Dublin had originally provided,[62] and it moved public opinion throughout the British Isles.

Two days later Lloyd George sent a letter to de Valera, now conveniently free again, asking him 'as the chosen leader of the great majority in Southern Ireland' and 'in the spirit of the King's words' to attend a conference in London.[63]

De Valera replied that he would consult 'such principal representatives of our nation as are available' and would consult with 'certain representatives of the political minority in this country' (by which he meant the Unionists). He was thus in fact already indirectly negotiating with Lloyd George by his choice of words, refusing to be drawn into a preliminary acceptance of partition or his own role as a mere representative of the South.

Griffith and Barton were released from prison to attend the consultation. Craig – also already negotiating by taking his stand firmly on the *status quo* in the North – refused to attend the conference. But the Southern Unionists, led by Lord Midleton, did so, and it was through their influence and the further conciliatory efforts of General Smuts that a truce was eventually arranged between the IRA and the government forces. It was agreed at the Dublin Mansion House on 8 July at a meeting which General Macready attended with some wariness, bringing a revolver in his pocket and being taken aback to be greeted by Larry O'Neill, the Lord Mayor, as if he were his 'long-lost brother'.*[64]

The truce which was to end all aggressive acts and provocative displays of force by either side was to come into force at noon on 11 July and was terminable at seventy-two hours' notice.

---

* The truce, though officially announced by the British on the evening of 8 July, was not formally agreed as to terms until 9 July.

Though operations by the Crown forces virtually ceased from the time of the truce conference, activity by the IRA continued up to the very last moment. On the day of the conference two spies were shot dead, one near Cashel and another near Tullamore, the latter bearing the slogan 'sooner or later we get them. Beware of the IRA.' The execution of a third man, a railway ganger, on the morning of Saturday, 9 July, was witnessed by a boy who heard him crying, 'Murder!' as he was forced to kneel beside the railway line and told to say his prayers. A girl had all her hair cut off at Wexford the same day, while threatened with a revolver, for 'spending all her time with Black and Tans'. Four unarmed soldiers were kidnapped in the streets of Cork on the night of Sunday, 10 July, and three of them were found blindfolded and shot dead in a field near a cemetery the next morning.

The last Black and Tan murder seems to have been that of a Cork JP, a supporter of Plunkett's Dominion Home Rule who had made an affidavit on behalf of IRA prisoners in Cork gaol. He was taken from his house and shot dead 'by armed men' on the night of Sunday, 10 July. The last of the 'enemy' to die at the hands of the IRA on the very last morning of this war of independence were, like the first in January 1919, two Irish Catholic policemen: Sergeant King, shot off his bicycle by two undisguised men in the street of Castlerea, and Constable Clarke shot dead in Skibbereen. The former had seen twenty-three years' service, the latter thirty-four years' service with the RIC.[65] Whereas the killing of Constables MacDonnell and O'Connell at Soloheadbeg had shocked the Irish nation, the deaths of Sergeant King and Constable Clarke barely caused the flicker of an eyelid except among those who mourned them. And too many people in Ireland were now mourners for much thought to be given to them.

That these last IRA actions were hardly those of irregular irresponsible individuals is indicated by the fact that as soon as the truce came into force, over most of Ireland where violent death had long been as routine as the rising-up and the going-down of the sun, there was in almost unearthly fashion suddenly a total absence of killing. Day after day at first there came the stunned realization that in this respect at least the truce was not being violated.* Only in the North was the truce welcomed in grim fashion. In Belfast ten people were killed and a thousand Catholics driven from their homes. It was a salutary reminder that for all the terrible events of the past two and a half years, the nature of that problem which had brought them about in the first place was quite unchanged. But with unarmed Auxiliaries and Black and Tan mixing freely with the people in the Dublin streets

* After four months of truce the British Government had complained of 595 breaches of the truce by the IRA altogether but none of them involved murder. 150 of them were concerned with the disputed issue of whether or not the terms permitted the IRA to drill publicly. 206 were concerned with the kidnapping of individuals but in over 150 of these cases the release of the victims was quickly secured by the IRA's truce liaison officers. (Hansard, H.C., 5th series, vol. 148, col. 389.)

and leather-gaitered men of the IRA coming down from the hills like heroes, the relief was too great for this to be widely remembered. It seemed almost more to the point that 'Mick' Collins had been offered £10,000 for his memoirs by an English publisher.[65]

11

Treaty (1921)

The responsibility of the leaders of the Republican movement was now awesome. They had to emerge from the blend of euphoric fantasy and day-to-day realism in which they had lived for the past five years and render account not only to the Irish people whom they had brought along with them but also, in their own view at any rate, to the past generations of Irish history. For the first time they faced the British Government as Redmond and Dillon had had to face them: round the negotiating table.

What were the realities with which they were confronted?

The truce had been a victory and a defeat for both sides. With it both sides acknowledged that they would prefer to fight no more. Inasmuch as the British Government were by far the stronger party and had always before been able to crush armed Irish rebellion, this represented a unique Irish victory. The government was treating its opponents as nominal equals. On the other hand they were not equals, and both sides knew it.

Far from having been able to drive the British out of Ireland, the IRA had been unable, as Mulcahy, the Chief of Staff, was soon to remind it, to drive them out of anything more than 'a fairly good-sized police barracks'.[1] If it came again to a mere test of strength – and contingency plans for the introduction of 250,000 British troops and even a blockade of Ireland were being discussed[2] – the IRA could never physically win. Moreover, in the sort of war the IRA had been fighting, a truce was much more harmful to their future capabilities than it was to that of regular professional forces. Key men had to come out into the open; the highly-strung tension on which so much of the successful morale of underground warfare depends was relaxed; and a population overwhelmed by relief automatically became less ready to resume the burdens of a war in which they had always been the chief sufferers. To offset this physical imbalance a most important political factor operated in favour of the Irish. The Irish leaders were unquestionably now representative of the vast majority of the Irish people, and British public opinion would only have been prepared to see the government's superior might made use of under certain circumstances.

This was really the strongest card in the Irish hand. Provided the terms they held out for did not seem outrageous to British public opinion, the government would have to forgo its physical advantage and submit to them.

There were two points around which all discussion of terms revolved. The first was the question of allegiance to the British Crown, carrying within it the very real issue of British security from some future enemy's attack through Ireland. The second was the question of North-East Ulster. The Crown in itself had never in the past been an important issue one way or the other in the priorities of the vast majority of Irishmen, concerned as they were with their everyday grievances. Attempts by political theorists like Tone and his Fenian descendants to make republicanism a panacea for those grievances had been ineffectual. The two great mass movements which had effectively sought to deal with grievances on the level of national aspirations, those of O'Connell and Parnell, had had no difficulty in acknowledging loyalty to the Crown. Those national aspirations which survived the resolution of practical grievances, reinforced by the cultural movement at the beginning of the century, continued to be expressed as far as the great majority of the people were concerned in the Home Rule movement. And this continued to accept without question the constitutional role of the Crown. Indeed, it would have been extraordinary if it had not done so. One of the great traditions of nationalism to which all Irish nationalism looked back, that of the Protestant colonists of the eighteenth century, had been based on a nominally independent Crown, Lords and Commons of Ireland – the Crown being shared with England. And it was this model which Arthur Griffith, now to head the Irish delegation to London, had realistically accepted as the only feasible one for the twentieth century.

Griffith's notion of the scale of autonomy required by Ireland had been far greater than that of the Home Rulers who formed the mass of Irish opinion, but on the question of the Crown itself there had been no dispute with them. Equally, the great majority of those who had voted for a Republic in 1918 had done so not as doctrinaire republicans but in the belief that to bid for a Republic was the most effective way of securing the largest measure of freedom the government could be forced to grant. Few of them then, or three years later, seriously believed that a British Government, whose prime concern for centuries had been the threat to Britain's security presented by an independent Ireland, would allow Ireland to abandon all form of nominal allegiance to the Crown. From the point of view of British public opinion, all-important to the negotiations, abandonment of the Crown could not be seen as a reasonable demand.

On the other hand, the leaders of the Irish delegation to London were in a peculiar difficulty as a result of their own rise to the position of negotiators for the Irish people. For they represented not only the Irish people but at the same time a minority clique of republican dogmatists who had been the active spearhead of the most recent phase of the nationalist movement. The

Republic for such people had become a Holy Grail, a sanctified symbol by which the suffering of the Irish people throughout history was to be redeemed – something inviolable and remote, and certainly not just a means to a political end. Anyone negotiating for Ireland at this moment was in the difficulty of simultaneously representing the Irish people and also representing this unrepresentative minority.

On the question of North-East Ulster there should have been no such complicating factor. This was after all the issue which had brought the mass of Irish opinion into support of minority republicanism in the first place. Only on a point of emphasis was there a difference of attitude. Since it was the all-embracing symbol of the Republic which was vital to out-and-out republican activists, the detail of North-East Ulster tended to assume a secondary position, whereas it was in fact, and always had been, the most important issue.

The early stages of the negotiations were handled by de Valera who, as the subtlest political mind on the Irish side, was well aware of all delicate considerations. He had once declared that he himself was no doctrinaire republican. He could not, however, ignore the fact that influential people both in the IRA and in his own ministry were doctrinaire republicans – among the latter Austin Stack and Cathal Brugha. De Valera was found at his desk by Griffith one day during this period, working out on paper what seemed like some geometric problem of right angles and curves and positions marked A, B, C and D. He explained that he was trying to devise some means by which he could get out of 'the strait-jacket' of the Republic and bring Brugha along with him.[3] To General Smuts in Dublin in July 1921 he had said – according to Smuts – 'If the status of a Dominion is offered me, I will use all our machinery to get the Irish people to accept it.'[4] And he had already admitted to Casement's brother, Tom, 'that a Republic was out of the question'.[5]

De Valera was in fact offered the status of a Dominion almost immediately but with fundamental reservations, most important of which was that the position of the six counties under the Parliament of Northern Ireland would remain as it was under the Government of Ireland Act. According to Lloyd George, de Valera replied with a demand for Dominion status inclusive of the North, with issues such as facilities for the British navy and air forces to be negotiated later between the two governments; alternatively, he demanded total independence for the rest of Ireland. On being told that these alternatives were unacceptable and meant the end of the truce, he turned very pale and demanded a respite for discussion in Dublin, which was granted. He asked Lloyd George not to publish the proposals and counter-proposals since this, he said, in a significant phrase, 'would increase my difficulties'.[6]

The Dail, on de Valera's recommendation, unanimously rejected the

British proposals, but with the air thus cleared he re-established contact with Lloyd George and after much haggling over terminology eventually accepted an invitation to a conference on terms which were without any pre-conditions whatever. They did not imply the sovereign independent status for the Irish delegates which de Valera had doggedly tried to establish. On the other hand, they did not imply any Irish obligation to the British Empire either. The invitation, which followed further conciliatory intervention by George v, asked him to come 'with a view to ascertaining how the association of Ireland with the community of nations known as the British Empire can best be reconciled with Irish national aspirations'.' The Conference began in London on 11 October.

On the Crown the Irish from the start adopted the ingenious compromise de Valera had worked out by geometry for Cathal Brugha's benefit and which he now called External Association. The actual use of the word 'external' came to him one morning after his first meetings with Lloyd George when he was tying his bootlaces in his house in Dublin.⁸ The term meant the voluntary association of an independent sovereign state with the British Empire, the membership of such association creating a special link with the Crown which was to be the head of the association.

Ironically, this was one day to become the standard constitutional pattern by which the British Empire or Commonwealth was enabled to survive, permitting African and Indian nationalist states to become wholly independent sovereign states while still linked to Britain. In 1921, however, such a formula seemed totally unacceptable to any British Government as disruptive of the Empire, and though it was to be presented over and over again by the Irish delegates it was always to be flatly rejected. Persistence with it did, however, successfully lead by way of compromise to at least a remarkable obfuscation in terminology of that allegiance the British regarded as indispensable. In any case the obvious Irish tactics were to break with the British, if break they must, not on the Crown – unimportant as it was to the Irish people as a whole and important to the British – but on Ulster.

On Ulster the Irish were on much stronger ground. Few people in Britain or Ireland liked partition. The Unionists as well as the Nationalists in the South were opposed to it. If a British Government were prepared, as they were, to give a form of Dominion status to the vast majority of the Irish people, why, it might be asked, should that status not apply to the whole of their country, including those sections of that vast majority who lived among a relatively small anti-nationalist minority in the north-east? The nationalists had after all already committed themselves in a statement of de Valera's to the principle of some autonomy within an Irish state for that minority. It was extremely unlikely that British public opinion would want to incur all the moral opprobrium and embarrassment of all-out war in Ireland for the sake of preventing that, particularly if further safeguards were to be given to Britain's security by the grant of special facilities to the British Navy in Irish ports.

It is easy now to see that the Irish delegation should have stuck rigidly to this position in their negotiations, making further concessions on the Crown, and on other matters if necessary, but on no account abandoning the basic principle of national unity for the preservation of which the Irish people had first called upon their party. We know now that given the evolutionary development of the British Empire that was to take place within even the next ten years, the widening of an Irish Dominion's internal powers and the eventual extension of its constitutional status would have presented no great difficulties and certainly would have involved no all-out war. But even without hindsight, to say this is to leave a number of vital contemporary factors out of account.

In the first place there was the simple personal factor. Lloyd George headed the British team, the 'Welsh wizard' by the lowest standards, and, by the highest, one of the most brilliant political manipulators of all time. Behind him were two men also of political stature in any age: Birkenhead and Winston Churchill. Only de Valera at the head of the Irish delegation might have been a match for Lloyd George, who had already paid him the compliment of saying that arguing with him was like trying to pick up mercury with a fork.* But for reasons which people have interpreted differently de Valera this time decided not to go to London. His enemies have said that it was because he knew there must be a compromise which would incur such odium among republicans in Ireland that he did not wish to be tainted by it. But this is wholly unjust.

It was indeed because de Valera knew there must be compromise that he remained in Ireland, but not in his own self-interest. By remaining in Ireland he was able to retain manoeuvre for two political situations at once. First, he was well positioned for the inevitable game of bluff needed to secure an acceptable compromise in London, with himself advantageously appearing an inflexible symbol of the Republic. Second, he was ready to deal with the delicate political situation that would arise at home with out-and-out republicans when the inevitable compromise on the Crown (embodied, he hoped, in some form of external association) went through. It was an example of the whole Republican movement's weakness as representative of Ireland in this crisis that the more important political problem should have appeared to arise not across the negotiating table in London but in the reaction to what happened in London among dogmatic republican circles in Ireland. For this reason, above all, Ireland's best player was, as Griffith put it, kept among the reserves.⁹ And self-imprisoned in the slight unreality of that

* 'Why doesn't he use a spoon?' was de Valera's riposte. See Frank Pakenham (now Lord Longford), *Peace by Ordeal*, London, 1935, p. 84. This fine work is the best account of the Treaty negotiations in detail.

Dublin situation de Valera inevitably applied to the negotiations in London something of its unreal perspective.

The other Irish negotiators, in addition to Griffith, were: Michael Collins, who had accepted the role most reluctantly, but whom the British, it could be assumed, would regard as representative of the hard-line IRA – and who conversely might be expected to lend a certain republican respectability to any necessary compromise in the minds of the IRA; Robert Barton, chosen partly for his economic interests, but also because as an ex-English public schoolboy and a land-owner he understood the background and mentality of men like Churchill and Birkenhead in the British delegation; E. J. Duggan, a solicitor who had acted as an intelligence front in Dublin for Collins in the past two and a half years, and George Gavan Duffy who had been a Sinn Fein representative in Paris. Erskine Childers, who had helped make such a brilliantly effective job of Sinn Fein's propaganda, was the delegation's secretary. The members of the delegation were defined in their credentials as 'plenipotentiaries', but they agreed to keep in touch with Dublin and also to submit the complete text of any draft treaty about to be signed with the British to Dublin and await a reply before signing.[10]

The full, complex, and detailed negotiations which led to the eventual signing of the so-called Anglo-Irish Treaty on the early morning of 6 December 1921 need not concern us. In the context of seven centuries of Irish history, or, more narrowly, in the context of a century and a half of different forms of Irish nationalism, what is important is what the negotiators brought back and why.

That as negotiators they were outclassed is undeniable. Their own private political difficulties in Dublin were certainly a handicap. But then the British delegation had an analogous handicap with many of their own party rank and file, of whom they were far in advance, in dealing with 'murderers' and assassins at all. The British, particularly Lloyd George, simply handled their own difficulties more subtly and skilfully.

The chief mistake the Irish delegation made was to allow the two all-important issues of the Crown and Ulster to become confused. They did not sufficiently single out Ulster as the issue on which to challenge the British to renew the war. This was largely because, though the unity of Ireland was more important than the issue of allegiance, to the people of Ireland in general, the issue of allegiance was of equal importance to the minority of republican dogmatists whom the delegates also represented. In the event they fought both issues either simultaneously or alternatively and lost over both. In terms solely of the tactics which the situation seemed to demand it is amazing to find that as late as ten days after the conference had begun the Irish were writing to de Valera through Childers for instructions as to which issue to give most weight to: Ulster or the Crown. When Griffith indicated that his natural inclinations were to offer concessions on the

Crown, de Valera wrote back that there could be 'no question of our asking the Irish people to enter an arrangement which could make them subject to the Crown, or demand from them allegiance to the British King. If war is the alternative we can only face it. . . .'[11]

It was to be de Valera's weakness throughout that, staying in Dublin where even External Association presented a problem, he should have been able to feel that he had made all the compromise necessary by (a) being prepared to give up the actual word 'Republic', and (b) by conceding a recognition of the Crown as head of the Commonwealth with which Ireland was to be associated. After Griffith had expostulated at de Valera's interference with the delegation's power of manoeuvre over the Crown, de Valera became less inclined to make further suggestions, and the dangers of future misunderstanding were enhanced by distance. The possibility that might have been open had the delegation felt wholly free to offer concessions on the Crown was revealed to Griffith by Lloyd George, who said that provided he had Irish reassurances on the Crown he would 'smite the Die-Hards and would fight on the Ulster matter to secure "essential unity" '.[12] And a few days later Griffith told de Valera that if Ulster proved unreasonable the British Government were prepared to resign rather than go back to war against the South.[13]

There were two difficulties. The first was that Griffith and Collins had only limited freedom of manoeuvre on the Crown. The second was that in the stage in the negotiations after Sir James Craig had shown himself uncomfortably intransigent towards any change in the 1920 *status quo*, Lloyd George had introduced a subtle device to try to get himself off both the Belfast and the Dublin hooks simultaneously. The device was a Boundary Commission which, along the lines of his original proposal for the Government of Ireland Bill,* would sit and adjust the borders in accordance with the wishes of the inhabitants. If this were to mean what it said, it could only mean that large areas of Counties Tyrone and Fermanagh, together with other areas of County Derry, South County Down and South County Armagh would be transferred to a Dublin government in return for small reverse border indentations in the Counties of Donegal, Cavan and Monaghan. On the grounds that any border adjustment of this sort would probably make the Northern Government politically and economically unviable, Griffith had privately agreed to accept it as a temporary solution of the Ulster difficulty when Lloyd George said that what he wanted was reassurances with which to calm his own right wing. When in the last hours of the negotiations, after it had seemed that they would break down altogether over the question of the oath, and the Irish delegates, on referring themselves to Dublin, had been sent back again with instructions to break on Ulster, Lloyd George suddenly produced Griffith's agreement to the Boundary

* See above. p. 90.

Commission, the delegates found they did not have Ulster to break on, only the Boundary Commission.[14] And to break on that would in the circumstances have come even more unreasonably from Griffith – who had agreed to it privately – than from Craig. It was a superb piece of political manoeuvre on the part of Lloyd George.

The very title of the agreement which the delegates brought back from London – 'Articles of Agreement for a Treaty Between Great Britain and Ireland' – announced a new era in Irish history, a change as fundamental in its way as that brought about by the arrival of the Norman barons seven centuries before. The use of the word 'Treaty' conferred a status Ireland had never before been granted.

'Who are our Ambassadors? What treaties do we enter into?' Sir Lawrence Parsons had exclaimed, deploring the hollowness of the Irish 'Nation' of Grattan's Parliament, 130 years before. Now she had a Treaty with the country that had disputed her nationality so long. By this document Ireland was given the constitution and status of Canada and the other Dominions 'in the community of nations known as the British Empire'. (As Collins was to point out, this automatically made the other Dominions guarantors of Ireland's status.) She was to be styled the Irish Free State – a literal translation of the Irish word *Saorstat* which Dail Eireann had been using as the Irish for Republic over the past two and a half years.

The 'representative of the Crown in Ireland' – a last-minute improvement secured by Collins over the word 'Governor-General' – was to be appointed and to act in accordance with the practice of the Canadian Governor-General. The oath to be taken by Members of the Parliament was set down in Clause 4 of the Treaty, and since it was to dominate the future of internal Irish politics for the next six years, is worth studying in full. In many ways it was a masterpiece of ingenuity, a compromise as brilliantly calculated to satisfy equally two diametrically opposed interpretations as any compromise of words could be.

'I ...,' the oath began, 'do solemnly swear true faith and allegiance to the Constitution of the Irish Free State as by law established ...' (Not, it may be noted, allegiance to the king.) It went on: '... and that I will be faithful to H.M. King George v, his heirs and successors by law, in virtue of the common citizenship of Ireland with Great Britain and her adherence to and membership of the group of nations forming the British Commonwealth of Nations.'[15] There was on a purely literal interpretation no oath to the king. The fact that 'allegiance' was subtracted from faithfulness where the king was concerned may even be said to have made this point emphatically. The faithfulness sworn was in respect of 'common citizenship' with Great Britain, and of Ireland's membership of the Commonwealth. The very use of the word 'Commonwealth' rather than the then current usage 'Empire' was in.

itself a mark of deference to Irish Republican susceptibilities. The phrase 'common citizenship' could be interpreted in two ways. In one interpretation it could be made to mean that Irish Free State citizens were still automatically subjects of H.M. King George v as English citizens were, and as Irishmen hitherto always had been. In another interpretation it could be made to seem that common citizenship specifically excluded subjection and was something voluntarily entered into by Irishmen with this Treaty. The whole past history of the close intermingling of the people of the two islands in their everyday lives made this a not undignified decision.

Amazing as it may now seem, Ireland was largely to destroy herself, to know again two rival reigns of terror – by government (though an Irish one this time) and by civilian guerrillas – to read again of executions by the roadside and in barracks yards, to see many more of her fine buildings consumed in flames and the highest hopes of those who had believed in Irish freedom for so long turned to ashes – all on the issue of whether or not the Treaty which contained this oath was a betrayal of all she had been struggling for.

On the question of Ulster, so much more fundamental to the concept of Irish nationalism, there were two major items. First, though the Treaty and the constitutional status similar to Canada's were conferred on Ireland as a whole, the powers of the Government of Northern Ireland established the year before were to remain unaffected until one month after the ratification of the Treaty by Act of Parliament. If within that month the Government of Northern Ireland so asked, then Northern Ireland was to continue to be excluded from the powers of the Free State. Second, if that happened – and everyone knew that it would – then a Commission was to sit to 'determine in accordance with the wishes of the inhabitants, so far as may be compatible with economic and geographic considerations, the boundaries between Northern Ireland and the rest of Ireland'.

Except for such adjustments as this Boundary Commission might give rise to, this was basically no improvement on the 'temporary' partition of the six counties to which Redmond had reluctantly agreed. Purely theoretically it might be said that since the six counties now had autonomy from Westminster, a sort of constitutional lip-service was thereby paid to the Irish nationalist principle. But in practice, given the known two-thirds anti-nationalist majority in the North, autonomy put paid to the national hopes of those who lived there more finally than subservience to Westminster had ever done. The Boundary Commission alone seemed to give some chance of a reprieve. For if the border were thus re-aligned then large tracts of Tyrone and Fermanagh at least and some parts of Derry, Armagh and Down would presumably be allotted to the Free State, and the question would inevitably arise as to whether 'Northern Ireland' could reasonably continue as a viable political and economic unit if so truncated. This was the hope to which Collins in particular clung, enabling him to convince himself that in the end the Treaty would not be found to have destroyed the All-Ireland principle. Just before the Treaty was signed Collins had an interview with Lloyd George in which the British Prime Minister allowed Collins to think that he too interpreted the significance of the Boundary Commission in this sense – i.e. in the sense that it would transfer large areas to the nationalist South.[16]

The constitutional status of Canada permitted Ireland to raise her own military and naval defence forces, but other clauses in the Treaty gave the British forces certain rights and facilities in four Irish ports. Some recognition, however, of the special strategic relationship between Britain and Ireland had always been made by Sinn Feiners and these rights could hardly be said to constitute a violation of Irish nationality in the circumstances.* Unquestionably the Treaty did not give Ireland the Republic many people had been fighting for. But hopes of getting that had been tacitly abandoned by entering into negotiations at all. Soon after they had begun in fact Collins had admitted in a private letter that Dominion status, though nowhere near a finalized solution, was 'the first step'. More than this could not be expected.[17] And de Valera himself had earlier made the same compromise. What the Treaty unquestionably did do was to end Ireland's old relationship with England for ever. And that for the vast majority of Irishmen and women after all they had gone through in the past two and a half years, after all their forefathers had gone through in seven centuries, was not a bad start. Ireland at last could now look to herself for salvation.

Of the five Irish signatories to the Treaty – Griffith, Collins, Duggan, Barton and Duffy – none had liked its compromises, but the first three had thought its advantages far outweighed its disadvantages. The essence of their position was that it gave, in Collins's phrase, the freedom to achieve freedom.

In London Collins, essentially a realist for all the extreme republican position from which he had started as a young man, had successfully adjusted fantasy to reality. Practical by temperament, he was able to maintain the adjustment on return to Ireland. The reality after all was greater than the majority of Irish nationalists only a few years before would have dreamt possible. On the other hand, Collins knew quite well the sort of mood he had to answer to among his former comrades. In the night hours in which the Treaty had been signed in London Churchill had noticed that Collins

---

* Nevertheless, there were extremists who so interpreted it and not even supporters of the Treaty, of course, liked the idea. Curiously, these rights, which constituted a difficulty between Britain and Ireland for eighteen years, were abandoned by the British Government in April 1938, a year before the outbreak of the Second World War in which they were to be so badly needed.

at one point looked as if he were going to shoot someone, 'preferably himself'. On his arrival by boat in Dublin on 8 December his first words to his intelligence agent Tom Cullen, who was first across the gangway, were: 'Tom, what are our fellows saying?' 'What is good enough for you is good enough for them,' came the reply.[18]

With Barton and Duffy the emphasis in their attitude to the Treaty was different. They had been appalled by its compromises, but thought them better than the alternative which was a breakdown, bringing, if not the 'terrible war' which Lloyd George threatened, at least a sterile and dangerous deadlock in which the Irish would have lost all advantage. (Collins, in whose political interest it was to play up the threat of war, in fact rather played it down.) Erskine Childers, the Secretary to the delegation, affected perhaps by the remorselessness of his own propaganda in the later phases of the military struggle, was by now an ascetically severe and dogmatic Republican, and had long been casting a baleful eye on the way things were going in London. Just before the end of the negotiations Collins had described Childers's advice and inspiration as being 'like farmland under water – dead. With a purpose, I think – with a definite purpose. Soon he will howl his triumph for what it is worth.'[19]

The remark is a good example of how Collins, realistic about the negotiations, was equally realistic about the potential political crisis over his shoulder in Dublin – in fact he had already once described Dublin as 'our over-riding difficulty'.[20]

Childers, uninhibited by any need to face the personal alternatives of signature or commitment to war, did much to reinforce the grievous doubts which de Valera himself felt when he first read the Treaty's details as outlined in the evening papers of 6 December. For the plenipotentiaries, though they had returned to Dublin to discuss with de Valera Britain's final offer on 3 December, when it was regarded by all as unacceptable, had signed, without further reference back, a Treaty that was only marginally improved.

The technicalities which have been endlessly argued over in Ireland ever since as to whether the plenipotentiaries really had full powers or whether they should have again referred back to Dublin before signing (which according to their original instructions they should have done) or whether the instructions were contradictory to their plenipotentiary status, are not in themselves nearly so important as they have sometimes been made to seem. They are important inasmuch as de Valera personally felt them to be important. He was in any case tensely prepared for the political situation he knew he would have to face over the inevitable compromise. Rightly or wrongly, he saw himself in Dublin as the central figure in control of the most delicate part of the political situation. And if that seems a parochial and dogmatic view in the context of the great drama being played out in terms of the lives of ordinary Irish people in London, it must be said that a dogmatic narrowness of view amounting at times to a sense of total unreality had long been one of the weaknesses of the Fenian and Republican movements. When, through what he regarded as a disregard of the technical arrangements he had made, he found himself by-passed in his control, an understandable personal resentment was added to what in any case was his own disappointment with the actual terms.

But that his own idea of what the minimum acceptable terms should have been were not in themselves so different from what were accepted could be immediately seen from the so-called 'Document No. 2' which he produced as an alternative in the great debate in the Dail that was inaugurated on 14 December 1921. For Document No. 2 did not mention the word 'Republic', though it spoke of the 'Sovereign Irish Nation', and inasmuch as it associated Ireland 'for purposes of common concern' with the British Commonwealth it recognized 'for the purposes of the Association ... His Britannic Majesty as head of the Association'. The fact that such a formula had been consistently turned down by the British negotiators from the very first hardly seemed to figure in his considerations. But in many ways the most remarkable feature of Document No. 2 was that on the most important question of all, that of Ulster, it actually accepted the provisions of the Treaty.[21]

The emotion with which de Valera and his supporters in the Dail now opposed Griffith and Collins and their supporters in debate was something which far out-reached the significance of the literal points on which they differed. Given the comradeship in difficult and dangerous times they had shared so long, and the courageous unanimity – unique in the history of Irish revolt – with which they had appeared to face the British Government, given the major national victory achieved by the removal of British rule from twenty-six of the thirty-two counties of Ireland, and the challenge that remained of vindicating the nationalist principle over the other six, it seems amazing that the movement should now have split as it did, so suddenly and ferociously. Part of the explanation of the intensely emotional character of this split must lie in the simple release of tension that automatically followed a period so long fraught with suppressed fears and anxieties on both the purely human and political levels. Individual personal rivalries and jealousies, too, that had long had to be restrained or concealed, could now leap out into the open.* Closer to the heart of the matter was the removal of the need for what had often been unnatural unanimity. There had always been moderates and extremists in the movement though the difference had been fairly efficiently concealed. More important: there had always been realists and fantasists and this difference was now often revealed clearly

---

* Cathal Brugha in a bitter and embarrassing speech in the Treaty Debate made little attempt to conceal his jealousy of Collins, whose nominal superior he had been in the IRA as Minister of Defence. He implied absurdly that Collins had merely been a publicity seeker and that his reputation had been largely forged in the newspapers.

for the first time as some of the toughest of the extremists in the past – Commandants of the IRA like MacEoin, of Ballinalee, and Mulcahy the Chief of Staff – followed Collins, the toughest of them all, in support of the Treaty. The women had perhaps the best reason to cling to fantasy: Mrs Pearse, mother of Padraic and Willie, Mrs Clarke, widow of Tom, Miss Mary MacSwiney, sister of Terence, and Mrs O'Callaghan, widow of the murdered Mayor of Limerick, all were passionate opponents of the Treaty. It was a struggle between those who were prepared to come down to earth from the loftiest flights of Irish nationalism and those who were not. And this, of course, was where the Irish people who had never been up there but had allowed their fate to be taken over by republican fantasists almost without realizing it, now suffered from being represented by an esoteric clique, which had to resolve its own contradictions in public.

The Dail in the end approved the Treaty by 64 votes to 57, a result which led to a number of near-theological political adjustments. De Valera resigned as President or Prime Minister and went into opposition to Griffith who took his place. The Treaty stipulated that a Provisional Government chosen by the Parliament of Southern Ireland was to implement its terms and produce the Constitution of the Irish Free State. But the mystical Republic continued in being for a time both in the minds of the supporters as well as of opponents of the Treaty. The Army, the pro-Treaty Mulcahy asserted in the last words of the entire twelve-day debate, remained the Army of the Republic.

The members of Dail Eireann were also nominally members of the so-called Southern Parliament, except for one man who represented only an Ulster constituency and therefore was only a member of the Dail. A momentary ghostly overlap of Parliaments thus became possible as the four Southern Unionists who alone had attended the Southern Parliament's one previous meeting joined pro-Treaty Dail members to elect a Provisional government. An even more curious ghostly overlap of governments thus came into being. This Provisional government had for form's sake to have a different leader from that of the fading Republic. Thus Collins, who retained his post as Minister of Finance in Griffith's government, became Chairman of the Provisional government with Griffith as his closest collaborator. Other ministers of Griffith's still Republican government became simultaneously ministers of Collins's Provisional Free State government: men like William Cosgrave, Kevin O'Higgins and Richard Mulcahy. Constitutionally the Irish Republic was disappearing like the Cheshire Cat in *Alice in Wonderland*.

But, of course, there were hard realities, and the chief of them was the Army.

12

Nemesis (1922–3)

It is more than likely that had the Republican movement been a genuine democratic political movement there would have been, as de Valera stoutly maintained there was, and as all hoped there would prove to be, a proper constitutional way of resolving its internal political differences. But the movement which had been outwardly democratic from 1917 to the General Election of 1918 had since been entirely taken over by violent undemocratic forces from within. Nothing in all the Treaty debate rang more hollow than the continued protestations on both sides that members' only responsibility was to their constituents. Collins himself, of all people, actually proclaimed: 'I would not be one of those to commit the Irish people to war without the Irish people committing themselves to war.'[1] And Kevin O'Higgins chose this moment to 'acknowledge as great a responsibility to the 6,000 people who voted against me in 1918 as to the 13,000 people who voted for me'.[2]

But, of course, it was the Volunteers, the 'Army', acting quite regardless of the people's approval, who had brought about the situation in which there was a Treaty to be debated at all. And not illogically, many of them failed to see why they should be any more responsible to the people now than they had been in the past two and a half years. The IRA had never been very respectful of its nominal allegiance to Dail Eireann and had often been remarkably independent even of its own headquarters leadership. The IRA was now better armed than ever before; its ranks were swelled by new eager young warriors anxious to emulate their elders; its veterans were flushed with what felt like victory over the British, and enjoying the public adulation which easily came their way. The IRA was the effective force in the country whatever happened on the political level.

For many of the most idealistic IRA leaders – men like Liam Lynch and Ernie O'Malley – the Republic may indeed have been a symbol, but it was a symbol which was solemn and very real. 'It is a living tangible thing,' declared Liam Mellows, the 1916 Galway leader, during the Treaty debate. 'Something for which men gave their lives, for which men were hanged, for which men are in gaol, for which the people suffered and for which men are still prepared to give their lives.'*[3] Even if only a word it was one which

* Mellows had been in America for most of the past three years. His words have a prophetic note in view of later events.

many men had sanctified with all they held most dear and to de-sanctify it was to betray themselves.

Pro-Treaty IRA men were just as agonized by the denial of something inside themselves which support of the Treaty required, none more so than Collins himself. One detail in the complex situation, however, made things easier: the continuing apparatus of the secret Irish Republican Brotherhood. Though in most ways superseded by the larger underground apparatus which Collins had developed in the IRA itself, the nucleus of the secret society still existed and Collins himself controlled it. He was able to throw it behind the Treaty with double advantage. First, it gave him a loyal organizational network within the IRA with which to rally material support to his side. Second, it enabled Republicans, even Collins himself, to feel that the establishment of the Free State was a temporary strategic requirement in continued pursuit of the still inviolate mystical Republic. With this factor in their favour Collins, Mulcahy and the Provisional Government were able to carry about half the IRA with them in support of the Treaty, arming them, giving them uniforms and, with a certain amount of ambiguity of Republican terminology, transferring them simultaneously into a Free State Army.

Roughly speaking, the IRA split down the middle, with units conforming to the pro- or anti-Treaty dispositions of their commanders. And since the IRA was officially taking over barracks from the evacuating British forces, pro- and anti-Treaty troops became distributed at random all over the country. Sometimes they occupied different premises in the same town, confronting one another in uneasy rivalry made all the more bizarre by the persisting comradeship of former times.

In March the anti-Treaty faction began to organize itself as a separate force. It repudiated its nominal allegiance to the Dail and in a press interview Rory O'Connor, who had been Director of Engineering in the old IRA and now headed the anti-Treaty section, left no doubt as to where the responsibility for future events was to lie. Asked if there were any government in Ireland to which he gave his allegiance, he responded, 'No.'

'Do we take it we are going to have a military dictatorship then?' went on his questioner.

'You can take it that way if you like.'⁴

The civil war which was soon to follow has often been popularly blamed on de Valera, but the responsibility was not his. His anti-Treaty attitude undoubtedly gave a coherence and a political point of focus to anti-Treaty opinion in the country. But anti-Treaty opinion inside the IRA, which was what was to bring about the civil war, organized and consolidated itself independently. It looked not to de Valera but to its own leaders.

On the night of 13 April O'Connor, supported by a new independent IRA executive including Liam Lynch, Ernie O'Malley, Sean Moylan and other battle-scarred combatants of the 'Tan war', occupied and set up military headquarters in the Four Courts, Dublin. Interviewed again by the press, O'Connor repeated that the IRA now had no political connections, merely adding that 'If the army were ever to follow a political leader, Mr de Valera is the man.' Independent gunmen had long been able to think that they were the only true guardians of Ireland's destiny and, with their occupation otherwise gone, saw no reason now to relinquish their sacred charge. Collins himself was now at the mercy of the very system he had created.

Politically de Valera still hoped to effect a compromise that would prevent civil war. He had prophesied its dangers clearly enough in near-hysterical words at Thurles in March, when he said that those who wanted to complete the work of the past four years would have to wade through the blood of Irish soldiers and even of members of the Irish Government to do so. It seems he meant this as a warning, though it sounded like a threat. Psychologically, de Valera was in the same position on the anti-Treaty side as Collins was on the pro-Treaty side: both desperate to avoid a split but committed to making a split inevitable.

To Collins's own anxieties over the anti-Treaty IRA were added complications over the situation in the North. There, the news of the Boundary Commission clause in the Treaty had been received badly by Protestants and had animated the worst sort of traditional tension between Protestants and Catholics. It immediately became clear that Lloyd George (by a trick similar to that with which he had reassured both Redmond and Carson with opposite interpretations of a single clause in 1916) had allowed both Collins and Craig to take totally contradictory impressions of what the Boundary Commission was meant to do. 'I will never,' said Craig in January 1922, 'give in to any re-arrangement of the Boundary that leaves our Ulster area less than it is under the Government of Ireland Act', emphasizing that Lloyd George had given him reassurances to this effect. Collins replied equally emphatically that there could be no dispute as to the fact that 'very large areas' in Tyrone, Fermanagh, Down, Derry and Armagh had been unquestionably understood as being involved in the agreement with the British delegation.[5] It was on this understanding that he had been able to convince himself that the Treaty did not at least make impossible the essential national unity of Ireland.

Rioting on a serious scale now broke out in the North. Neither pro- nor anti-Treaty IRA there hesitated to support in arms the Catholic minority or cease to regard the North as national territory. The recently-created force of Ulster A and B specials did not hesitate to support the Protestants. In three weeks in February 138 casualties were reported from Belfast, of whom ninety-eight were Catholics. Thirty people were killed there in a single night. Catholic refugees streamed south of a border that began to look as if it were not going to be changed after all.

Collins's own personal position was extremely ambivalent. Technically bound by the Treaty to regard the northern area as outside the Free State's powers, he could not possibly bring himself to stand by and watch Irish nationalists subjected to violence because they were Irish nationalists. What, after all, had he been fighting for all these years? He therefore found himself in the ambiguous position of being on the verge of civil war with anti-Treaty IRA in the South, while virtually recognizing no differences in the IRA in the North and even supplying them with arms regardless of whether they were anti-Treaty or not. In a meeting with Craig in London he had done what he could by negotiation, calling off the Dail's Ulster boycott in return for Craig's promise to reinstate expelled Catholic shipyard workers in Belfast. But the disagreement over the Boundary Commission left him in an appalling state of frustration. 'I am really and truly having an awful time,' he wrote in January to the Irish girl in County Longford to whom he was engaged, 'and am rapidly becoming quite desperate. Oh Lord, it is honestly frightful.' And after Craig's uncompromising statement on the Border, 'This is the worst day I have had yet – far, far the worst. May God help us all.'[6]

Events in the North and the South interacted upon each other disastrously. A year before, at the time of the Northern Ireland election and at the height of the conflict between British forces and the IRA, there had been a preparedness by Northern leaders to consider some eventual cooperation with the South and some gesture towards the principle of a united Ireland.[*] It had been inspired more by pragmatic doubts about 'Northern Ireland's' future viability than by consideration for the South's susceptibilities, but it had been a positive attitude. Now there was only a cold and self-preserving shutting of the mind to everything but the ancient principle, rooted in fear, of 'What we have, we hold'.

The change had started as a negotiating position at the time of the opening of the Treaty talks in London. Craig had correctly understood that it was in his tactical interest to take the firmest possible stand on 'the rock of Ulster' as planted in the new Government of Ireland Act. To a large extent his tactics had succeeded and he now only had the Boundary Commission to fight, with Northern Ireland Protestant opinion solidly behind him, expressed in the new Parliament which had had nearly a year's viable existence. With its assistance he had created his own para-military force of some 25,000 A and B Specials, many of them fanatical Orangemen from Carson's old Ulster Volunteer Force, and had introduced a Special Powers Bill giving him power to inflict flogging and the death penalty for unauthorized possession of arms. A feeling that the Six-County State of Northern Ireland was sacrosanct, and somehow part of the natural order of things, took root among Northern Protestants, though the British Government had been prepared to make it negotiable only a few months previously and were still nominally

* See above, pp. 140–41.

committed to adjust its form. Similarly, a sense of helplessness and desperation began to overwhelm northern nationalists, who, as the prospects of a genuine Boundary Commission receded, saw their only support in the IRA. In March, sixty people were killed in Belfast, and Craig appointed Sir Henry Wilson, arch-enemy of Irish nationalism, as his adviser to help provide law and order.

Rory O'Connor's anti-treaty republican headquarters in the Four Courts, openly tolerated by Collins, further increased the Northern Protestants' sense of threat and their determination to defend their new establishment. As anti-Catholic riots continued, sometimes supported in ugly fashion by uniformed forces who were supposed to be preserving law and order, it seemed to Irish nationalists both inside and outside the IRA that in the North something like the Tan war was still in progress. By the middle of June, 264 people had been killed altogether in the six counties of Northern Ireland since the signing of the Treaty – 93 of them Protestants and 171 Catholics. Thousands of refugees streamed south to Dublin and a thousand even across the water to Glasgow.[7]

This Northern situation made it even more imperative for Collins to try to avoid the danger of civil war in the South and was a contributory factor to a curious political event which now took place there. A general election was due to give democratic status to the Provisional Government and its new Constitution based on the Treaty. Collins and de Valera, in their mutual anxiety to avoid civil war, worked out an electoral Pact by which the old Sinn Fein party was to stand for election as one party on a single panel. Candidates were to be distributed on the panel between the two sides in the proportion of 64 pro-Treaty to 57 anti-Treaty, being the proportion in which the vote had been distributed on the Treaty in the Dail. Candidates of other parties, or independents, were of course free to stand as they chose, but the panel would nevertheless undoubtedly result in a far greater number of anti-Treaty candidates being returned than was representative of the true state of opinion on the Treaty in the country. Furthermore, by the terms of the Pact, it was provided that after the election there should be a Coalition Government composed of five pro-Treaty Ministers and four anti-Treaty Ministers.

In some respects the Collins–de Valera Pact actually increased Collins's difficulties. For news of it was heard with alarm in London and at the same time drove Craig in the North into an intransigent frenzy. He seized it as an opportunity to denounce privately to the British Government the whole idea of the Boundary Commission, feeling not without some justification that if Collins and de Valera could agree politically, then the Treaty was being undermined. Publicly, Craig declared that if the clause on the Boundary Commission were now enforced it would lead to civil war.[8] On the Government side the evacuation of British forces from Southern Ireland was suspended. Churchill declared that should a new Coalition Government such as might emerge from a Pact election set up a Republic in defiance of the Treaty it would produce a situation comparable to that which gave rise to the American civil war: 'We should no more recognize it than the Northern States of America recognized secession.'[9]

Collins's motives in agreeing to the Pact with de Valera – which strained his own relations with Griffith to the limit – were mixed. He was desperate to avoid civil war, partly for straightforward emotional reasons, partly because he wished to retain an effective unity with which to confront the situation in the North. In this sense he undoubtedly wanted, against all the odds, to try to reconcile two irreconcilable positions. On the other hand, he had always been the most practical realist of them all. And there was an element of strict realism in the de Valera Pact. The explanation which he gave to the British Government, namely that it was the only way of allowing Ireland to have an election at all, had good sense in it and may well have been his principal motivation. The split in the IRA and the dissociation of the anti-Treaty elements had led to conditions of increasing anarchy in the South over which the government had no control. It was not just that fusillades between pro- and anti-Treaty IRA forces, sudden and furious as hailstorms, though usually as harmless, swept the streets of towns like Sligo and Kilkenny. Far more serious was the breakdown of law and order on an everyday detailed level over much of the area in which any local Brigade Commander was an anti-Treatyite.

Some of the lawlessness was honestly undertaken. Sean Moylan, for instance, commended once for his chivalry in action after an IRA ambush of British forces,* actually boasted proudly in the Dail that he had robbed nineteen Post Offices in one day in the neighbourhood of Kantark in March 1922. He told how he had 'collected' dog taxes with relish from pro-Treaty citizens and others, to clothe and provide food, tobacco and – 'We are not all Pussey footers' – a drink or two for his men. He would do it again, he said, because in doing such things he was 'standing up for and defending the Republic'.[10] It can be imagined what opportunities such a state of affairs provided also for those who were just standing up for themselves. In the three weeks from 29 March to 19 April, 323 Post Offices were robbed in the South of Ireland; and forty consignments of goods were seized from the Dublin and South-Eastern Railway between 23 March and 22 April, though in only thirty of the cases was the seizure even stated to be 'by order IRA'. When a big pro-Treaty meeting was held at Wexford on 9 April special trains were stopped by armed men and the crews forcibly prevented from running them; telephone and signal wires were cut and sleepers and rails removed.[11] Murders of former RIC men, ex-servicemen, or other individuals against whom old scores of one sort or another needed to be settled occurred

* See above, p. 126.

weekly, sometimes daily. There were constant forced levies of money from people too frightened to resist or to inquire too closely the exact nature of the cause to which they were contributing. All these activities to which it had been so easy to give a patriotic gloss in the days of the 'War of Independence' were resumed now in the anti-Treaty cause with even less punctiliousness than before. Not for nothing were the anti-Treaty forces becoming known as 'irregulars'.

It was difficult to think of an election taking place successfully in such an atmosphere. Ordinary public opinion in the country was overwhelmingly for the Treaty, but at the mercy of anti-Treaty men with revolvers who often had long training in the arts of intimidation. Prior to the Pact, de Valera himself, though he expressed disapproval of interference with political freedom of speech, used a number of constitutional excuses to try to have the election postponed, principally complaining that the electoral register which had not been revised since October 1918 was unfair. By the Pact Collins secured de Valera's and the political republicans' active participation in the election. For quite apart from any genuine hopes Republicans might have of a bold change of face on the part of Collins, it was obviously in their interest to take advantage of an election presented to them in such advantageous terms.

That a certain Machiavellian realism at least overlapped Collins's more emotional conflict of loyalties was shown by his electioneering behaviour. For although early in the campaign he addressed a number of meetings on behalf of the panel as a whole, speaking on the same platform as de Valera, yet on the eve of the poll itself, when the Pact had done its work and secured at least a coherent election, he made a speech in Cork which undermined the Pact's whole intention. A large number of independents and candidates of other parties had in fact presented themselves on nomination day to oppose the panel, and all were pro-Treaty. Now in this speech in Cork Collins advised his audience to vote not necessarily for the Sinn Fein panel but for the candidate they thought best. 'The country must have the representatives it wants,' he continued. 'You understand fully what you have to do and I call on you to do it.'[12]

Voting took place on 16 June and the results were declared on 24 June. A surprisingly high number of pro-Treaty candidates outside the panel had been elected: thirty altogether – without the four Unionists from Trinity College. Ninety-four out of the total of 128 members of the new Dail were for the Treaty. Collins made no move towards implementing the Coalition clause of the Pact, though de Valera waited for an invitation. Collins now had unmistakable democratic sanction for the Treaty.

Such clear expression of the people's will had been accomplished in the nick of time. For on 22 June there came a piece of news which transformed the entire post-Treaty situation.

Sir Henry Wilson, on returning by taxi to his house on the corner of

Eaton Place and Belgrave Place on the afternoon of 22 June, having just unveiled a memorial at Liverpool St to the employees of the Great Eastern Railway Company who had lost their lives in the war, was attacked on his doorstep by two men with revolvers. He made a spirited attempt to defend himself with his sword but fell, mortally wounded by their bullets. His assailants were IRA men named Joseph O'Sullivan and Reginald Dunne and both had previously served in the British Army. O'Sullivan had lost a leg at Ypres and his consequent slowness in making a getaway led to the almost immediate capture of himself and his companion.

The killing had been carried out on the order of Collins, the last of the long series of such killings for which he had been personally responsible since 1919. Dunne and O'Sullivan, though they eventually revealed their own identity and membership of the IRA, said nothing of Collins. Whether or not their orders had been issued recently or had been given before the Treaty and the men were now acting on their own initiative in the light of Catholic suffering in Northern Ireland is still uncertain. It seems at least possible that Collins himself had issued the order expressly as a result of recent events in the North. He was anguished by what was happening there and at the extent to which his ability to act was hampered by his obligations to the Treaty. During the Tan war he had been opposed to the assassination of British political figures and there seems little reason why he should then have selected Wilson as an exception. He certainly now did what he could to save Dunne and O'Sullivan from the gallows, though to no avail. The question of responsibility for the deed at this time is however only of academic interest. What was important was its consequence.

Ironically, the British Government automatically put the blame on the anti-Treaty Republicans with their headquarters in the Four Courts. Their first instinct was to order General Macready, who was still in Dublin, to attack the building and force O'Connor's surrender. But sensibly advised by Macready that the result would be to unite pro- and anti-Treaty men solidly against the British and thus destroy all hopes for the Treaty, the government eventually issued an ultimatum to Collins and Griffith as heads of the Provisional Government to take action at last and do the job themselves. If they did not they would regard the Treaty as abrogated.

The Provisional Government's own relationship with the men in the Four Courts was at that moment particularly tense. The result of the election and the imminent assembly of the new pro-Treaty Dail had brought about a situation in which the anti-Treaty men would soon be forced to act if they wanted to make themselves effective. There was talk in O'Connor's executive about an immediate attack on the British, and of a move against the North. For several days there was tension while Collins played for time with the British demand, asking for proof of association between the Four Courts and Wilson's assassins. There at least he knew he was on strong ground.

Relatively trivial incidents set off the explosion. The Four Courts men 'commandeered' sixteen cars from a garage in Dublin, but the officer in charge of their operation was arrested by Collins's forces. The Four Courts men retaliated by kidnapping one of Collins's generals, 'Ginger' O'Connell. At 3.40 a.m. on the morning of 28 June Collins decided. He sent an ultimatum to the Four Courts to surrender within twenty minutes. There was no reply. At seven minutes past four, two field guns which Collins had borrowed from General Macready, opened fire on the building from across the Liffey. The government's soldiers wore the new green uniform of what was soon to be the Free State Army. They were so inexperienced that one of the gunners blew a hole in the banks of the Liffey on his own side.[13]

Most of the available shells were shrapnel and it took two days to reduce the building, though it was only a few hundred yards away, but on 30 June the Four Courts surrendered and the anti-Treaty IRA executive, including Rory O'Connor, Liam Mellows, Ernie O'Malley and a hundred others, were taken prisoner. O'Malley escaped, as he had once done from the British, and made his way south to join Liam Lynch, Seumas Robinson and other legendary IRA figures in a new war for the Republic on a line of resistance that ran roughly from Wexford to Limerick. South and west of that line had been all the most aggressive of the IRA Brigades which Collins had helped to organize against the British. Now they were organized against him.

The rest of the story has something of the quality of the last act of *Hamlet*.

There were other individual anti-Treaty IRA units installed in different buildings in Dublin. In the first serious fighting after the Four Courts surrender, the opposite side of O'Connell Street to that which had been destroyed in Easter Week was burned and battered to the ground. Out of one of the blazing buildings in which a group of anti-Treaty men had eventually surrendered there emerged after a pause, into the dust and rubble, a small dark man carrying a Thompson sub-machine gun. He had shaken off a St John's Ambulance man who tried to make him give himself up, and suddenly started firing.[14] It was Cathal Brugha. He was brought down in a hail of bullets, and died two days later. Altogether some sixty people were killed and three hundred wounded in the eight days' fighting in Dublin.[15]

Beaten in Dublin, the anti-Treaty IRA who began to be referred to simply as Republicans or, from the government side, 'irregulars', consolidated in the South. De Valera, temporarily an irrelevant figure, joined them, as did Erskine Childers whose virulent propaganda techniques were now effectively displayed against the Free State. For the Free State, Collins, liberated suddenly from the insidious toils of politics into the field of action, threw himself into the campaign with his old gusto. Though the Republican forces had the initial military advantage in the South, with many of the best brigades of the old IRA in arms, it was inevitably only a matter of time before the superior resources of the Free State, with the official machinery of government at its disposal, began to tell. Collins received considerable supplies of rifles from the British Government.* To the nucleus of the pro-Treaty sections of the old IRA he recruited new raw young Irish country boys, many of whom only learnt to load their rifles shortly before going into action,[16] together with ex-professional Irish elements from the British and even American armies and some former members of the RIC.

At the end of July 1922, units of the new Free State Army were sent round by sea to the South and West of Ireland and by 10 August Cork, the only large town occupied by Republicans, had fallen into Free State hands. From then on the Republicans were more and more forced to fight a guerrilla war of ambushes and flying columns in the countryside similar to that which they had fought against the British. The major difference now, however, was that the support of the ordinary people in the countryside could no longer be counted on and without such support a guerrilla movement is doomed. 'The Republic' and many of the dreams that had been made to go with it began to disappear from view in increasingly senseless acts of gunmanship and in the roar of flames of country houses burned as often as not in vindictive impotent rage as for any 'military' purpose. In the course of the fighting in July and August 1922 about five hundred men were killed on both sides.

Military success in any civil war is a bitter thing. In Ireland after the historic climax to seven hundred years which had just been achieved, victory seemed more than ever like self-destruction, and death ate into every triumph like acid. Though Cathal Brugha had made a savage attack on Collins in the Treaty debates his death caused him only sadness. 'Because of his sincerity,' he wrote, 'I would forgive him anything. At worst he was a fanatic though in what has been a noble cause.'[17]

One of the worst consequences of the Treaty for Collins had been his disagreement over it with his old friend and companion of happier days, Harry Boland. When the civil war fighting broke out Boland took the Republican side. 'Harry – it has come to this! Of all things it has come to this!' Collins wrote to him on 28 July 1922.[18] Three days later, in the middle of the night, Free State Army troops went to arrest Boland in the Grand Hotel, Skerries, where he was staying. The soldiers who came into his bedroom seem to have been nervous. Boland insisted on seeing the officer in charge of the raid and moved towards the bedroom door. A soldier fired, hitting him in the stomach. He died soon afterwards, asking to be buried beside Cathal Brugha. Collins passed the hospital that night. 'My mind went in to him lying dead there,' he wrote. '... I only thought of him with the friendship of 1918 and 1919.' A few days later he wrote, 'There is no one who

* 10,000 according to a British cabinet document of the time. (See Younger, *Ireland's Civil War*, p. 318.)

feels it all more than I do.' But Nemesis, of which he seems to have been unconscious, was at work. 'My condemnation,' he continued, 'is for all those who would put themselves up as paragons of Irish Nationality and all the others as being not worthy of concern.'[19]

A week later, on 12 August 1922, the day after the Free State troops had taken Cork, a new and completely unexpected blow struck Ireland. Arthur Griffith, now Prime Minister of the new Free State Government, who had been spending a few days recovering from overwork in a Dublin nursing-home, suddenly collapsed and died. Collins, who, as Commander-in-Chief of the Free State Army, had been touring positions in the South and West, returned to Dublin for the funeral where he marched beside Mulcahy, MacEoin and other IRA heroes of the past, all in their new uniforms. Two of his men, Dunne and O'Sullivan, had just gone to the gallows for the killing of Sir Henry Wilson. 'Oh! Pray for our poor country,' wrote Dunne in his last letter.[20]

Ten days later Collins himself was dead.

He was killed in an ambush at Bealnamblath on the Macroom–Bandon road in his own home county of Cork. The ambush party, which had learnt of his presence in the neighbourhood quite accidentally that morning, had been waiting for him all day. They had just given up hope and were dispersing in the fading evening light when the convoy of a motor-cycle outrider, Collins's open touring Rolls, a Crossley tender and an armoured car drove up into the position. The fight, in which Collins took part with a rifle, lasted about half an hour and he was hit towards the end of it by a ricochet bullet in the back of the head.*

But Nemesis was only just beginning. Leadership of the Free State Government, which had just lost its two principal leaders, was now assumed by William Cosgrave and Kevin O'Higgins, both former Ministers of Griffith and earlier of de Valera. Saddled with their sudden responsibility, the one over-riding task in their own eyes seemed understandably to be to preserve the new State from disintegration at all costs and to restore law and order. Both had long been identified with the movement. Cosgrave had been out in Easter Week and condemned to death; O'Higgins, a young law student, had been imprisoned in 1918, and elected at the General Election. Earlier for a time he had been a member of the IRB. But both were less immediately entangled in the conflicting loyalties which had tortured Collins, and thus less concerned with reconciliation as an end in itself than he might have been if he had lived. They had the staunch support of Collins's old Chief of Staff, Richard Mulcahy, new Minister of Defence. Mulcahy obtained, through

---

* Forester, *Collins*, pp. 332–9. Many myths and suspicions have accumulated round the manner of Collins's death. This most recent account seems the best summary of all available evidence. Dr Oliver St John Gogarty carried out a post-mortem and confirmed the nature of the wound.

the new pro-Treaty Dail, emergency powers to set up military courts and Cosgrave specifically stated that the government were not going to treat rebels as prisoners of war. They offered an amnesty for surrender before a certain date and thereafter, armed with their emergency powers, set out to break the Republican guerrilla war of attrition with a sternness which was sometimes to cause even their supporters to gasp.

Unauthorized possession of a revolver was now punishable, as it had been in the final phases of the conflict with the British in martial law areas, by death. On 10 November Erskine Childers, who had been conducting Republican anti-Treaty propaganda with all his old single-minded zeal, was trapped by Free State troops and arrested in County Wicklow. He was armed with a revolver which had been given him by Collins as a token of comradeship in arms in other times. On the day he was tried by court-martial *in camera* it was suddenly announced by the government that four rank-and-file members of the Dublin anti-Treaty IRA who had been arrested at night under arms in the streets of Dublin had been shot by a firing squad.

The emergency powers had been granted two months before and these were the first executions under them. Mulcahy explained the decision to a shocked Dail. 'We are faced,' he said, 'with eradicating from the country the state of affairs in which hundreds of men go around day by day and night by night to take the lives of other men.'[21] Another Minister, Ernest Blythe, the old Sinn Fein organizer, who in his day had vigorously incited Volunteers to kill policemen in *An t Oglach*, declared that there was now no such thing in reality as a Republican movement but only a movement of anarchy; so-called Republicans were for the most part criminals and stern measures were essential to put down the 'conspiracy of anarchy'.[22] But Kevin O'Higgins, Minister for Home Affairs, gave a more ominous-sounding explanation of the four unknown men's execution, though none of the uneasy members of the Dail then picked him up on it. 'If,' said O'Higgins, 'If you took as your first case some man who was outstandingly active or outstandingly wicked in his activities the unfortunate dupes throughout the country might say, "Oh, he was killed because he was a leader", or, "He was killed because he was an Englishman."...'[23]

It was a common gibe among opponents of Erskine Childers that he was an Englishman, though his mother was Irish, and, having been brought up in Ireland, he had given many years of his life to the cause first of Irish Home Rule and then of a Republic. But even Griffith had jeered at him as an Englishman in the Dail. Now in O'Higgins's use of the term, though he did not name Childers, there was a sinister ring.

A week later Childers was taken from his cell and shot at dawn at Beggars Bush barracks. A week after that three more rank-and-file Republican IRA were executed, bringing the total number of executions for the month to eight. Even more shocking news was to come.

Ever since the surrender of the Four Courts in July the government had held in prison the hundred or so men captured there, including the members of the then Republican executive: Rory O'Connor, Liam Mellows, Joseph McKelvey and Richard Barrett. These men, of course, in the nature of things had no direct responsibility for what was being done now in November, though Mellows was in fact nominated 'Minister for Defence' in a new underground government which de Valera set up in agreement with the IRA in October. But it was a military and not a political situation in this period and the effective military personality was the Republican Chief of Staff, Liam Lynch. There was a particular poignancy typical of the Irish tragedy of the time about Rory O'Connor's imprisonment, for in the days of the fight against the British he had been the much loved and highly praised secretary of Kevin O'Higgins himself. O'Connor had even been best man at O'Higgins's wedding.

On 30 November 1922 Liam Lynch issued an order which the government captured, stating that all members of the government or members of the Dail who had voted the emergency powers were to be shot on sight. On 7 December two deputies were shot at as they were leaving their hotel for the Dail and one of them, Sean Hales, whose brother was actually a Brigade Commander on the Republican side, was killed. As a deterrent to more such shootings Mulcahy asked the rest of the cabinet to take an unprecendentedly severe form of action, to which after considerable discussion they agreed – O'Higgins, to do him justice, one of the last.[24] During the following night Rory O'Connor, Liam Mellows, Joseph McKelvey and Richard Barrett were woken in their cells and told to prepare themselves for death. They were shot without trial in the yard of Mountjoy gaol at dawn.

Altogether, in just over six months the new Free State Government executed seventy-seven Republicans by shooting, more than three times the number executed by the British Government in the two and a half years of the 'Anglo-Irish war'. Thirty-four of the Free State's executions were in the month of January 1923 alone. The executions ended when de Valera, speaking as political head of a movement whose one chance of success had appeared to rest on its military effectiveness, and whose military effectiveness had patently collapsed, issued with IRA agreement an order to dump arms. 'Soldiers of the Rearguard,' he told the 8,000 or so gunmen who were by May 1923 now the only free scattered remnants of the anti-Treaty IRA, 'other means must be sought to safeguard the nation's right.' There were also by then some 13,000 Republican prisoners, including Ernie O'Malley, who had been severely wounded. But one former hero was not among them. Liam Lynch, refusing stubbornly to face up to the realities of the Republicans' hopeless situation, had been killed in a running fight with Free State troops in the Knockmealdown mountains of Tipperary on 10 April 1923.

The last few months of the civil war, though they presented no serious threat to the political stability of the new Free State Government, presented a continuous and horrible threat to the peace and order of ordinary citizens' everyday lives. With only the newly-created police force, the unarmed 'Civic Guard', and a Free State Army of some 35,000 men it was often impossible to eliminate or even contain the small bands of irregulars who created for themselves fastnesses in mountainous country and descended from time to time to rob and terrorize and kill on behalf of the Republic. One of the many individuals murdered by the Republicans in this time was O'Higgins's own father. And in such an atmosphere, and in the atmosphere created by the government's ruthless severity, other things besides human values got lost sight of. For all the corpses and all the burned houses, the worst casualty of the civil war from the point of view of the ideals of Irish nationalism was the cause of One-Ireland.

In the first place such events in the South hardened a determination among the Protestants of North-East Ulster to retreat into the self-protected isolation offered by their border. The long tradition of fear and prejudice on which the division between the two sections of the population was based became still more deeply entrenched. O'Higgins himself expressed this aspect graphically and bitterly:

We had an opportunity [he said, referring to the North-East] of building up a worthy State that would attract and, in time, absorb and assimilate those elements. We preferred the patriotic way. We preferred to burn our own houses, blow up our own bridges, rob our own banks, saddle ourselves with millions of debt for the maintenance of an Army and for the payment of compensation for the recreations of our youth. Generally, we preferred to practise upon ourselves worse indignities than the British had practised on us since Cromwell and Mountjoy and now we wonder why the Orangemen are not hopping like so many fleas across the Border in their anxiety to come within our fold and jurisdiction.[25]

It was a reproof, however, which could have been extended to other Republicans besides those who now got called 'irregular'. On the question of national unity, O'Higgins put his faith in the Boundary Commission clause of the Treaty which still had to be implemented. Like Collins, he believed that the Commission's findings must lead to such a substantial adjustment of the Border in favour of the Free State that the remaining Northern Ireland territory would cease to be viable and eventual national unity be assured. It would be the ultimate vindication of the Treaty. But unlike Collins, O'Higgins was temperamentally inclined to trust the British Government.[26] If Collins had lived it is difficult to think that he would have accepted the disastrous collapse of the Boundary Commission principle with which the Free State were soon to be presented as a *fait accompli*.

The minds of O'Higgins and Cosgrave had in any case been seriously deflected from the Boundary Commission by the need to fight for the very existence of the infant Free State. Again, if Collins had lived this might not have happened, either because he would not have allowed it to or because he would have achieved the end of the civil war earlier. In fact it was not until 1924 that the Free State asked the British Government to constitute the Boundary Commission as prescribed.

Differences of opinion as to what exactly the Commission's function was to be had existed between North and South from the beginning, and Sir James Craig for the North had, of course, specifically repudiated it altogether in 1922. He now refused to nominate one of the three members of the Commission as stipulated by the Treaty – the other two to be nominees of the British and Free State Governments.

Craig was not a signatory of the Treaty. But the British Government was and thus found itself unable to honour its word. The clause was in fact reasonably precise, defining the Commission's function as being to determine the border 'in accordance with the wishes of the inhabitants, so far as may be compatible with economic and geographic conditions'. There could be no doubt that the inhabitants of large parts of Tyrone and Fermanagh, and smaller parts of Derry, South Down and South Armagh wished to be incorporated with their fellow nationalists in the Free State, while the inhabitants of a strip of East Donegal and North Monaghan wished to be incorporated in Northern Ireland. And with the reservation, accepted by the Treaty clause, that economics and geography laid down certain limitations, there was no practical reason why such a rearrangement of the Border should not be made. The clause had been instrumental in bringing the Irish to sign the Treaty. It could not simply be ignored.

The British Government therefore appointed an extra Commissioner of their own, reasonably enough in the circumstances an Ulsterman who was a close friend of Craig's named Fisher. The Free State Commissioner was to to be Eoin MacNeill, himself an Ulsterman from the Catholic and nationalist part of County Antrim. The other British nominee, the Chairman, was a South African judge, Mr Justice Feetham, a former protégé of Lord Milner's and therefore a man whose mind was cast politically in an imperial mould. Deadlock between Fisher, who wished to preserve as much of Northern Ireland as possible, and MacNeill, who wished the reverse, was inevitable and it would be Feetham's role to resolve it. He assumed the task in an atmosphere conditioned by statements from Birkenhead and Austen Chamberlain, both signatories of the Treaty, to the effect that the clause had been intended to consolidate the Northern Ireland Government's jurisdiction over the six counties, and to affect only a few parishes. A voice by which he was less likely to be influenced was that of the *Irish Independent* which declared that but for the Boundary Commission and the interpretation Collins and Griffith had placed on it the Treaty 'would never have received five minutes' consideration in this country'.

The Commission sat for a year during which MacNeill proved a most ineffectual advocate of the Collins' and Free State Government interpretation of its function. At the same time the Free State Government allowed itself to become curiously out of touch with what was transpiring. Finally, in November 1925, after an accurate leak to a newspaper had revealed that only very minor adjustments of the Border were intended and that these would actually include a transfer of territory in East Donegal from the Free State to Northern Ireland, MacNeill resigned in an embarrassingly late protest. It was Mr Justice Feetham's conclusion that the Commission could not recommend any adjustment of the border which would affect materially the political integrity of Northern Ireland."

The Commission's findings were in fact never officially published or implemented. Instead, Cosgrave, O'Higgins and Ernest Blythe went to London and negotiated an amendment to the Treaty by which the Boundary Commission was revoked in its entirety in return for a revocation of the Free State's financial obligations to the United Kingdom under the Treaty. In a phrase which now seems curiously unfortunate, Cosgrave told the Dail he had got from the British what he wanted: 'a huge O'.

The financial part of the transaction could legitimately be regarded as a success. But it was difficult for nationalists in Tyrone, Fermanagh, Derry, South Down and South Armagh not to feel that they had been sold. As for the eventual collapse of partition which had been so implicit to Collins in the Boundary Commission concept, that could be a hope no longer. All-Ireland unity had been abandoned more permanently than in any compromise Redmond had ever considered. In order to survive at all the movement had had to forsake for all practical purposes that very principle which had enabled it to claim the support of the Irish people in the first place.

This, surely, was the final act of Nemesis.

Epilogue

In his last message to the 'Soldiers of the Republic, Legion of the Rear-guard', de Valera had assured them that their sacrifices and the deaths of their comrades had not been in vain, and that in a little time the civilian population who were now weary and needed a rest would recover and rally again to the standard. 'When they are ready,' he wrote, 'you will be, and your place will be again as of old with the vanguard.'[1]

This analysis of future events was to prove in one sense correct, though it was a prophecy to be fulfilled so much more in the letter than in the spirit that the heroic tone in which it was uttered has a hollow ring today. The divisions of the civil war continued to scar Irish political life for nearly half a century. In the course of that half century, Ireland, or rather the greater part of her, evolved into a totally independent sovereign republic, technically a realization of all the most extreme nationalist had ever dreamed of. Certainly it was a serious blemish that six counties of the North escaped the realization altogether. But a piece of political casuistry by which this Republic's constitution is made to apply theoretically to the whole of Ireland even enables some Irishmen to overlook that blemish and thus fosters the illusion that, on the issue of a united Ireland, Republicans have been able to do better than Redmond.

This achievement came about largely thanks to the political skill and perseverance of Eamon de Valera himself. He was to spend some thirty years tidying up the aftermath of the Treaty and bringing reality into line as far as possible, and on paper at least, with the aspirations with which the Republican movement had gone into the General Election of 1918. And on paper at least, with a literal consistency and a mathematical zeal transcending fanaticism, he can be said to have been successful.

After the end of the civil war in 1923, de Valera and the Republicans actually took no part in the official political structure for many years. They made use of the General Election for the Dail of August 1923 to establish that they were no insignificant force in public opinion, but their forty-four successful candidates (out of a total Dail membership of 153) refused to enter the Dail because to do so meant acceptance of the oath to the King. At this election, de Valera himself, standing for his old seat of Clare, was arrested by Free State troops while attempting to address his constituents at Ennis. He was held prisoner for nearly a year, though he had won the seat by an overwhelming majority. Later in 1924, though prohibited from entering the Six Counties by the Northern Ireland Government, he went to address an election meeting in Newry, was arrested and spent a month in Belfast gaol.

In the South, thanks to the stern single-mindedness and courage of men like Cosgrave, O'Higgins and Blythe, which won them many enemies, law and order was consolidated. Many Republicans chose to emigrate rather than stay where unemployment was high in what seemed the waste-land of their ideals and dreams. But there were still occasional acts of violence. One in 1927 had something of the epic horror of old. For on a Sunday morning in July of that year, while walking alone to Mass, Kevin O'Higgins was fired at with a revolver at point-blank range by a man who stepped out of a waiting motor-car. Turning and trying to run for cover from the bullets, as so many men had done in Ireland in the past eight years, O'Higgins was set upon by two other men who emptied their revolvers into him as he lay dying on the ground. His murderers were never caught and there is a mystery about them to this day.[2]

Also in 1927, de Valera, recognizing the sterility of leaving a sizable proportion of Irish public opinion disfranchised, caused a further split among Republicans by finally entering the Dail after all. He did so expressly to abolish the oath of allegiance, and took with him a new party he had formed: Fianna Fail (Warriors of Ireland). He got round the embarrassment of taking the oath himself after all this time by simply signing his name in the book as required while pushing away the Bible which lay beside it and declaring categorically that he was taking no oath. However, as the only physical requirement for the taking of the oath was the placing of his signature in the book, this secured him entry even though he insisted that all he had done was to contribute his autograph.[3]

The band of die-hard Republicans who regarded this entry into the Dail by de Valera as a betrayal continued to call their militant wing the Irish Republican Army which, surviving further internal disruptions, has thus continued its existence in Ireland as a clandestine and illegal organization, from the time of the Fenians to the present day.

In a General Election in 1933, de Valera's prophecy of ten years before began to be fulfilled as the Irish people, reacting against ten years' government by one set of men moved round to support him. They elected himself and Fianna Fail to power, and in 1937 he produced a new Constitution to replace that created by the Treaty. This was the Constitution of Eire (Ireland) which abolished the oath of allegiance and claimed sovereignty over all thirty-two counties while recognizing that in six of them the claim could not be implemented for the foreseeable future. It recognized as in Document No. 2 the king as Head of the Commonwealth. The office of king's representative in Ireland created by the Treaty and first occupied by the aged anti-Parnellite Parliamentarian Tim Healy was now abolished, and in a further acknowledgement of the continuity of Irish history Douglas Hyde, first President of the Gaelic League, was nominated first President of Eire.

The British Government, embarrassed by this unilateral re-styling of the Treaty, recognized that it made little real difference where its own essential interests were concerned. The new Constitution did not alter the former Free State's membership of the Commonwealth and the position of Northern Ireland remained in practice unaffected. Advantage was taken of the unfamiliarity of the term 'Eire' in English ears to make it apply, for British Government purposes, to the twenty-six counties only, though it was of course nonsensical to pretend that the six counties in the North were somehow not part of 'Ireland'. However, having already made what, to many Unionists, was 'the great surrender' in 1921, the British Government continued to make up for past intransigence with a cooperative attitude towards the new Ireland.

In the following year, 1938, the British Government even agreed to a further most important modification of the 1921 Treaty. This concerned the clauses permitting military and naval bases to British forces in certain areas of Ireland, specifically at Berehaven in Bantry Bay and at Cobh (Queenstown), the port of Cork. Rights to these bases were now abandoned. Since one of the chief arguments even against Home Rule and later against any attempt to take Ireland outside the British Empire had rested on the need for British bases in time of national emergency, there was something bitterly ironical about the timing of this generous-hearted concession. For within two years Britain was to be at war in the greatest crisis of her history and desperately handicapped by lack of the Irish bases from which to protect her western approaches against enemy submarines and aircraft. One line of reasoning might be to blame this handicap on the ineptitude of the Chamberlain government of the day. But it is at least as reasonable to blame the short-sighted Unionist imperialism of 1914. For it is not unlikely that if Home Rule for all Ireland had been allowed to progress beyond the statute book in 1914 the southern Irish bases would have been available to Britain in 1940 as a matter of course.

It was de Valera's skill and determination in keeping Eire neutral in the Second World War which more than any constitutional nomenclature signified the real degree of political independence that Ireland, or more than three-quarters of her, had at last achieved. By a further ironical twist of the sort in which Irish history abounds, it was while de Valera himself was temporarily out of office that 'Eire' finally received the sacred appellation of Republic and was taken outside the Commonwealth. The change was brought about as an internal political manoeuvre by a temporary coalition of the old pro-Treaty party (Fine Gael) and a new legal republican party (Clann na Poblchta) headed by Sean MacBride, son of John MacBride and Maud Gonne. In the British Government's Ireland Act of 1949 this further *fait accompli* was accepted with a good grace. But a valuable acknowledgement was made to past realities by the refusal, while accepting the Republic's sovereign and independent status, to treat citizens of that Republic as aliens. A further clause in the Act spelt out that the British Government would never consent to the placing of Northern Ireland outside the Crown's dominions without the consent of the Parliament of Northern Ireland.

Few Irishmen today would accept that what Irish nationalists have achieved represents a true fulfilment of that near-mystical ideal for which, in one form or another, Irishmen had striven for so long. Every mystical ideal is diminished by being translated into reality but the sense of diminishment in Ireland has been profound. One reason, in addition to the missing counties, is perhaps that the real substance of the aspirations that had made Irish history so tumultuous for a century and a half had already been achieved before the climax of these last years was reached.

What had kept the green flag flying throughout the period which Patrick Pearse saw as 'a hopeless attempt by a mob to realize itself as a nation' had been no doctrinaire concept of nationality but a much more simple human desire for a decent life, for an assurance of life at all, in the beautiful country in which Irishmen were born. The goal of 'freedom' was as vague as that and embraced a wide and diffuse political emotion. With the social revolution begun by the Land Acts and ending in the massive transfer of land-ownership through the long Land Purchase operation the greater part of this goal was quietly achieved. There remained only what might be called a debt to history, to be paid in the form of an award of that political self-respect which went with some form of Home Rule. For long years Irishmen had not been particularly insistent about this. And yet refusal to pay it, and a contemptuous refusal at that, stirred old memories and eventually led to an extraction of the debt after much bitterness and bloodshed in a compromise form of payment. In the course of this bitterness and bloodshed all the old emotions had been re-aroused.

James Connolly and other socialists had hoped to give the new nationalism a dynamic of its own, but socialism made little appeal to a nation of Catholic peasant proprietors with the traditions of an ancient Gaelic aristocracy deep in its folk memory. Even the cause of a united Ireland slumbered for nearly half a century before other, social grievances among the Catholic minority in Northern Ireland raised it again to embarrass not only the British Government, but this time the Republic too.

An incident from the battle of Fredericksburg early in the American Civil War epitomizes the emotion which once surrounded Ireland's old green flag.

Meagher's Irish Brigade with the Union army had been making repeated assaults on the Confederate positions across the Rappamahoch river but had been consistently repelled, and, in the course of the fighting, one of the Brigade's colour-bearers had fallen and with him the green flag. Its fall had been noted by an Irish Confederate soldier named Michael Sullivan, fighting opposite Meagher with the Georgia Irish Brigade. Under cover of darkness Sullivan returned to the spot, and after taking the green flag and wrapping it round his body under his shirt swam across the river to the Union lines. He was hit by a bullet in the thigh as he went, fired from Confederate outposts who supposed him to be a deserter.

On arrival in the Union lines Sullivan indeed gave himself up and asked to be taken to General Meagher to whom he presented the flag. Meagher had Sullivan's wound dressed and, though he was now technically a prisoner, offered to let him go a free man on Union soil. Sullivan, however, having done his duty to Ireland now wished to continue to do it to his adopted cause. He asked to be allowed to return to the Confederate lines. And this Meagher, against all the normal conventions of war, permitted him to do.[5]

Many other brave men tried to give the new tricolour flag and the notion of 'the Republic' the same sanctity, but much of the substance of that emotion was wasted in the bitterness of civil war and its aftermath. As a mere political formula the Republic had only been for a very short time an important reality of Irish life. Its final literal achievement could not help but be a sort of anti-climax.

This strange historical anti-climax has left us with certain facts which cannot be altered and must be lived with. The logical and reasonable solution to the Irish problem was Home Rule for all Ireland with special safeguards, and even a degree of internal autonomy for parts of North-East Ulster. But that solution itself passed from the realm of reality over fifty years ago. And though relatively few in Ireland had ever seriously wanted a republic and the literal rejection of allegiance to a British king had been historically of little urgency to the Irish people, yet these things became in this century symbols essential to an expiation of the past. For the majority of Irishmen today these symbols, in the light of that past, can only be permanently revered.

There is another phenomenon in Ireland today which is not natural to Ireland and yet which in fifty years has also acquired by right of survival a natural status. This is the concept of a 'Northern Ireland' whose problems can somehow be kept separate from those of the rest of Ireland. How these two unnatural realities – 'The Republic' and 'Northern Ireland' – can be re-adjusted in future to a new reality compatible with the unity of Ireland is a matter which is not yet the concern of the historian.

References

1 Executions and Negotiations

1 O'Broin, *Dublin Castle*, p. 121.
2 Gwynn, *Redmond*, p. 475.
3 ibid., pp. 475–6.
4 ibid., p. 480.
5 'Personal Recollections of the late Father Aloysius, O.F.M.', *Capuchin Annual*, 1966, p. 288.
6 O'Broin, op. cit., p. 130.
7 ibid., p. 139.
8 *Capuchin Annual*, 1966, pp. 304–5.
9 Martin, *Studia Hibernica*, no. 7, p. 10.
10 Lynch, *The I.R.B. and the 1916 Rising*, p. 25.
11 Gwynn, op. cit., p. 483.
12 ibid., p. 483.
13 *Rebellion Handbook*, p. 269.
14 T. M. Healy, *Letters and Leaders of My Day*, vol. ii, p. 563.
15 Lyons, *Dillon*, p. 379.
16 Countess of Fingall, *Seventy Years Young*, London, 1937, p. 375.
17 O'Broin, *Dublin Castle*, p. 141.
18 *Sinn Fein Rebellion Handbook*, p. 99.
19 C'Broin, op. cit., p. 132.
20 Gwynn, op. cit., p. 488.
21 ibid., p. 485.
22 *Capuchin Annual*, 1966, p. 306.
23 O'Broin, op. cit., p. 133.
24 Hansard, H.C. Debates, 5th series, vol. 82, cols. 935–51.
25 *Capuchin Annual*, 1966, p. 290; Greaves, *Connolly*, p. 34.
26 *Capuchin Annual*, 1966, p. 302.
27 O'Broin, op. cit., p. 136. (A letter which Maxwell did not allow to be sent.)
28 *Capuchin Annual*, 1966, p. 306.

29 ibid., p. 301.
30 Gwynn, op. cit., pp. 491, 502.
31 *Rebellion Handbook*, pp. 69, 87–91.
32 ibid., p. 182.
33 Gwynn, op. cit., p. 493.
34 Roy Jenkins, *Asquith*, p. 147.
35 Alison Phillips, *The Revolution in Ireland*, London, 1920, p. 108.
36 Gwynn, op. cit., p. 499.
37 Jenkins, op. cit., p. 448 (paperback).
38 Gwynn, op. cit., pp. 497–9.
39 ibid., pp. 500–501.
40 ibid.
41 ibid., p. 501.
42 Lyons, *Dillon*, p. 384.
43 ibid.
44 ibid., p. 385.
45 Gwynn, op. cit., p. 506.
46 For full headings of the draft proposals see Gwynn, op. cit., pp. 517–18.
47 Hyde, *Carson*, p. 403.
48 Lyons, op. cit., p. 396.
49 ibid., p. 401.
50 Hansard, H.C. Debates, 5th series, vol. 84, col. 1434.
51 Denis Gwynn, *The Life and Death of Roger Casement*, pp. 16–17.
52 René MacColl, *Roger Casement*, p. 296.
53 ibid., p. 293.
54 Cited Lyons, op. cit., p. 394.
55 ibid., p. 403.

2 Rebellion to de Valera's Election at Clare (July 1917)

1 *Irish Times*, 27 June 1916.
2 *Irish Independent*, 6 July 1916.
3 ibid., 14 August 1916.
4 ibid., 7 October 1916.
5 ibid.
6 ibid., 11 November 1916.
7 Margery Forester, *Michael Collins: The Lost Leader*, London, 1971, p. 61.
8 Rex Taylor, *Michael Collins*, London, 1958, pp. 77–8.
9 The O'Mahony, *Irish Independent*, 19 January 1917; 1 February 1917.
10 *Irish Independent*, 3 February 1917.
11 ibid., 31 January 1917.
12 ibid.

13 ibid., 6 February 1917.
14 Taylor, op. cit., p. 82.
15 *Irish Independent*, 10 April 1917.
16 Beaslai, *Collins*, vol. i, p. 152.
17 Sean O Luing, *I Die In A Good Cause: a study of Thomas Ashe*, Dublin, 1970, p. 122.
18 *Irish Independent*, 8 May 1917.
19 Gwynn, *Redmond*, pp. 543–5.
20 *Irish Independent*, 15 June 1917.
21 See, particularly for the return of Countess Markievicz, the contemporary news film included in Gael Linn's film *Mise Eire*, directed by George Morrison.
22 *Irish Independent*, 23 June 1917.
23 ibid., 25 June 1917.
24 ibid.
25 ibid., 9 July 1917.
26 ibid.
27 *Daily Mail*, 9 October 1917.
28 *Irish Independent*, 12 July 1917.
29 ibid.
30 ibid., 16 July 1917.
31 ibid.

3 The New Sinn Fein (July 1917–April 1918)

1 *Irish Independent*, 16 July 1917.
2 ibid., 14 July 1917.
3 ibid., 12 July 1917.
4 ibid., 17 July 1917.
5 ibid., 5 September 1917.
6 Sean O Luing, *I Die In A Good Cause*, p. 124.
7 *Irish Times*, 2 October 1917; *Daily Mail*, 15 October 1917.
8 *Irish Independent*, 25 September 1917.
9 All details of these proceedings from the inquest on Thomas Ashe reported in the *Irish Independent*, 28 September 1917–2 November 1917.
10 *Irish Independent*, 30 October 1917.
11 ibid., 9 October 1917.
12 ibid., 2 November 1917.
13 ibid., 1 October 1917; Beaslai, *Collins*, vol. i, p. 166.
14 *Irish Independent*, 1 October 1917.
15 ibid.
16 ibid., 26 October 1917.
17 ibid.

18 ibid.
19 ibid., 29 October 1917.
20 ibid., 26 November 1917.
21 ibid., 3 December 1917.
22 Ernie O'Malley, *On Another Man's Wound*, London, 1936, p. 57.
23 Dan Breen, *My Fight for Irish Freedom*, Dublin, 1950, pp. 6–10.
24 *Irish Independent*, 26 November 1917.
25 ibid.
26 ibid., 10 December 1917.
27 ibid., 12 December 1917.
28 ibid., 15 January 1918.
29 ibid., 25 January 1918.
30 ibid., 23 February 1918.
31 ibid., 26, 28 February; 4, 15, 19 March 1918.
32 ibid., 2 March 1918.
33 ibid., 9 March 1918.
34 Gwynn, *Redmond*, p. 579.
35 ibid., p. 568.
36 *Irish Independent*, 2 February 1919.
37 ibid., 20 March 1918.
38 ibid., 22 March 1918.
39 Election and post-election details, ibid., 16, 23, 24, 26 March 1918.

4 *Conscription Crisis to General Election (December 1918)*

1 *Irish Independent*, 10 April 1918.
2 ibid.
3 ibid., 19 April 1918.
4 ibid.
5 Richard Laide and John Browne.
6 Breen, *My Fight for Irish Freedom*, pp. 15–16.
7 Florence O'Donoghue, *No Other Law*, Dublin, 1954, pp. 8, 22–3.
8 *Manchester Guardian*, 13 May 1918.
9 Taylor, *Collins*, p. 93.
10 See, e.g., *Irish Independent*, 9, 14 December 1918.
11 ibid., 20 August 1918.
12 ibid., 29 August 1918.
13 David Hogan (Frank Gallagher), *The Four Glorious Years*, Dublin, 1953, pp. 34–8.
14 *Irish Independent*, 5 October 1918.
15 ibid., 31 October 1918.
16 ibid., 28 December 1918.
17 *Irish Times*, 28 December 1918.

18 *Irish Independent*, 14 November 1918.
19 ibid., 12 November 1919.
20 The total Irish electorate in December 1918, as given by *The Times*, was 1,937,245. There were, in the uncontested seats, 474,778 electors. This leaves a possible electorate of 1,462,467. Of these, 1,071,086 voted, making a percentage of seventy-three per cent (*The Times*, 4 January 1919 and 7 January 1919). For the abstention theory see *The Times*, 17 January 1919; also W. Alison Phillips, *The Revolution in Ireland*, London, 1923, pp. 152–3 and Edgar Holt, *Protest in Arms*, London, 1960, p. 168. Holt for some reason gives the poll in 1918 as sixty-nine per cent. A. J. P. Taylor, *English History 1914–1945*, Oxford, 1965, even less explicably gives it as sixty per cent (p. 154n.).
21 *The Times*, 4 January 1919.
22 P. S. O'Hegarty, *The Victory of Sinn Fein*, Dublin, 1924, p. 32.
23 *Irish Independent*, 31 December 1918.

5 Sinn Fein in a Vacuum (January–May 1919)

1 Cited in *Irish Independent*, 4 January 1919.
2 ibid., 7 January 1919.
3 O'Donoghue, *No Other Law*, p. 35; *Irish Independent*, 7 January 1919.
4 Sean O'Murthuile (John Hurley). ibid., 8 January 1919.
5 Margery Forester, *Michael Collins: The Lost Leader*, p. 97.
6 *Daily News*, 16 January 1919.
7 *Daily Mail*, 22 January 1919.
8 *Manchester Guardian*, 24 January 1919.
9 Macardle, *Irish Republic*, p. 273.
10 ibid., pp. 274–5.
11 ibid., p. 925.
12 *Irish Independent*, 22 January 1919.
13 *Freeman's Journal*, 22 January 1919.
14 *Irish Independent*, 21, 23 January 1919.
15 Breen, *My Fight For Irish Freedom*, pp. 34–40.
16 *Irish Independent*, 23 January 1919.
17 *Irish Times*, 24 January 1919.
18 *Tipperary Star*, 25 January 1919.
19 *Irish Times*, 27–8 January 1919.
20 *Irish Independent*, 27 January 1919.
21 O'Donoghue, *No Other Law*, pp. 44–5.
22 *Irish Independent*, 27 January 1919.
23 Beaslai, *Collins*, vol. i, pp. 274–5.
24 ibid., p. 277.
25 ibid., p. 276.

26 *Irish Independent*, 21 February 1919.

27 Beaslai, op. cit., pp. 269–70.

28 *Irish Independent*, 13 March 1919.

29 ibid., 17 March 1919; Beaslai, op. cit., p. 304.

30 ibid., 17 March 1919.

31 *Irish Times*, 12 March 1919.

32 *Irish Independent*, 21 March 1919.

33 *Irish Times*, 12 March 1919. The prisoner who had died was Pierce McCann.

34 *Nationality*, 21 February 1919.

35 *Irish Independent*, 26 February 1919.

36 ibid., 4 March 1919.

37 Cited ibid., 22 March 1919.

38 *Freeman's Journal*, 2 June 1919.

6 Michael Collins and Others (*April–December 1919*)

1 *Irish Times*, 2 April 1919; *Mayo News*, 20 March 1918, 28 June 1919.

2 O'Donoghue, *No Other Law*, p. 44.

3 Lord Longford and T. P. O'Neill, *Eamon de Valera*, London, 1970, p. 90.

4 On 17 May 1919. Taylor, *Collins*, p. 105.

5 *Irish Independent*, 1 April 1919.

6 ibid., 10 April 1919.

7 ibid., 10–11 April 1919.

8 ibid., 22–3 April 1919.

9 ibid., 23 April 1919.

10 ibid.

11 *Daily News*, 31 May 1919.

12 Tom Barry, *Guerrilla Days in Ireland*, Cork, 1950, pp. 1–2, 5.

13 Forester, *Collins*, p. 102.

14 *Irish Independent*, 12 May 1919.

15 *Irish Times*, 10 May 1919.

16 *Irish Independent*, 12 May 1919.

17 ibid., 16 May 1919.

18 ibid., 21 May 1919.

19 Breen, *My Fight for Irish Freedom*, pp. 83–105.

20 *Glasgow Herald*, 31 May 1919.

21 Forester, op. cit., pp. 103–4.

22 *Irish Independent*, 11 April 1919.

23 Taylor, *Collins*, pp. 126–8 and p. 130.

24 *Freeman's Journal*, 14 February 1920.

25 *Daily Telegraph*, 31 May 1919.
26 Denis Gwynn, *De Valera*, p. 77.
27 Seven such cases between 31 July and 5 October 1920 alone, taken from police records, are given in 'I.O.' (Major C. J. Street), *The Administration of Ireland, 1920*, London, 1921, pp. 234–5. There were many others.
28 ibid., pp. 64–7.
29 Forester, op. cit., pp. 103–4.
30 Longford and O'Neill, op. cit., p. 90.

7 The Campaign of Killing (1919–20)

1 *Freeman's Journal*, 25 June 1919; *Irish Times*, 26, 27 June 1919; *Tipperary Star*, 21, 28 June 1919.
2 *Irish Times*, 30 June 1919.
3 *Freeman's Journal*, 25 June 1919.
4 *Irish Times*, 30 June 1919.
5 *Freeman's Journal*, 16 June 1919.
6 ibid., 28 June 1919.
7 *Observer*, 13 July 1919.
8 *Freeman's Journal*, 14 July 1919.
9 ibid.
10 Taylor, *Collins*, p. 286.
11 Sir Ormonde Winter, *Winter's Tale*, London, 1955, pp. 299–300.
12 *Irish Times*, 4 August 1919.
13 *Freeman's Journal*, 6, 9, 15 August 1919.
14 Beaslai, *Collins*, pp. 302–4, 333–5.
15 *Freeman's Journal*, 11 August 1919.
16 ibid., 12 August 1919.
17 *Irish Times*, 22 August 1919.
18 *Freeman's Journal*, 22 August 1919.
19 Forester, *Collins*, p. 123.
20 *Freeman's Journal*, 15, 16 September 1919.
21 O'Donoghue, *No Other Law*, p. 48.
22 *Irish Times*, September 1919 (Inquest proceedings). For an inside account of the raid see O'Donoghue, *No Other Law*, pp. 48–54, in which the number of rifles taken is given as fifteen.
23 ibid.
24 ibid., 12 September 1919.
25 ibid., 9 September 1919.
26 ibid.
27 *Freeman's Journal*, 1 December 1919.
28 As published, for instance, in the *Killarney Echo*, 20 September 1919.

This and other papers, notably the staid Nationalist *Cork Examiner*, were suppressed by the authorities for a few issues for publishing such advertisements.

29 *Freeman's Journal*, 3 November 1919.
30 *Irish Times*, 27 September 1919.
31 ibid., 16 September 1919.
32 *Clare Champion*, 25 October 1919.
33 ibid., 25 October 1919.
34 *Irish Times*, 22 December 1919.
35 Taylor, *Collins*, p. 106.
36 *Irish Times*, 22 December 1919.
37 Breen, *My Fight For Irish Freedom*, pp. 143–4.
38 O'Hegarty, *The Victory of Sinn Fein*, pp. 46–8.
39 Macardle, *Irish Republic*, pp. 304–5.
40 O'Malley, *On Another Man's Wound*, p. 145.
41 See captured document quoted in court-martial proceedings, *Irish Times*, 22 October 1920. Also O'Donoghue, *No Other Law*, pp. 42–3.
42 O'Donoghue, op. cit., p. 35.
43 ibid., p. 86.
44 Barry, *Guerrilla Days in Ireland*, p. 100.
45 See captured document cited in the trial of Sean Morrisey, *Irish Times*, 22 October 1920.
46 *Freeman's Journal*, 27 November 1919.
47 *Clare Champion*, 13 December 1919.
48 *Freeman's Journal*, 8 December 1919.
49 *Irish Times*, 23 December 1919.
50 ibid.

8 Enter Black and Tans (1920)

1 *Irish Times*, 22, 26 January 1920.
2 ibid., 22, 26 January 1919.
3 *Freeman's Journal*, 16 February 1920.
4 ibid., 26 February 1920.
5 *Cork Examiner*, 17 March 1920.
6 *Freeman's Journal*, 23 March 1920.
7 *Cork Examiner*, 19 March 1920.
8 *Freeman's Journal*, 26 February 1920.
9 ibid., 15 April 1920.
10 ibid, 16 April 1920.
11 ibid., 31 July 1920.
12 Hansard, H.C., 5th series, vol. 139, col. 238; vol. 140, col. 436.

13 *Freeman's Journal*, 28 September 1920.
14 Parliamentary Papers, H.C., 1922, Cmd. 1618, XVII, p. 785.
15 *Freeman's Journal*, 19 March 1920.
16 Hansard, H.C., 5th series, vol. 153, col. 257.
17 *Freeman's Journal*, 27, 12, 18 March 1920.
18 ibid., 15 March 1920.
19 *Tipperary Star*, 3 April 1920.
20 *Freeman's Journal*, 17 April 1920.
21 General Sir Nevile Macready, *Annals of an Active Life*, London, 2 vols., 1924.
22 Brigadier F. P. Crozier, *Impressions and Recollections*, London, 1930; *Ireland For Ever*, London, 1932.
23 Edward Maclysaght, *Master of None* (MS. of an autobiography shown to the author in 1954).
24 Inquest details. *Irish Times*, 27 March 1920.
25 ibid., 31 March 1920.
26 *Freeman's Journal*, 20 April 1920.
27 H. of C., 1922, XXIX, Cmd. 1534, pp. 398-9.
28 ibid.
29 *Freeman's Journal*, 5 August 1920.
30 *Irish Times*, 31 May, 2 June 1920.
31 Hugh Martin, *Insurrection in Ireland*, London, 1921, pp. 69–70.
32 ibid.
33 O'Donoghue, *No Other Law*, pp. 63–5. *Freeman's Journal*, 16 June 1920.
34 *Freeman's Journal*, 4 June 1920.
35 *Freeman's Journal*, 9 June 1920.
36 *Irish Times*, 21, 23 June 1920.
37 *Freeman's Journal*, 20 July 1920. *Irish Times*, 10 August 1920.
38 O'Malley, *On Another Man's Wound*, p. 168.

9 *Murder by the Throat (1920)*

1 Florence O'Donoghue, *Tomas MacCurtain*, Dublin, 1958, photograph facing p. 202.
2 Callwell, *Wilson*, vol. ii, p. 246.
3 *Galway Express*, 24, 31 July 1920.
4 *Tipperary Star*, 2 August 1920.
5 *Irish Times*, 4 September 1920.
6 ibid., 23 August 1920.
7 ibid., 11 September 1920.
8 ibid., 7 September 1920.
9 ibid., 1 October 1920.

10 *Freeman's Journal*, 22 September 1920.

11 ibid., 11 October 1920.

12 See O'Malley, *On Another Man's Wound*, pp. 189–94; O'Donoghue, *No Other Law*, pp. 99–101.

13 *Irish Times*, 28 September 1920.

14 ibid., 20 April 1921.

15 James Gleeson, *Bloody Sunday*, London, 1962, pp. 56–78.

16 D. O'Hannigan (one of the IRA officers concerned), 'Origins and Activities of the First Flying Column', in J. M. MacCarthy (ed.), *Limerick's Fighting Story*, Tralee, pp. 85–7.

17 O'Donoghue, *No Other Law*, p. 334.

18 Hansard, H.C., 5th series, vol. 135, cols. 507–8 (captured IRA documents).

19 *Irish Times*, 18 October 1920.

20 ibid., 19 October 1920. Also see *Galway Observer*, 9, 23 October, 13 November 1920.

21 Hansard, H.C., 5th series, vol. 135, col. 544.

22 *Irish Times*, 2, 7 October 1920.

23 ibid., 1 October 1920.

24 ibid., 13 October 1920.

25 ibid., 11 October 1920.

26 ibid., 20 April 1921.

27 ibid., 1 April 1921.

28 ibid., 13, 16 April 1921.

29 *Freeman's Journal*, 25 September 1920.

30 *Irish Times*, 21 October 1920.

31 For General Strickland's statement, *Evening Standard*, January 1921.

32 *Irish Times*, 16 November 1965. Three articles based on Moylett's papers appeared on that date and on 15 and 17 November 1965.

33 For a detailed description of all these events compiled from contemporary newspapers and other sources, see James Gleeson, *Bloody Sunday*.

34 Forester, *Collins*, p. 172, where the diary of a Castle official, Mark Sturgis, is cited.

35 Winter, *Winter's Tale*, p. 323.

36 Forester, op. cit., p. 174.

37 *Irish Times*, 16 November 1956.

38 ibid., 12 January 1921.

39 Barry, *Guerrilla Days in Ireland*, p. 46.

40 Callwell, *Diaries of Sir Henry Wilson*, vol. ii, p. 265.

10 War and Truce (1921)

1 Hansard, H.C., 5th series, vol. 133, col. 1582; vol. 139, cols. 2245, 2384.
2 31 March 1920 to 14 April 1921 ibid., vol. 140, cols. 16, 1277. 1 January 1919 to 31 May 1921 ibid., vol. 143, col. 2172. Also White Paper cited *Irish Times*, 4 March 1921. Casualties 1 January 1921 to 11 July 1921 see *Freeman's Journal*, 12 July 1921, citing official sources.
3 Hansard, H.C., 5th series, vol. 140, col. 1277.
4 ibid., vol. 135, col. 2447.
5 *Freeman's Journal*, 12 July 1921.
6 Holt, *Protest in Arms*, p. 241 and see newspapers passim.
7 Cited *Irish Times*, 4 February 1921.
8 MacCarthy (ed.), *Limerick's Fighting Story*, pp. 107-28.
9 *Irish Times*, 1, 15, 21 February. For Mourne Abbey see O'Donoghue, *No Other Law*, pp. 135-6; for Clonmult see Barry, *Guerrilla Days*, pp. 78-86. Barry has an interesting account (pp. 78-86) of a successful IRA break-out from a similar trap at Burgatia House, Rosscarberry, in the same month. In this the Crown claimed six IRA dead but there were in fact none. See also *Irish Times*.
10 For Sixmilebridge see *Irish Times*, 25 January 1921. For MacEoin, see *Irish Times*, 8 August 1921.
11 See captured IRA document, asking for GHQ guidance on this point, cited *Irish Times*, 28 February 1921.
12 *Irish Times*, 6 June 1921.
13 ibid., 7 May 1921.
14 See Hansard, H.C., 5th series, vol. 135, col. 508.
15 *Irish Times*, 25 January 1921.
16 ibid., 7 February 1921.
17 See advertisement, *Irish Times*, 14 March 1921.
18 *Irish Times*, 26 November 1920.
19 ibid., 10 February 1921.
20 ibid., 16 February 1921.
21 ibid., 12 July 1921.
22 ibid., 15 April 1921.
23 ibid., 20 April 1921.
24 O'Malley, *On Another Man's Wound*, p. 316.
25 *Irish Times*, 21 February 1921.
26 *Irish Times*, 20 June 1921.
27 ibid.
28 ibid., 14 March 1921.
29 MacCready, *Annals*, vol. ii, pp. 488-9.
30 *Irish Times*, 13 June 1921.
31 ibid., 22 April 1921.

32 ibid., 4 June 1921.
33 ibid.
34 ibid., 1 June 1921.
35 ibid., 18 June 1921.
36 ibid., 15 March 1921.
37 Captured IRA document dated 7 February 1921, cited in *Irish Times*, 26 March 1921.
38 Cited in Lyons, *Dillon*, p. 467.
39 *Freeman's Journal*, 12 July 1921.
40 *Irish Times*, 1 March 1921.
41 ibid., 1, 2 March 1921.
42 ibid., 29 April 1921.
43 Winter, *Winter's Tale*, p. 302.
44 Beaslai, *Collins*, vol. ii, p. 193.
45 O'Malley, op. cit., pp. 328–32.
46 Douglas V. Duff, *The Rough with the Smooth*, London, 1940, pp. 79–80.
47 O'Malley, op. cit., p. 311.
48 ibid.
49 ibid., p. 326.
50 *Irish Times*, 16 April 1921; 6 July 1921.
51 O'Donoghue, *No Other Law*, p. 173.
52 In Downing Street to Sir Hamar Greenwood after the signing of the Treaty. L. S. Amery, *My Political Life*, 3 vols., London, 1953, vol. ii, p. 230. Greenwood was Amery's brother-in-law.
53 Longford and O'Neill, *De Valera*, p. 121.
54 T. P. O'Neill (ed.), Introduction to Frank Gallagher, *The Anglo-Irish Treaty*, London, 1965, pp. 21–4.
55 Longford and O'Neill, *De Valera*, pp. 115–16.
56 Hansard, H.C., 5th series, vol. 140, cols. 2044–5.
57 *Irish Times*, 18 October 1920.
58 ibid., 31 January 1921.
59 ibid., 4 May 1921.
60 Longford and O'Neill, *De Valera*, p. 123.
61 ibid., p. 125.
62 Sir Harold Nicolson, *King George V*, London, 1952, pp. 348–54.
63 Macardle, *Irish Republic*, p. 471.
64 MacCready, *Annals of an Active Life*, p. 572.
65 *Irish Times*, 11, 12 July 1921. *Freeman's Journal*, 12 July 1921.
66 *Irish Times*, 16 July 1921.

11 Treaty (1921)

1 Dail Eireann Official Report, Treaty Debates, p. 143.
2 For the figure of 250,000 see Sir Geoffrey Shakespeare, *Let Candles Be Brought In*, London, 1949, p. 88.
3 O'Hegarty, *The Victory of Sinn Fein*, p. 87.
4 Nicolson, *George V*, p. 356.
5 Forester, *Collins*, p. 196. The source is a diary entry of Tom Casement's, dated 14 June 1921.
6 Nicolson, op. cit., p. 351.
7 Pakenham, *Peace by Ordeal*, p. 88.
8 Longford and O'Neill, *De Valera*, p. 139.
9 ibid., p. 143.
10 ibid., pp. 149-50.
11 ibid., pp. 152-3.
12 ibid., p. 157.
13 Pakenham, *Peace By Ordeal*, pp. 315-16.
14 ibid., pp. 218, 299-300.
15 For text of Treaty see Macardle, *Irish Republic*, pp. 953-8.
16 Forester, *Collins*, pp. 249-50. Source: a Collins minute of the interview. In the Dail Debate on the Treaty, Collins declared it as his belief that the way in which the Treaty dealt with the problem of the North-East would bring it under an Irish Parliament. Dail Eireann Official Report, p. 35.
17 Taylor, *Collins*, p. 163.
18 Forester, op. cit., p. 260.
19 Taylor, *Collins*, p. 175.
20 ibid., p. 165.
21 For Document No. 2 see Macardle, *Irish Republic*, pp. 959-63.

12 Nemesis (1922-3)

1 Dail Eireann Official Report, Treaty Debate, p. 34.
2 ibid., p. 46.
3 ibid., p. 229.
4 Cited Macardle, *Irish Republic*, p. 678.
5 ibid., pp. 658-60.
6 Forester, *Collins*, pp. 287-8.
7 ibid., pp. 729-30.
8 Forester, *Collins*, p. 306. Hansard, H.C., 5th series, vol. 154, col. 2149.
9 ibid.
10 Dail Eireann Official Report, 28 April 1922, p. 340.
11 ibid., 26 April 1922, pp. 256-7. Report by Richard Mulcahy.

12 Macardle, op. cit., p. 721.
13 Calton Younger, *Ireland's Civil War*, London, 1968, p. 3 8.
14 Taylor, *Collins*, p. 235.
15 Macardle, op. cit., p. 754.
16 Calton Younger, op. cit., p. 401.
17 Taylor, *Collins*, p. 236.
18 ibid., pp. 238–9.
19 Forester, *Collins*, p. 329.
20 ibid., p. 332.
21 Dail Eireann Official Report, vol. i, p. 2264.
22 ibid., p. 2274.
23 ibid., p. 2267.
24 T. de Vere White, *Kevin O'Higgins*, paperback ed., Tralee, 1968, p. 131.
25 ibid., pp. 206–7.
26 ibid., p. 203.
27 For MacNeill's statement and Feetham's views see Macardle, op. cit., pp. 886–7.
28 ibid., p. 892.

Epilogue

1 Macardle, *Irish Republic*, p. 858.
2 For a reasoned speculation about their identity see T. P. Coogan, *Ireland Since the Rising*, London, 1966. pp. 261–2.
3 ibid., p. 65.
4 *Freeman's Journal*, 26 November 1913.
5 For this story see *Freeman's Journal*, 28 March 1914.

Index

ALL for Ireland League, 17 fn
Amending Bill to Third Home Rule
    Bill, 18
America—
    changing opinion of Irish rebellion
        (1916), 9
    de Valera fails to gain recognition
        by, 136–7
American Commission for Irish
        Freedom—
    help to Republican cause from,
        70–7
    President Wilson and, 70
Anderson, Sir John, 120, 137–8
Anglo-Irish Treaty (1921)
    Boundary Commission, 151–2
    compromise oath, 152–3
    constitutional status of Irish Free
        State, 152, 154, 157
    Dail approval for, 157
    independent association suggested
        for, 148
    Irish delegation's errors, 150–1
    London Conference (1921), 147
    national unity abandoned in, 149
    Ulster conditions, 153
Anglo-Irish war, 124–5
An t Oglach, Irish Volunteers'
    newspaper, 61–2, 64, 80
Arbitration Courts, 79
    function under Volunteer guard,
        104
Armagh South by-election and Sinn
        Fein, 42
Ashe, Thomas—
    arrest, 32–3
    funeral, 34
    Longford by-election, 24–5

Ashtown, attempt on life of Lord
    French at, 85
Asquith, Henry Herbert—
    and rebel executions, 3, 5
    defeated by Lloyd George, 20
    new plans for Home Rule, 9
    visit to Dublin (1916), 8–9
Auxiliary Division of Royal Irish
        Constabulary, 107
    Bloody Sunday, 119–20
    effect on IRA, 114–15
    final struggle, 125–35
    first mobile column, 113–14
    horror of reprisals, 116–18
    IRA ambush, 120–1

BALBRIGGAN, County Dublin, sacked
    by Black and Tans, 112
Bannister, Gertrude, 14
Bantry, IRA and RIC fury in, 102–3
Barrett, Richard, execution, 169–70
Barrington, Miss, 127
Barry, Kevin, execution, 121–2, 132
Barry, Tom, and ambush of
    Auxiliaries, 70, 121–2, 128
Barton, detective, 84
Barton, Robert—
    escape from Mountjoy gaol, 71
    favours compromise Treaty, 155
    Irish delegate to Treaty
        negotiations, 150
    released from gaol, 142
Bealnamblath, 168
Beaslai, Piaras—
    editor of An t Oglach, 61
    imprisonment and escape, 64, 77 fn
Beds. and Herts. Light Infantry, 128
Belfast, casualties in (1922), 160–62

194

Bell, Alan, murdered in Dublin
    street, 101
Birkenhead, Lord (F. E. Smith)—
    and Boundary Commission, 172
    at Treaty Conference, 149
    on Home Rule Act, 72
    prosecutor against Casement, 12–13
    'war' statement boosts IRA, 127
Birrell, Augustine, report to Asquith, 1
Black and Tans—
    and RIC Auxiliaries, 97
    and RIC resignations, 107
    killings and, 127–35, 143
    naming of, 96–7
    reprisals on IRA, 97–8, 102–3,
        110–14
    truce, 143
Bloody Sunday (1920), 119–20
Blythe, Ernest—
    and Boundary Commission, 173,
        175
    and Free State executions, 169
Boland, Harry—
    and Nationalists, 54
    avoids arrest, 47–8
    confidence in victory, 50
    de Valera and America, 76
    killed by Free State Army, 167
    part in de Valera's escape, 63
    Peace Conference and President
        Wilson, 54
Bonar Law—
    Carlton Club and Ulster, 12
    in War Cabinet (1916), 21
Boundary Commission—
    a political manoeuvre, 151–2
    collapse of principle, 171–2
    Nationalists and, 161
    objects of, 153–4
    Protestant reactions, 160
Brady, constable, murder of, 83
Breen, Dan—
    at Knocklong, 72, 74, 116 fn, 134
    at Soloheadbeg, 58
British Army—
    Catholic leaders and, 77–8
    shows power, 69–70
British Government—
    and Casement Diaries, 14
    and Irish conscription, 44

Conservatives and Home Rule,
    11–12
Dail Eireann declared illegal, 82
discipline of Crown forces, 116–18
Dominion status offered to Ireland,
    147–9
effect of reprisals, 117–18
effects of military repression,
    69–70
failure of Boundary Commission,
    172–3
'German plot', 46–7
internment, 108–9
IRA executions, 132
Ireland Act 1949, 176–7
Lloyd George and Home Rule,
    90–1
London Treaty Conference (1921),
    147–52
McSwiney's hunger strike, 122–3
modifications to Treaty, 176
reaction to Collins–de Valera pact,
    162–3
reaction to Wilson's murder, 165
truce negotiations, 138–9
voluntary recruiting in Ireland, 49
Broy, Edward, detective, 74
Brugha, Cathal (Charles Burgess)—
    and de Valera, 147–8
    as Sinn Fein executive, 36
    Collins on, 167
    death in Dublin, 166
    Defence Minister, 57
    dual identity, 60
    Easter Week wounds, 33
    evades arrest, 47–8
    message to free nations, 61
    secret direction to Volunteers, 61
    Volunteers' Chief of Staff, 37
Buckingham Palace Conference
    (1914), 10, 140
Burgess, Charles, see Brugha, Cathal
Burke, Head Constable, murdered,
    112
Byrne, murdered Volunteer, 69

CAHERGUILLAMORE House, Limerick,
    IRA dance at, 125
Canterbury, Archbishop of, and
    Casement, 14

Carrowkennedy, Co. Mayo, IRA
    victory at, 128
Carson, Sir Edward—
    and Home Rule negotiations, 10–11
    call for repeal of Home Rule Act,
        79
    in Lloyd George Government, 20
    resigns Ulster leadership, 140
Casement, Sir Roger, trial and
    execution, 12–14
Cashel, Archbishop of, condemns
    Soloheadbeg murder, 58
Catholic Church—
    and conscription, 45
    denounces ambushes, 98
    priests at de Valera's election
        meetings, 28
    reaction to shooting of police and
        soldiers, 59–60, 61
Catholics, Irish—
    and Ulster Special Constabulary,
        130
    refugees from North after riots, 165
    tension with Protestants, 160
Cavan East by-election (1918), 45–7
Ceannt, Eamonn (Edmund Kent),
    execution of, 5–7
Chamberlain, Austen, on Boundary
    Commission, 172
Childers, Erskine—
    and Irish Bulletin, 104
    and IRA shootings, 133
    arrested and executed, 169
    in Treaty negotiations, 150
    joins IRA, 166
    reaction to Treaty, 155
Christensen, Adler, and Casement
    Diaries, 13
Churchill, Winston Spencer—
    at Treaty conference, 149, 153–4
    'cowardly assassins', 138–9
    reaction to Collins–de Valera pact,
        163
Civil War (1922–3), executions by
    Free State Government in, 166,
    169–70
Clancy, George, murdered, 135
Clancy, MP, J. J., 77 fn
Clancy, Paedar, killed by Auxiliaries,
    119–20

Clare, Co.—
    County Council debate, 89
    de Valera wins election at, 26
Clarke, Thomas J., execution of, 1–2
Clarke, Katharine—
    against Treaty, 157
    and National Aid Association, 22
Cloney, Thomas, 112
Clonmore, Co. Kerry, IRA successes
    at, 128
Clonmult, IRA reverse at, 126
Clune, Conor, Gaelic League, death,
    120
Cohalan, Dr, Bishop of Cork, 98
Colbert, Cornelius, executed, 5
Coleman, Richard, Volunteer, dies
    in prison, 63
Collins, Michael (IRB)—
    and Ashe's funeral, 34
    and Boundary Commission, 154,
        160
    and Dail Eireann, 55–6
    and de Valera's escape from gaol,
        63
    and double agents, 74
    and Irish White Cross relief fund,
        127
    and Longford by-election, 24–5
    and memoirs 144
    and murder of Dublin detectives,
        81–2
    and Provisional Government, 157
    and Republican Loan, 79, 81–2
    attempt to assassinate Lord
        French, 85
    British Government ultimatum to,
        165
    campaign against anti-Treaty
        Republicans, 166–7
    control of underground movement,
        47–8
    Dail Finance Minister, 57
    de Valera's return, 67–8
    dual identity, 60
    Dublin conference with IRA, 107
    electoral pact with de Valera, 162
    helps de Valera to get to America,
        76
    in Dublin, 100–1
    killed in Cork ambush, 168

on arms raids, 40
on executions of New Volunteers, 33
on Sinn Fein Convention council, 35–6
orders assassination of Sir Henry Wilson, 164–5
organizes arms raid and gaol escapes, 64
organizes gunmen squads, 73–4
reaction to Treaty, 155–6
receives arms for Free State Army, 167
release from Frongoch Camp (1916), 21
reorganizer of Cork Volunteers, 55
scorn of Sinn Fein Executive, 73
Secretary of National Aid Society, 22
support for Plunkett, 22–3
terror against RIC, 77
Volunteers and Dail oath, 87
Volunteers' organizer, 37
Collinstown aerodrome, raid on, 64
Colonial Home Rule, 30
  Home Rule concept and, 19
  Irish Independent adopts, 24
Connaught Rangers, 104 fn
Connolly, James—
  executed, 6–7
  hopes for Ireland, 177
Conscription Act (1916)—
  and Ireland, 44
  campaign against, 48–9
  conference on at Dublin Castle, 45
  effect on unity of Ireland, and Sinn Fein, 44, 45
Cork—
  Auxiliaries sack, 116–17
  Collins in, 55
  Collins's speech on pact, 164
  hunger-strikers, 122
  in Civil War, 167
  IRA in, 99, 104, 108, 113, 128
  murder of McCurtain, 95–6
  police accused of killings in, 95
  reprisals and executions in, 132–4, 143
  Volunteers in, 68, 80, 82, 84, 86
Cork, Bishop of, on the Dail, 127

Cork Examiner, 28
Cosgrave, William—
  and Free State, 157, 168, 171
  death sentence commuted, 4
  Kilkenny by-election, 31
  Minister in Dail, 57
Council of Ireland, 140–1
County Council elections (1920), 106
Craig, James—
  and Boundary Commission, 172
  and Collins–de Valera pact, 162
  and Treaty negotiations, 151–2
  Henry Wilson an adviser to, 162
  leader of Ulster Unionists, 138
  meeting with de Valera fails, 141
  position after Treaty, 161–2
  rejects truce conference, 142
Croke Park, 119
Crossbarry action at, 128
Crozier, Brigadier-General, 100
Curzon, Lord, member of War Cabinet (1916), 21

DAIL Eireann (Irish National Assembly)—
  Arbitration Courts, 79
  attitude to shootings, 72–3
  Constitution of, 56–7
  County Councils declare allegiance, 105
  Declaration of Independence, 57
  declared illegal by Britain, 82
  divisions over Treaty, 157
  IRA and, 136–7
  Lloyd George and, 138–9
  message to free nations, 57
  oath of allegiance to, 86–7
  reaction to Free State executions, 169
  rejects Dominion Status, 147–8
  Republican Loan, 79
  Republicans refusal to enter, 174
  Second Dail, 139
  writ replaces King's writ, 104
Daily Express, on Ashe's death, 35
Daily Mail, and Sinn Fein, 35
Daily News, on Black and Tans, 103
Daly, Edward, executive, 2
Derby, Lord, and peace settlement, 138–9

de Valera, Eamon—
  American failure, 136–7
  amnesty, 26–7
  and boycott of RIC, 75
  and External Association, 148
  and London Conference, 149
  and Treaty negotiators, 155–7
  and Volunteers violence, 86
  arrest and release of, 141
  arrest at Clare, 174
  arrest of, 46
  arrives in New York, 76
  consription conference, 45
  defeat of Dillon at election, 52
  death sentence commuted, 7
  election to Dail, 28
  escape from Lincoln prison, 63
  Griffith, and interference by, 151
  joins anti-Treaty IRA, 170
  meeting with Craig, 140–1
  negotiations with Lord Derby,
    138–9
  on constitutional position of IRA,
    88 fn
  pact with Collins, 162–4
  President of Dail, 47
  President of Irish Volunteers, 37
  President of Sinn Fein, 35–6
  produces Constitution of Eire, 175
  rejects Dominion Status, 147–8
  resigns as Dail President, 157
  responsibility for IRA actions, 137
  St Patrick's Day message, 63–4
  truce conference, 142
  Waterford by-election, 42
Devlin MP, Joe, at conscription
    conference, 45
Devoy, John and de Valera, 136
Dillon MP, John—
  and burning of Dublin Customs
    House, 131–2
  and execution of rebels, 1
  and Irish political situation, 15
  conscription conference, 45
  defeat by de Valera, 52
  in House of Commons, 6
Dineen, Co. Clare, 112
Downing, Constable, shot dead, 83
Dromkeen, ambush at, 125

Dublin—
  Active Service Unit in, 131
  American Commission reception,
    71
  anti-conscription conference, 45
  Bloody Sunday, 119–20
  Civil War in. 166
  IRA officers' conference, 107
  Plunkett's 'Irish Assembly' in, 23
  Sinn Fein Convention, 35–6
  truce conference, 142
Dublin Customs House, burned
    down by IRA, 131–2
Duggan, E. J., 150
Dunne, Reginald—
  execution of, 168
  murder of Sir Henry Wilson, 165

EIRE—
  Constitution of (1933), 175
  named Republic, 176–7
  neutral in Second World War, 176
Ennis, Co. Clare, de Valera arrested
    at, 174
Ennistymon, Co. Clare, 112
External Association, 147–8

FEETHAM, Mr Justice, 172
Fermoy, Co. Cork, raid by Lynch at,
    82–3
Figgis, Darrell (Sinn Feiner)—
  campaign in Waterford, 42
  on Collins and Sinn Fein, 68 fn
Finnegan, Constable, shot dead at
    Thurles, 93
Finlay, Dean, shot by IRA, 129
Fisher, H. A. L., 118–19
Flying Columns, beginnings of, 114
Free State Army—
  Boland killed by, 167
  defeats anti-Treaty Republicans,
    166–7
French, Lord, Viceroy, 46, 47
Frongoch camp, 21

GALWAY, Bishop of, condemns
    killing of police, 80
Garvin, J. L., 9, 78
George V—
  conciliatory intervention by, 148

position of in Treaty vote, 152–3
speech at opening on Northern
   Ireland Parliament, 142
Ginnell, Lawrence, MP, 77 fn
Glasdrummon, Co. Leitrim, ambush
   at, 128
Government of Ireland Act (1920),
   139
Greenwood, Sir Hamar—
   and Auxiliary Division, 117
   Chief Secretary in Dublin, 99
   on Collins, 127
Grey, Constable, 98
Griffith, Arthur—
   and breakdown of negotiations,
      137–8
   and Longford by-election, 25
   and Provisional Government, 157
   arrested, 45–6
   at anti-conscription conference, 45
   attitude to violence of Volunteers,
      86–7
   Free State Prime Minister, 168
   gaoled, 137
   leads Irish delegation at Treaty
      negotiations, 149–50
   Minister in Dail, 57
   peace moves, 118–19
   post-treaty position, 156–7
   quarrels with Collins, 24
   release from Reading gaol, 21
   released from gaol for truce
      conference, 142
   support for Plunkett, 22–3
Grigg, Sir Edward, 142

HALES, Sean, Dail deputy, shot dead,
   176
Hall, Admiral Sir William, and
   Casement Diaries, 14
Hardwicke, Constable, 98
Harrison, Henry, Nationalist MP, 70
Harty, Dr, Archbishop of Cashel,
   denounces RIC shootings, 72
Headford, ambush at, 126
Healy, F. J., by-election candidate, 20
Healy, Tim, 20, 175
Heuston, Sean, 5, 7
Hoey, Detective Constable, shot in
   Dublin, 81

Hogan, Sean—
   at Soloheadbeg, 58
   rescued at Knocklong, 72
Home Rule—
   Asquith's plan for, 9
   Lloyd George and initial
      agreement on, 10–11
   Redmond assurances fail, 15
   strength of Nationalism, 20
Hyde, Douglas, first President of
   Eire (1933), 176

IRISH BULLETIN, 104
Irish Department of Agriculture, 37
Irish Free State (Saorstat Eireann)—
   and Boundary Commission, 171–3
   becomes Eire (1937), 175
   constitutional status of, 152, 154
   executions by, 169, 170
   name conferred on (1921), 152
Irish Independent—
   and national mood 24, 31
   and Sinn Fein, 38–9
   condemnation of assassination
      attempt on Lord French, 85
   criticism of British military, 70
   report on de Valera election
      victory, 28
Irish National Volunteers—
   and Sinn Fein, 50
   call for reconciliation with Sinn
      Fein, 31
   raid on headquarters of, 31
Irish Nation League, 19
Irish Parliament, creation of
   Northern and Southern, 139
Irish Republic—
   and General Election (1918), 50,
      52–3
   Collins and, 36
   compromise under Treaty, 154 ff
   de Valera and Sinn Fein allegiance
      to, 30
   Sinn Fein and, 35
   Volunteers oath of allegiance to, 86
Irish Republican Army (IRA)—
   anarchy in the South, 163
   and murder of Wilson, 165–6
   anti-Catholic riots, 162
   anti-Treaty garrison, 159–60, 166

arms dumping, 170
as illegal organization, 175
attack on RIC, 103
Auxiliaries ambushed by, 120–1
Auxiliaries' attacks on, 114–15
Bloody Sunday, 119–20
Brig.-Gen. Lucas captured by, 102
calling of Irish volunteers, 70
civil war, 159 ff
continued under Treaty, 157
Customs House fire, 131–2
Dail attitude to, 158
flying columns, 114
guerilla warfare, 101–2
internment and executions, 132
labels attached to corpses, 75
Lynch, and Dail shootings, 170
oath to Dail, 86
persuasive methods, 84–5
reprisals, 133
Irish Republican Brotherhood (IRB)—
and Ashe, 32
and Longford by-election, 24–5
Collins and Volunteers, 37
Collins's membership of, 21
continued under Collins after
Treaty, 159
de Valera, Brugha and, 36
execution of leaders, 2–6
reorganization of, 21–2
Irish Times—
and permanent partition, 18–19
reaction to Home Rule proposal
(1919), 91
Irish Transport and General Workers'
Union, 34, 112
Irish Volunteers—
and authority of courts, 40
and Lord French, 85
at Soloheadbeg, 58
by-election activities, 28
de Valera elected President of, 37
Dublin headquarters, 80
executions of, 2, 3, 5, 6
funeral of MacCurtain, 96
oath to Dail, 87
police patrols, 105–6
raids by, 39, 45, 64, 82–3
reorganization, 21
Sinn Feiners and, 37–8

KAVANAGH, James, Collins's
detective, 74
Kent, Thomas, execution of, 6
Kildare, Bishop of, 115
Kilkenny, by-election, 31
Kilmainham gaol executions, 1–6
Kilmallock, Co. Limerick, 103
Kilmichael, ambush at, 120–1
King's Shropshire Light Infantry,
82
Knockjames, 85
Knocklong, rescue of Volunteer at, 72

LAHINCH, Co. Clare, 112
Lansdowne, Lord, opposes Home
Rule, 8
Limerick, murders of Lord Mayors
of, 135
Lindsay, Mrs, IRA shoot, 132–3
Lloyd George, David—
and amnesty, 26
and Convention (1918), 41
and Irish Convention (1917), 25–6
and Partition, 44
becomes Prime Minister, 20–1
Boundary Commission, 151–2,
160
end to truce talks, 120
government attitude to truce,
138–9
negotiation issues and de Valera,
138–9
on police provocation, 116
peace moves, 118–19, 137–8
proposals for new Home Rule
Bill, 90–1
releases rebels (1916), 21
Logue, Cardinal—
and Irish White Cross relief fund,
127
condemns conscription, 44–5
on killings, 85
Pastoral Letter, 94
warning against Sinn Fein, 38
Long, Walter—
Colonial Secretary, 20–1, 79 fn
opposition to Home Rule, 8, 12
Longford by-election (1917), 24
Lucas, Brigadier-General, capture by
Liam Lynch, 102

Lynch, Colonel Arthur, recruits for
  British Army, 49
Lynch, Liam (Volunteer)—
  and bank robbers, 104–5
  and civil war, 166
  and IRA, 87, 158–60
  arrest and release, 108
  captures Brig.-Gen. Lucas, 102
  Cork commander, 80
  Fermoy raid, 82–3
  killed in running fight, 170
  orders shooting of Dail members,
    170
  preparation for armed struggle
    (1918), 45
  raid on Mallow barracks, 113

MACBRIDE, John, 176
  executed, 3–4
MacBride, Sean, 176–7
McCartan, Patrick—
  and South Armagh by-election, 42
  Sinn Fein Ambassador in America
    (1919), 64
MacCurtain, Lord Mayor of Cork—
  death and funeral, 90–6, 98, 129
  on police activities, 96
MacDermott, Sean, Execution of, 6
MacDonagh, Thomas, poet—
  execution of, 1–2
  last letter, 6
MacDonagh, District Inspector, shot
    dead, 94
MacDonald, Constable, killed by
    Volunteers 58
MacEntee, Sean, 31–2
MacEoin, Sean, 124, 157, 158
McGarry, Sean, 63 fn
MacGrath, Joe, prison escape, 64
MacGuinness, Joe, Longford by-
    election, 24
MacKelvey, Joseph, executed, 169–70
McKee, Richard—
  at MacCurtain's funeral, 109
  imprisoned, 40
  murdered, 119–20
Macnamara, Patrick, Collins's
    detective, 74
MacNeill, Eoin—
  and Volunteers' violence, 73

Boundary Commission, 172–3
  campaigns for de Valera, 27
  Dail Minister, 57
  life sentence, 7
  Sinn Fein Executive, 36
Macpherson, Ian, Chief Secretary, 96
Macready, General—
  Commander-in-Chief army in
    Ireland, 99–100
  and anti-Treaty Republic and,
    165–6
  at Truce conference, 142
  on Ulster Special Constabulary,
    130
Macroom—
  Auxiliaries ambushed at, 120–1
  Auxiliaries at, 114
  disarming of soldiers at, 59, 62
MacSwiney, Terence, Lord Mayor of
    Cork—
  arrested, 108
  death, 122
Mallin, Michael, 5–6
Mallow, Co. Cork, IRA at, 127
Manchester Guardian, 129
Markievicz, Constance—
  at Ashe's funeral, 34
  life sentence, 5
  Minister of Labour in Dail (1919),
    57
Martin, Hugh, Daily News
    correspondent, 103
Martyn, Edward, visits from Sinn
    Feiners, 39
Maxwell, General Sir John—
  and burial of Pearse, 2
  and German-inspired rebellion, 4
  and rebel executions, 5–6
Maynooth, 77–8
Mayo East, de Valera election, 52
Meagher, Thomas, presented with
    green flag, 178
Mellows, Liam—
  and the Republic, 158
  executed, 169–70
  taken prisoner, 166
Midleton, Co. Cork, reprisals at, 132
Midleton, Lord—
  and Redmond, 26
  attends Truce conference, 142

Milling, R. M., shot dead, 67–8
Milroy, Sean, 63 fn
Miltown Malby, Co. Clare, 112
Monteagle, Lord, 105
Mountjoy gaol, 32, 64, 89
Mourne Abbey, IRA reverse at, 126
Moylan, Sean, 124, 128, 157, 159, 163
Moylett, businessman, and peace
    negotiations, 118–20, 138
Mulcahy, Richard—
    and military courts, 160
    at Griffith's funeral, 168
    pro-treaty, 157
    Volunteers Chief-of-Staff, 57, 73,
        145
Municipal Elections (1920), 92

NATIONAL Aid Association, 22
National Brotherhood of St Patrick,
    22
National Parliamentary Party—
    and Partition, 10, 15
    by-election results (1917–18), 22–5,
        28, 31, 41–3
    General Election (1918) and, 52
Neligan, David, Collins's detective,
    74
Northcliffe, Lord, 9
Northern Ireland Parliament, 139,
    177

OATHS—
    of allegiance to Crown, 152–3
    of Volunteers to Dail Eireann,
        86–7
O'Brien, MP, William—
    anti-conscription conference (1918),
        45
    supports Sinn Fein, 50
O'Brien, William, associate of
    Larkin, 45
O'Callaghan, Michael, murdered, 135
O'Callaghan, Mrs Michael, 135, 157
O'Connell, constable, killed by
    Volunteers, 58
O'Connell, General 'Ginger', 166
O'Connor, Rory—
    anti-Treaty leader, 159–60
    executed, 169–70
    taken prisoner, 166

O'Connor, T. P., 15
    and executions, 132
O'Flanagan, Father Michael, 53
O'Hanrahan, Michael, execution of,
    2–3
O'Higgins, Kevin—
    and Boundary Commission, 171,
        172–3
    and executions, 169–70
    and Free State, 157–8, 168
    shot dead, 175
O'Kelly, James J., death, 22
O'Kelly, Sean, and President Wilson,
    64–6
O'Malley, Ernie—
    administers Dail oath, 87
    executes British officers, 133–4
    in civil war, 170
    joins anti-Treaty IRA, 158–9
    on attitude to IRA, 135
    organizer for Collins, 80
    prison and escape, 166
    raid on Mallow barracks, 113
O'Neill, Laurence—
    and murder of police, 81, 84
    and truce, 142
O'Sullivan, Joseph—
    and murder of Sir H. Wilson, 165
    execution of, 168
Oxford and Bucks. Light Infantry, 128

PARIS Peace Conference (1919)
    American Commission for Irish
        Freedom at, 66
    Irish Hopes of, 22, 30, 32, 50, 59
    no official place for Ireland at, 55–6
    President Wilson refuses
        interference in Irish affairs,
        65–6
Parsons, Sir Lawrence, 152
Partition of Ireland, 139–40
    Griffith and, 9
    plans for, 43–4, 90–1
    Southern Unionists against, 19, 20
Peake, IRA reverse at, 126
Pearse, Mrs, mother of Patrick, 157
Pearse, Patrick H.—
    executed, 1–2
    last letter, 6–7
    on Irish nationalist aspirations, 177

Pearse, Willie, executed, 2–3
Perth (Australia), Archbishop of, in
  peace negotiations, 137–8
Plunkett, Count—
  and Royal Dublin Society, 22
  convenes 'Irish Assembly', 23
  Minister in Dail, 57
  stands down for de Valera, 35
  wins Roscommon by-election
    (1917), 22–3
Plunkett, Horace, forms Irish
  Dominion League (1919), 57
Plunkett, Joseph Mary, executed, 2
Power, John O'Connor, elected MP, 4
Protestants, Irish—
  Boundary Commission tension
    with Catholics, 160
  support Craig, 161
  Ulster Special Constabulary and
    deaths, 130
Provisional Government
  Collins Chairman of, 157
  Collins–de Valera pact and, 162
  ultimatum to after murder of Sir
    H. Wilson, 165

Quinlisk, Sgt. Timothy, shot by
  Collins as spy, 99 fn

Rathmore, Co. Kerry, ambush at,
  128
Redmond, Assistant Commissioner
  of Police, murdered in Dublin, 93
Redmond, John—
  and Casement's execution, 12
  and convention of Irishmen, 25–6
  and political survey, 15
  and rebel executions, 2
  agreement with Asquith on
    treatment of rebels (1916), 1
  humiliation and death, 41
  intervenes for de Valera, 7
  recommends new Home Rule
    terms, 10–11
  Roscommon by-election set-back,
    22–3
Redmond, Captain, elections, 42, 52
Republican Loan—
  announced by Dail, 79
  success of, 101

Restoration of Order in Ireland Act,
  1920, 109
Robinson, Seumes—
  and civil war, 166
  at Knocklong, 68
  At Soloheadbeg, 58
Roscommon by-election (1917), 22–3
Rosscarbery, fight for police
  barracks at, 128
Royal Irish Constabulary (RIC)—
  and Black and Tans, 96, 107–35
  Auxiliary Division, 97
  Collins's terror campaign against,
    77
  de Valera and boycott of, 75
  IRA attack on Kilmallock
    barracks, 103
  murder of MacCurtain, 95–6
  Soloheadbeg shootings, 57–8
  violence by in Thurles and Cork,
    93–4
  Westport shooting, 67
Ryan, Monsignor, condemns
  Soloheadbeg killing, 58

Selborne, Lord, and Home Rule, 8,
  12
Shortt, Chief Secretary, 46
Sinn Fein—
  and arms raids, 39–40
  attitude to Volunteers killings, 59
  ban on hunting in Ireland, 62–3
  banned in Tipperary, 78
  Collins castigates, 73
  conscription and, 44
  de Valera reconstructs (1917), 30
  effects of military repression, 70
  election successes and reverses,
    31, 41–3, 52, 92, 105, 139
  General Election manifesto, 50
  'German Plot', 46
  militant members avoid arrest, 47–8
  political aspects of, 35–6, 64–5
  repudiates murder, 69
  Volunteers and reconciliation, 31,
    37–8
  wreck of HQ, 50
Sixmilebridge, ambush at, 126
Smuts, General, 142, 147
Smyth, detective shot in Dublin, 81

'Soldier's Song', 31
Southern Ireland Parliament, 139, 157
Southern Unionists—
  disapproval of Partition, 18, 26
  Midleton and, 41
  Redmond and, 26
South Mayo Flying Column, 126
'Spies', execution of, 84, 88, 99,
  128–30
Stack, Austin, and forcible feeding in
  Mountjoy gaol, 32–3
Stockley, Professor, 95, 96
Strickland, General, 117 fn, 118
Sullivan, Serjeant, defends Casement,
  13
Swanzy, District Inspector, 96

Templemore, Co. Limerick, 111
Thomson, Captain, executed by
  IRA, 128
Thurles, Co. Tipperary—
  Black and Tan retaliation at, 98–9
  killings at, 93
Times, The, 38
Tipperary, Soloheadbeg killings at,
  58
Tourmakeady, IRA action at, 128
Traynor, Oscar, imprisoned, 44
Treacy, Sean—
  at Knocklong, 72
  at Soloheadbeg, 58
  death, 116, 134
Tuam, murders at, 109–10
Tuam, Archbishop of, 77, 78, 110,
  127
Tudor, General H. H., and RIC,
  99–100
Tullow, 121
Tyrone East by-election, 43

Ulster—
  conditions in Treaty agreement
    (1921), 153
  effects of Boundary Commission,
    153–4
  refugees after riots, 161
  IRA and support for Catholic
    minority, 160

Ulster Special Constabulary, 129–30
  160
Ulster Unionists—
  and nine county exclusions, 10
  attitude to United Ireland, 140–1
  dislike of Dail, 106
  election results, 52–3, 139–40
  errors in Lloyd George's proposals,
    11
Ulster Volunteer Force, vengeance on
  Sinn Fein Irishmen, 106–7
Upton, ambush at, 127

Vicars, Sir Arthur, shot by IRA, 129

Walsh, Dr W. J., Archbishop of
    Dublin—
  and American Commission, 71
  and Longford by-election, 25
Waterford by-election (1918), 42
West Cork by-election, 17, 20
Westmeath Independent, 27
Westminster Gazette, 30, 38
Westport, Co. Mayo—
  American Commission held up by
    military at, 71
  murder of RIC Inspector at, 67, 68
Wilson, District Inspector, shot dead,
  111
Wilson, Sir Henry, Director of
    Military Operations—
  adviser to Craig, 162
  alarmed by Ulster Special
    Constabulary, 130
  assassination of by Collins's orders,
    164–5
  criticism of Government, 109
Wilson, President Woodrow—
  embarrassed by Irish question, 65–6
  Irish hopes founded on, 55
Wimborne, Lord, Viceroy (1915), on
  'German Plot', 46–7
Woods, Sir Robert, 56 fn
Worcester Regiment, 141

Yeats, W. B., poem on executions, 14

FOR THE BEST IN PAPERBACKS, LOOK FOR THE

In every corner of the world, on every subject under the sun, Penguin represents quality and variety – the very best in publishing today.

For complete information about books available from Penguin – including Puffins, Penguin Classics and Arkana – and how to order them, write to us at the appropriate address below. Please note that for copyright reasons the selection of books varies from country to country.

In the United Kingdom: Please write to *Dept E.P., Penguin Books Ltd, Harmondsworth, Middlesex, UB7 0DA.*

If you have any difficulty in obtaining a title, please send your order with the correct money, plus ten per cent for postage and packaging, to *PO Box No 11, West Drayton, Middlesex*

In the United States: Please write to *Dept BA, Penguin, 299 Murray Hill Parkway, East Rutherford, New Jersey 07073*

In Canada: Please write to *Penguin Books Canada Ltd, 2801 John Street, Markham, Ontario L3R 1B4*

In Australia: Please write to the *Marketing Department, Penguin Books Australia Ltd, P.O. Box 257, Ringwood, Victoria 3134*

In New Zealand: Please write to the *Marketing Department, Penguin Books (NZ) Ltd, Private Bag, Takapuna, Auckland 9*

In India: Please write to *Penguin Overseas Ltd, 706 Eros Apartments, 56 Nehru Place, New Delhi, 110019*

In the Netherlands: Please write to *Penguin Books Netherlands B.V., Postbus 195, NL–1380AD Weesp*

In West Germany: Please write to *Penguin Books Ltd, Friedrichstrasse 10–12, D–6000 Frankfurt/Main 1*

In Spain: Please write to *Alhambra Longman S.A., Fernandez de la Hoz 9, E–28010 Madrid*

In Italy: Please write to *Penguin Italia s.r.l., Via Como 4, I-20096 Pioltello (Milano)*

In France: Please write to *Penguin Books Ltd, 39 Rue de Montmorency, F-75003 Paris*

In Japan: Please write to *Longman Penguin Japan Co Ltd, Yamaguchi Building, 2–12–9 Kanda Jimbocho, Chiyoda-Ku, Tokyo 101*

Modern Ireland 1600–1972   R. F. Foster

'Takes its place with the finest historical writing of the twentieth century, whether about Ireland or anywhere else' – Conor Cruise O'Brien in the *Sunday Times*

Death in Hamburg   Society and Politics in the Cholera Years 1830–1910
Richard J. Evans

Why did the cholera epidemic of 1892 kill nearly 10,000 people in six weeks in Hamburg, while most of Europe was left almost unscathed? The answers put forward in this 'tremendous book' (Roy Porter in the *London Review of Books*) offer a wealth of insights into the inner life of a great – and uniquely anomalous – European city at the height of an industrial age.

British Society 1914–1945   John Stevenson

A major contribution to the *Penguin Social History of Britain*, which 'will undoubtedly be the standard work for students of modern Britain for many years to come' – *The Times Educational Supplement*

A History of Christianity   Paul Johnson

'Masterly ... a cosmic soap opera involving kings and beggars, philosophers and crackpots, scholars and illiterate *exaltés*, popes and pilgrims and wild anchorites in the wilderness' – Malcolm Muggeridge

The Penguin History of Greece   A. R. Burn

Readable, erudite, enthusiastic and balanced, this one-volume history of Hellas sweeps the reader along from the days of Mycenae and the splendours of Athens to the conquests of Alexander and the final dark decades.

Battle Cry of Freedom   The American Civil War
James M. McPherson

'Compellingly readable ... It is the best one-volume treatment of its subject I have come across. It may be the best ever published ... This is magic' – Hugh Brogan in *The New York Times Book Review*

The Penguin History of the United States   Hugh Brogan

'An extraordinarily engaging book' – *The Times Literary Supplement*. 'Compelling reading ... Hugh Brogan's book will delight the general reader as much as the student' – *The Times Educational Supplement*. 'He will be welcomed by American readers no less than those in his own country' – J. K. Galbraith

The Making of the English Working Class   E. P. Thompson

Probably the most imaginative – and the most famous – post-war work of English social history.

Galileo: Heretic   Pietro Redondi

'A powerful and brilliantly evocative book, possibly the most important, certainly the most controversial, contribution to Galileo studies for many years' – *The Times Literary Supplement*

The City in History   Lewis Mumford

Often prophetic in tone and containing a wealth of photographs, *The City in History* is among the most deeply learned and warmly human studies of man as a social creature.

The Habsburg Monarchy 1809–1918   A J P Taylor

Dissolved in 1918, the Habsburg Empire 'had a unique character, out of time and out of place'. Scholarly and vividly accessible, this 'very good book indeed' (*Spectator*) elucidates the problems always inherent in the attempt to give peace, stability and a common loyalty to a heterogeneous population.

Inside Nazi Germany   Conformity, Opposition and Racism in Everyday Life
Detlev J. K. Peukert

An authoritative study – and a challenging and original analysis – of the realities of daily existence under the Third Reich. 'A fascinating study ... captures the whole range of popular attitudes and the complexity of their relationship with the Nazi state' – Richard Geary

The Victorian Underworld Kellow Chesney

A superbly evocative survey of the vast substratum of vice that lay below the respectable surface of Victorian England – the showmen, religious fakes, pickpockets and prostitutes – and of the penal methods of that 'most enlightened age'. 'Charged with nightmare detail' – *Sunday Times*

Citizens Simon Schama

The award-winning chronicle of the French Revolution. 'The most marvellous book I have read about the French Revolution in the last fifty years' – Richard Cobb in *The Times*. 'He has chronicled the vicissitudes of that world with matchless understanding, wisdom, pity and truth, in the pages of this huge and marvellous book' – *Sunday Times*

Stalin Isaac Deutscher

'The Greatest Genius in History' and the 'Life-Giving Force of Socialism'? Or a tyrant more ruthless than Ivan the Terrible whose policies facilitated the rise of Nazism? An outstanding biographical study of a revolutionary despot by a great historian.

Jasmin's Witch Emmanuel Le Roy Ladurie

An investigation into witchcraft and magic in south-west France during the seventeenth century – a masterpiece of historical detective work by the bestselling author of *Montaillou*.

The Second World War A J P Taylor

A brilliant and detailed illustrated history, enlivened by all Professor Taylor's customary iconoclasm and wit.

Industry and Empire E. J. Hobsbawm

Volume 3 of the *Penguin Economic History of Britain* covers the period of the Industrial Revolution: 'the most fundamental transformation in the history of the world recorded in written documents.' 'A book that attracts and deserves attention ... by far the most gifted historian now writing' – John Vaizey in the *Listener*

PENGUIN POLITICS AND SOCIAL SCIENCES

Political Ideas   David Thomson (ed.)

From Machiavelli to Marx – a stimulating and informative introduction to the last 500 years of European political thinkers and political thought.

On Revolution   Hannah Arendt

Arendt's classic analysis of a relatively recent political phenomenon examines the underlying principles common to all revolutions, and the evolution of revolutionary theory and practice. 'Never dull, enormously erudite, always imaginative' – *Sunday Times*

Ill Fares the Land   Susan George

These twelve essays expand on one of the major themes of Susan George's work: the role of power in perpetuating world hunger. With characteristic commitment and conviction, the author of *A Fate Worse than Debt* and *How the Other Half Dies* demonstrates that just as poverty lies behind hunger, so injustice and inequality lie behind poverty.

The Social Construction of Reality   Peter Berger and Thomas Luckmann

Concerned with the sociology of 'everything that passes for knowledge in society' and particularly with that which passes for common sense, this is 'a serious, open-minded book, upon a serious subject' – *Listener*

The Care of the Self   Michel Foucault
The History of Sexuality Vol 3

Foucault examines the transformation of sexual discourse from the Hellenistic to the Roman world in an inquiry which 'bristles with provocative insights into the tangled liaison of sex and self' – *The Times Higher Education Supplement*

Silent Spring   Rachel Carson

'What we have to face is not an occasional dose of poison which has accidentally got into some article of food, but a persistent and continuous poisoning of the whole human environment.' First published in 1962, *Silent Spring* remains the classic environmental statement which founded an entire movement.

Comparative Government   S. E. Finer

'A considerable *tour de force* ... few teachers of politics in Britain would fail to learn a great deal from it ... Above all, it is the work of a great teacher who breathes into every page his own enthusiasm for the discipline' – Anthony King in *New Society*

Karl Marx: Selected Writings in Sociology and Social Philosophy
T. B. Bottomore and Maximilien Rubel (eds.)

'It makes available, in coherent form and lucid English, some of Marx's most important ideas. As an introduction to Marx's thought, it has very few rivals indeed' – *British Journal of Sociology*

Post-War Britain   A Political History   Alan Sked and Chris Cook

Major political figures from Attlee to Thatcher, the aims and achievements of governments and the changing fortunes of Britain in the period since 1945 are thoroughly scrutinized in this readable history.

Inside the Third World   Paul Harrison

From climate and colonialism to land hunger, exploding cities and illiteracy, this comprehensive book brings home a wealth of facts and analysis on the often tragic realities of life for the poor people and communities of Asia, Africa and Latin America.

Housewife   Ann Oakley

'A fresh and challenging account' – *Economist*. 'Informative and rational enough to deserve a serious place in any discussion on the position of women in modern society' – *The Times Educational Supplement*

The Raw and the Cooked   Claude Lévi-Strauss

Deliberately, brilliantly and inimitably challenging, Lévi-Strauss's seminal work of structural anthropology cuts wide and deep into the mind of mankind, as he finds in the myths of the South American Indians a comprehensible psychological pattern.

BY THE SAME AUTHOR

Volume I and II of his highly acclaimed trilogy

Robert Kee's *The Green Flag* stands as the most comprehensive and illuminating history of Irish Nationalism yet published.

The Green Flag: Volume I
The Most Distressful Country

In this opening volume he asks the question. 'Who are the Irish?', and covers events from Ireland's earliest beginnings to the Great Famine of 1845.

'Historians tend to be either quarriers or masons: Kee contrives to succeed as both ... I cannot recall any work giving so agreeably objective a picture' – Brian Inglis in the *Guardian*

'His common sense cuts through to the truth ... Robert Kee has established himself as a very considerable analyst of Ireland's troubles' – Edward Norman in the *Spectator*

The Green Flag: Volume II
The Bold Fenian Men

Volume Two in Robert Kee's monumental history covers events from the founding of the Fenian Movement to the Dublin Rising of 1916.

'Wholly admirable ... a highly topical book ... The English have always turned a blind eye to the history of Ireland, because they behaved worse there than anywhere else; and the Irish, in both the Republic and the North, love to dwell upon their past – which they embroider with legends. Robert Kee's new history may therefore vex all three parties ... he is so beautifully objective and thorough' – *Sunday Times*

'If there had been more Englishmen with Kee's perception part of our tragedy would never have happened' – *Irish Independent*